The Young Child and Mathematics

Second Edition

Juanita V. Copley

**National Association for the
Education of Young Children**
Washington, DC

NATIONAL COUNCIL OF
TEACHERS OF MATHEMATICS

Reston, Virginia

National Association
for the Education
of Young Children
1313 L Street NW, Suite 500
Washington, DC 20005-4101
202-232-8777 • 800-424-2460
www.naeyc.org

NAEYC Books

Director, Publications and
Educational Initiatives
Carol Copple

Managing Editor
Bry Pollack

Design and Production
Malini Dominey

Editorial Associate
Melissa Hogarty

Editorial Assistant
Elizabeth Wegner

Permissions
Lacy Thompson

Through its publications program, the National Association for the Education of Young Children (NAEYC) provides a forum for discussion of major issues and ideas in the early childhood field, with the hope of provoking thought and promoting professional growth. The views expressed or implied in this book are not necessarily those of the Association or its members.

For help accessing the DVD, see Appendix A on page 162.

Book Permissions

The poem "two friends" (p. 75) from *Spin a Soft Black Song: Poems for Children* (Rev. ed.), by Nikki Giovanni and illustrated by George Martins (New York: Hill & Wang), is reprinted with permission of Hill & Wang, a division of Farrar, Straus and Giroux, LLC. © 1971, 1985 by Nikki Giovanni.

The cube diagrams (p. 117) are reproduced from *Mathematics Institute for Pre-Kindergarten and Kindergarten: A TEXTEAMS Project*, by Juanita V. Copley (Austin: University of Texas at Austin, 2001).

The graphs (p. 147) and text from *Principles and Standards for School Mathematics*, by the National Council of Teachers of Mathematics (Reston, VA: NCTM), are adapted with permission. © 2000. All rights reserved.

The excerpt (pp. 155–56) from the National Research Council's *Mathematics Learning in Early Childhood: Paths Toward Excellence and Equity*, edited by Christopher T. Cross, Taniesha A. Woods, & Heidi Schweingruber; Committee on Early Childhood Mathematics, Center for Education, and Division of Behavioral and Social Sciences and Education (Washington, DC: National Academies Press, 241), is reprinted with permission. © 2009 by the National Academy of Sciences.

DVD Permissions

Excerpts from *Principles and Standards for School Mathematics* (pp. 29–31, 392, 394, 396, 398, 400, and 402), by the National Council of Teachers of Mathematics (Reston, VA: NCTM), are reprinted with permission. © 2000. All rights reserved.

Excerpts from *Curriculum Focal Points for Prekindergarten through Grade 8 Mathematics: A Quest for Coherence* (pp. 5–6, 11–14), by the National Council of Teachers of Mathematics (Reston, VA: NCTM), are reprinted with permission. © 2006. All rights reserved. No portion of the *Focal Points* material may be excerpted, published, or reproduced in any format for commercial or nonprofit use without prior permission from NCTM. Submit requests to: permissions@nctm.org.

Credits

Photographs copyright © by: *Nancy P. Alexander*, 75; *Juanita V. Copley*, 50, 93, 111, 116 (top), 130, 140; *Stephanie Feeney*, 16; *William Geiger*, 26; *Getty Images*, 40; *Rich Graessle*, 7; *iStockphoto*, 3; *Natalie Klein*, 4; *Jimmie Lanley*, 116 (bottom); *Jeane Claude Lejeune*, 2, 106; *Elisabeth Nichols*, 144; *Karen Phillips*, 8, 31, 92, 136 (top), 150; *Daniel Raskin*, 122; *Shari Schmidt*, 5, 136 (bottom); *Ellen B. Senisi*, 21, 33, 58, 115, 125; *Subjects and Predicates*, 70, 159

Children's art provided by Juanita V. Copley
Illustrations by Natalie Klein

The Young Child and Mathematics, 2d ed.
Copyright © 2010 by the National Association for the Education of Young Children. All rights reserved. Printed in the United States of America.

A copublication of the National Association for the Education of Young Children and the National Council of Teachers of Mathematics, 1906 Association Drive, Reston, VA 20191-1502.

Library of Congress Control Number: 2009940171

ISBN: 978-1-928896-68-5 (book and DVD)

NAEYC Item# 167

NCTM Stock# 13861

About the Author

Juanita Copley is a professor emerita at the University of Houston. She has taught middle school mathematics in the public schools, served as a mathematics specialist in two urban school districts, and taught math education courses at the University of Houston. She currently spends at least one day a week teaching in prekindergarten and elementary school classrooms. For more than a decade, Dr. Copley directed the innovative Early Childhood Mathematics Collaborative, a professional development project that has trained more than 2,000 preservice teachers and 250 inservice teachers. She has also worked with the Head Start Bureau in developing a mathematics initiative for teachers and young children. As professor emerita, she continues to devote much of her time and energy to professional development in early mathematics teaching.

Dr. Copley has written and edited a number of books about early childhood mathematics, three of which are copublications of NAEYC and NCTM (National Council of Teachers of Mathematics). Her research on early childhood math and on effectiveness of professional development models for teachers in mathematics has been published in journals and presented at national early childhood and mathematics education conferences.

Acknowledgments

The author extends special thanks to the children, families, teachers, and administrators of: **Farias Early Childhood Center** (teachers *Pam Morse* and *Yadira Suriano*, instructional specialist *Maria Nevarez-Solis*, principal *Ali Oliver*), **Oates Elementary School**, and **Herod Elementary School**, Houston (Texas) Independent School District; **E.A. Lawhon Elementary School** (second grade teacher *Laura Wheat*, first grade teacher *Maria Sears*, curriculum and instruction math specialist *Valerie Johse*, principal *Marlo Keller*), Pearland (Texas) Independent School District; and **Hearne Elementary School**, Alief (Texas) Independent School District.

To these neighborhood centers in Houston, Texas: **Cook Road Center** (teacher *Fehintola Ayoola*, manager *Tracy Joseph*), **New Horizon Center** (teacher *Vera Hurst*, manager *Monique Shobo*); **Albury Center** (teacher *Karen Walker*, manager *Dana Anglin*); **Klein Center** (teacher *Raquel Doneley*, manager *Markeysha Hinderman*); and **Sharp Center** (teacher *Jacquelyn Wilson*, manager *Parel Washington*).

And to 3-year-olds teacher *Mimi Lodowski* and prekindergarten teacher *Susan McDaniel*, **River Oaks Baptist School**, Houston, Texas; and kindergarten teachers *Michell Harper* and *Karen Walker*, Katy (Texas) Independent School District.

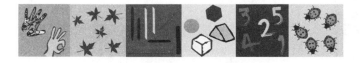

Contents

Chapter 1

The Child Learns, the Child Teaches

An 8-year-old with spiky hair, an impish demeanor, and a seemingly permanent pout, Timmy entered my life late one October. He was referred to me because he demonstrated few skills in reading or mathematics, seemed unmotivated to attempt new tasks, and seldom—if ever—completed a readable assignment.

Jessica, age 8, was quiet and compliant. She never caused problems, never showed any particular gift for mathematics, and never volunteered in class. In fact, I had difficulty finding anything specific to say to her parents during parent-teacher conferences.

With hands up in the air and a grin a mile wide, 5-year-old Armand, an enthusiastic ball of energy, entered the science lab with his kindergarten class and announced, "I'm here! I love science! I can't wait!" Within an hour I found Armand on the floor holding an earthworm, surrounded by dirt from the earthworm farm, every inch of bare skin and most of his clothing covered with dirt.

I have been a teacher for 38 years. I have taken courses, read books, earned degrees, conducted research, and published articles. I have learned how to do mathematics, how to teach mathematics, how to assess mathematical understanding, how to understand child development, and more. My teachers and mentors have been wonderful. They have taught me much, given me ideas, and broadened my beliefs about teaching. However, the lessons I learned from children—from Timmy, Jessica, Armand, and others—are the ones that have made the most difference in my teaching.

The Young Child and Mathematics focuses on children from age 3 through 8 and their mathematical learning. The placement of the phrase *young child* before the word *mathematics* in the book's title is not accidental. It comes first because I believe that the child should be the focus of early education. In this chapter I share some of the lessons that I have learned about children and their understanding of mathematics. Some of my ideas about how to teach mathematics come from textbooks, some from watching other teachers teach, and some from experts. However, most, if not all, of the ideas were greatly influenced by children themselves. In some cases their strategies changed the activities for my lessons, their interests changed the scope of the content, or their particular strengths or weaknesses changed the sequence of my instruction. Whatever the case, I have found that when I make the child the focus of my teaching, I teach mathematics well.

Learning from Timmy

Let's talk about Timmy. After looking at his work and his records, I understood his teacher's frustration. Indeed, Timmy was a child with whom teachers found it difficult to work. He had demonstrated a very short attention span, and he showed little promise in mathematics or any other subject. I admitted him to a special program for "slow learners."

Because of an unexpected assignment, I didn't have time to work with Timmy that first day he appeared in my classroom. To keep him busy, I gave him a large box of electrical equipment from the sixth grade electricity unit: switches, batteries, wire, and small light bulbs. I asked him to sort the box's contents and told him that I would return in a while.

Thirty minutes later, when I walked back into the room, I discovered that Timmy had created a working electrical system! Six bulbs were lit, three switches were incorporated, and within the connection he had produced a working model of both a parallel and a series circuit. I watched and listened as this challenging, unmotivated, and unskilled 8-year-old shared with me his creation, which was much more complicated than anything I could build. Timmy explained why certain bulbs were half the brightness of other bulbs, he told me how to predict whether a bulb would light or not light, and he told me about resistance and the advantages and disadvantages of series and parallel circuits.

Timmy taught me an important lesson: Spend time observing, listening, and watching children. Pay attention to what they like, listen to their reasoning, ask them to explain their creations, challenge them with tasks that seem impossible, and give them the opportunity to show you what they can do in the way they want. If I encourage children in these ways, I provide them a greater opportunity to reach their true potential in mathematics!

A lesson from Jessica

Quiet Jessica was one of my students during my second year of teaching. At the end of the year, I asked each child in my class to give me a report card for being a teacher. I stressed the fact that they should tell me good things as well as things I could improve.

Jessica took my directions seriously. Her block-print note with her own spelling stated,

> Ms Copley. You were real good with the dumd kids. They needed you and you halped them. You were real good with smart kids. You always keeped them buzy. but you should do better with the plane kids like me. I need to learn to!
>
> Luv, Jessica

She was right; I had spent most of my time with the special children, and I had ignored the "plain" kids. I learned an important lesson from that note: Remember that every child is important! It is my job to do my best teaching for those children who have special gifts; those who need concentrated help to overcome difficulties; *and* those quiet, plain children who have the right to learn.

The joy of Armand

Armand's fascination with earthworms began that first day in the science lab. He spent countless hours observing them, "reading" earthworm books in the library, and asking questions. During his study he became obsessed with finding the eyes of earthworms. Assuring me that "They gots to have eyes! They gots to see!" Armand kept asking for bigger magnifiers so that he could find their eyes.

Instead of discouraging Armand and correcting his misconception, I helped him set up experiments to test his hypothesis. During the last two months of the school year, Armand spent every free minute conducting experiments with colored mats, homemade earthworm houses, and colored lights. As he boarded the bus for his final trip home as a kindergartner, he yelled out the window, "I still think they gots eyes, Mrs. Copley!"

That statement taught me a great deal. Because I allowed him to investigate his hypothesis—and in fact encouraged his exploration—Armand learned more about earthworms than anyone in the school. Because he had a need to know, Armand read fourth and fifth grade–level books about earthworms and could use the proper terminology to describe their body parts. More important, because he was in charge of his own learning, Armand continued to be a powerful, excited learner.

When I heard Armand's final statement, I was reminded how important it is not to jump to correct every misconception. Instead, encourage investigation, and remember that children construct their own knowledge. What an valuable lesson for someone teaching mathematics!

My three lessons

These three lessons should be in evidence throughout this book. First, spend time observing, listening, and watching children. Some of the many vignettes and dialogues I have recorded, videotaped, and remembered appear in every chapter. I believe that you can learn most from children and classroom examples; thus, such examples are abundant and presented as realistically as possible.

Second, remember that every child is important. This volume offers a variety of examples and suggested activities that work for children with all types of needs in diverse settings. Because I have been privileged to teach in multicultural settings; in urban and rural communities; in private and public schools; and in 4-year-old, kindergarten, first grade, and second grade classrooms, the ideas here reflect those contexts.

Third, encourage investigation and remember that children construct their own knowledge. I value the joy of learning, exploration, and discovery. While mathematics is often considered a subject of right answers and prescriptive instruction, the ideas presented in this book foster investigation in the way children learn.

1. The intuitive mathematical knowledge of the young child

Young children are natural learners. They construct their own understanding about quantity, relationships, and symbols. They approach new tasks with curiosity and a sense of experimentation. Counting is a natural task, *more* is a word 2-year-olds know readily, and the process of adding and subtracting can describe and explain to children situations that they encounter in their world. When a new idea or piece of information doesn't make sense to a child, Jean Piaget theorized that the experience creates dissonance— mental conflict that the child seeks to resolve. Thus, the child develops and assimilates knowledge, making it her own.

The intuitive, informal mathematical knowledge of young children often surprises early childhood teachers. Yet, kindergarten curriculum tends to reflect the belief that 5-year-olds enter school as blank slates, with no mathematics concepts and no experience with quantities, patterns, shapes, or relationships! Instead, research strongly indicates that young children have a strong, intuitive understanding of informal mathematics.

Block Shapes

Three-year-old Jeffrey discusses a new set of blocks with his teacher:

Ms. Wright: Tell me about these new blocks. What do you call them?

Jeffrey: Blocks with different shapes.

Ms. Wright: What can you tell me about these different shapes?

Jeffrey: This yellow one is a star. The blue one is a triangle.

Ms. Wright: Wow! Have you ever seen shapes like this before?

Jeffrey: [sighing loudly] Yeah, at my house, my Granna house, my Daddy house, outside.

Ms. Wright: You have all these shapes at everybody's house?

Jeffrey: No. . . . [picking up the orange circle] This is like my Uncle Dee's basketball, but [frowning] it won't bounce up and down. This is a piece of pizza [indicating a purple, wedge-shape block], this is a table [a pink square], this is my best book [a rectangular block].

Jeffrey proceeds to separate the blocks into two groups: five shapes on one side and one shape on the other side. The star-shaped block is alone, and the others—triangle, square, pizza slice, circle, and rectangle—are heaped together in a pile.

Ms. Wright: Why did you put the star on the other side?

Jeffrey: [with a deep, long sigh that sounds as if he has lost his patience] These belong in a house and this one [the star] doesn't. It belongs in the sky!

Did you notice Jeffrey's verbal labeling of the block shapes, his connection of the blocks to items he regularly sees, and his clarification of differences between the basketball and the round block? While his particular classification system (belongs in the house, doesn't belong in the house) is not found in state objectives, his system is perfectly correct and indicates greater consistency than young children typically show.

Identification of two-dimensional shapes is an objective in kindergarten programs; Jeffrey has already shown that ability at age 3. The identification of shapes in the everyday world is also a standard objective in kindergarten curricula; again Jeffrey demonstrates that ability. I am not proposing that all 3-year-olds have Jeffrey's understanding and use of language; however, I do believe that many early childhood programs and teachers view young children as incapable, when in fact they already grasp many mathematical concepts at an intuitive level.

While reviewing research studies is not the purpose of this book, I have listed below some important points supported by research (Copley 1999; Clements & Sarama 2007; NRC 2009) that illustrate the intuitive mathematical knowledge of the young child:

● Young children have the ability to learn mathematics. Through everyday experiences they acquire a wealth of informal knowledge and strategies to deal with situations that have a mathematical dimension.

● The operations of addition, subtraction, multiplication, and division are often understood by young children. While they may not be able to complete a written equation such as $5 - 2 = 3$, they can easily tell you how many buttons you would have on your shirt if you started with 5 and 2 fell off. Accordingly, they can figure out how many pieces of candy to purchase for a birthday party if everyone attending got 3 pieces.

● Children's understanding of rational numbers, while incomplete, is often more accomplished than expected. Their common sharing experiences, their use of the term *half*, and their fair distribution of quantities among friends are natural by-products of everyday experiences.

● The development of geometric concepts and spatial sense can often be observed when young children participate in free play. The young child directing a building block project uses words and motions to tell his friend how to make a castle. "Do it like me. You need a square block" (his description for a cube). "No, not that way. Turn it over!" When his friend says, "It doesn't matter, it's always the same," the child reaffirms his own understanding by saying, "Well that's 'cause now it's right!" Both children are experimenting with beginning concepts of rotation and the language of geometry.

● A natural fascination with large numbers is evident with young children. While they frequently invent nonsensical numbers (a million-dillion-killion), they often show a partial understanding of quantity and the need for counting.

Do we need to directly teach young children all they need to know about mathematics? Do we need to start from the beginning, drill in those basic facts, and fill all the holes in their understanding? Do we need to tightly define as developmentally appropriate only very easy mathematical concepts?

The answer to all of these questions is a resounding *No!* Instead, we need to remember that young children possess a vast amount of intuitive, informal mathematical knowledge. Our job is to assess their prior knowledge, build upon their strengths, facilitate their learning, and enjoy the process.

2. The constructed mathematical concepts of the young child

Young children continually construct mathematical ideas based on their experiences with their environment, their interactions with adults and other children, and their daily observations. These ideas are unique to each child and vary greatly among children the same age. Some of the ideas are perceptually immature, many of the problem-solving strategies are inefficient, and the verbal information necessary to discuss mathematics is often incorrectly labeled or modeled. The child who perceives more candy to be in the larger bag, the child who always adds together two sets of items using the counting-all strategy, and the child who counts "6, 7, 8, 9, 10, oneteen, twoteen, threeteen," all illustrate mathematical ideas that would be labeled incorrect for an adult but are developmentally correct for a young child.

An early childhood teacher who frequently listens to ideas expressed by young children can provide materials and an environment conducive to the development of mathematical concepts. More important, by observing young children, the teacher can ask questions that prompt them to make new discoveries and form their own questions. To illustrate this point, the vignette below shows how some prekindergartners respond to a problem presented by their classroom teacher.

Six Legs, Five Fingers

Miss Riley: I just bought this bee puppet [shows a bee puppet attached to a black, six-fingered glove] and I have a problem. When I put my hand into the glove, I always have an empty leg on the puppet. I don't have enough fingers for all of the legs. I have only five fingers and there are six legs on this puppet. I don't know what to do! Maybe I'll just take it back to the store.

The children seem to be thinking about this problem. Some count their fingers, others talk to their partners, and still others shrug their shoulders.

Russell: Well, maybe you got your fingers in wrong.

Miss Riley: Maybe. Let's see. [The teacher puts her hand in and out of the puppet a few times, each time showing the leg without the finger.] No, it's still there.

Marta: Just cut it off.

Miss Riley: Well, that's an idea, but it's brand new. I don't want to cut up a brand new puppet!

Svetlana: I know. Let me show you. [Svetlana tries to put one of the legs inside the glove. It leaves a hole, and Svetlana shrugs and sits down.]

Miss Riley: Good try, Svetlana, but it still seems like it's not quite right.

Duane: Hey, maybe the guy who made it had six fingers!

This idea seems to satisfy many of the children, who nod. The children are excited about a possible solution.

Miss Riley: Maybe so. Let's see. How many fingers do you have on one hand?

Everyone spends time counting and recounting the fingers on their hands. Some repeat the counting three or four times.

Miss Riley: Does anyone have six fingers on a hand?

The children shake their heads no or respond verbally, saying they have five fingers. Others act like they do have six fingers, count aloud as they touch them, and then say that they have only five. After a few minutes they seem to be satisfied that no one in the class has six fingers.

Linda: [excitedly raising her hand] Umm . . . umm . . . maybe bees have six legs!

Duton: No, I have lots of bees at my house and they all have five legs! [Linda looks disappointed; because Duton is a class leader, most students believe he is right.]

Miss Riley: Maybe Linda has a good idea. How could we find out?

The children suggest many ideas, including going to the library center. After a brief discussion, the children disperse to different activity centers, some looking for books with bee pictures and others becoming involved in other activities. Angelica is still sitting, counting her fingers over and over again.

Angelica: [calling out after about five minutes] Teacher, teacher, look! If I count my fingers real fast, I get six!

This brief classroom vignette illustrates beautifully the variability and wonderful creativeness of young children as they attempt to solve a real problem. Russell's notion— that if the teacher's fingers are taken out and put back into the glove again, there would no longer be an extra leg—demonstrates a lack of number conservation, a characteristic common in many 4-year-olds. Russell seems to believe that if the appearance of the fingers in the puppet changes, the number of legs will change as well. Marta's and Svetlana's subtraction methods were expedient yet did not take into account any reason for the extra leg. Duane's creative idea about six-fingered people may indicate his lack of experience with other people's number of fingers. The class's ready belief that Duton's five-legged house bees are like all bees reveals faulty reasoning based on insufficient evidence. Finally, Angelica's humorous response illustrates an inefficient and incorrect "fast-counting" strategy and also reveals her ability to persist in seeking solutions.

Many research studies report findings consistent with the idea that children construct their mathematical knowledge through experiences. In addition, studies have suggested that the teacher's significant roles of observing, facilitating, supporting, and questioning are essential to that construction.

● Mathematics is for *everyone*. If mathematics is taught properly at the early childhood and elementary levels, all children should develop proficiency in it. Instances that appear to be learning disabilities in mathematics are often caused by inappropriate teaching rather than intellectual inadequacy.

● Few, if any, differences in young children's ability to learn mathematics relate to gender or socioeconomic status. Rather, *opportunity* to learn is the primary factor in the development of that ability.

● Young children make sense of mathematical situations in different ways. Not all children in a group represent or solve problems in the same way. Not all children follow the same specific developmental sequence. However, there are some *general trajectories or paths* that children travel and that teachers can follow that will give children experiences with a variety of thinking strategies and modeling procedures. (See Appendix B for a chart of these learning trajectories.)

Should we immediately correct young children's misconceptions about mathematics? Can we expect all children to solve problems in identical ways? Should we expect all the young children in a group to "get it" at the same time? Again, the answer to all these questions is *No!* As teachers, we need to remember that young children construct mathematical understanding in different ways, at different times, and with different materials. Our job is to provide an environment in which all children can learn mathematics.

3. The power of positive attitude

In 1990 President George H. W. Bush and the nation's governors established a list of national education goals to be reached in the year 2000. Goal one states, "By the year 2000, all children in America will start school ready to learn." While I understand that the panel was concerned about the physical, social, and emotional needs of the young child, my experience, supported by countless research studies, has demonstrated that the young child has long been more than ready to learn mathematics. In fact, by the time she starts school, she is already learning more complex mathematics than we might expect.

Young children are typically motivated to learn quantitative and spatial information. Their dispositions allow them to be positive and confident in their mathematical abilities. The highly prized characteristics of persistence, focused participation, hypothesis testing, risk taking, and self-regulation are often present, but seldom acknowledged, in the young child.

After describing a young child's strong motivation to learn mathematics, the National Research Council (1989; 2001) stated that a gradual change occurs in the early primary grades and described it as a shifting disposition from enthusiasm to apprehension and from confidence to fear. Unfortunately, this gradual change is often completed by third grade. In *Adding It Up*, members of the Council stated,

> Most U.S. children enter school eager to learn and with positive attitudes toward mathematics. It is critical that they encounter good mathematics teaching in the early grades.

Otherwise, those positive attitudes may turn sour as they come to see themselves as poor learners and mathematics as nonsensical, arbitrary, and impossible to learn except by rote memorization. (NRC 2001, 132)

After spending two years researching the motivation of 7- and 8-year-olds as they solve spatial tasks, I was amazed at the differences in motivation of children in that age group. Let me illustrate the two contrasting situations by describing two children's actions during a spatial task.

According to the cognitive ability measure in the example below, Roberto and Mei-Chi possessed almost the same analytical and quantitative ability. English was the first language for both children, and they both participated in a program for gifted students. To assess their specific motivation to solve problems, each child was given the choice of doing "easy" or "hard" symmetry tasks during a ten-minute session. Each task consisted of asking the child to place a mirror (held vertically) adjacent to a picture card (laid flat on the table) such that the image created by the picture and its reflection in the mirror looked like the image on the task card presented by the teacher. Unknown to the children, the easy tasks were quite easy and could be solved in less than fifteen seconds by the average 7-year-old, and the hard tasks were impossible because of the target image's nonsymmetrical characteristics.

See how Roberto's and Mei-Chi's responses differ in this problem-solving task:

A Matter of Motivation

Mrs. Evans: Mei-Chi, you may choose to do either the hard tasks or the easy ones. I don't care which ones you do, and you may stop at any time and change to another task. I will tell you if you have solved the problem or if you haven't solved the problem. But you do not need to solve the problem to move on to another task. It will be your choice. Understand?

Mei-Chi: I will take an easy one.

The task card is given to Mei-Chi, and she solves it in approximately fifteen seconds. The teacher states that it is correct.

Mei-Chi: I will take another easy one.

Again, Mei-Chi quickly solves it, and the teacher states that it is correct.

The activity continues for ten minutes. Mei-Chi solves more than thirty-five easy tasks, never asking for a hard one. Each time she solves one, she looks at the teacher and asks if it is correct.

Mrs. Evans: Mei-Chi, before you go . . . I noticed that you never tried a hard task. I was wondering why not. Could you tell me?

Mei-Chi: Yeah, I might get it wrong! You told me they are hard!

Mei-Chi leaves and Roberto enters. The same directions are given to Roberto.

Roberto: I will take a hard one.

Roberto eagerly takes the task card. He maneuvers the card and mirror, trying to complete the task in a variety of ways. Roberto works on the one hard task during the entire ten minutes, ignoring the teacher and never completing the task.

Mrs. Evans: Roberto, I am sorry, our time is up. You will need to leave the task here for now and go back to class.

Roberto: Aw, I was just about to get it. Can't I stay a little longer?

Mrs. Evans: No, I'm sorry. I promise to let you try again on another day.

As Roberto starts to leave, the teacher is busy preparing for another student. She glances up and sees Roberto placing the task card in his back pocket.

Mrs. Evans: Roberto, I need that card. I'm sorry, you will need to leave it with me.

Roberto: If you would just let me take it home, I know I could get it!

What different responses! Mei-Chi completes many tasks successfully; Roberto never successfully completes one task. Mei-Chi requires a teacher's acknowledgment of success; Roberto seems to ignore the teacher. Mei-Chi attempts short, easy tasks; Roberto demonstrates great persistence on only one task. Mei-Chi takes no risks; Roberto even risks taking the task card against the teacher's wishes.

Both of these children are smart, capable mathematics learners. However, on this task they demonstrate quite different motivational characteristics. Mei-Chi worked for the teacher's approval, performing many tasks but never trying hard ones. Her motivation could be termed *performance-oriented*. Roberto, on the other hand, worked to complete the task, persisting at a hard task in spite of his continual failure. His motivation could be termed *task-learning–oriented*.

Research indicates that disposition is very important to the long-term learning of mathematics (Renga & Dalla 1993). Disposition concerns more than attitudes toward mathematics alone; persistence, risk taking, hypothesis making, and self-regulation are all important to a motivated disposition.

● All children seem strongly motivated to perform well in school mathematics. By about third grade, however, important differences in both motivation and achievement begin to emerge.

● Performance-oriented children are motivated by others' approval and often "perform" to be successful. They frequently underestimate their successes and overestimate their failures. In addition, they demonstrate little persistence and, when confronted with a problem, can exhibit a state of "learned helplessness."

● Task-learning–oriented children are motivated by learning and view each task as something to be mastered. They seldom express interest in what others think; in fact, they often ignore feedback about success or failure. They frequently take risks, demonstrate great persistence, and often continue a task in spite of many obstacles.

● Teachers can directly influence performance-oriented children. When teachers stress learning rather than performance, significant differences are observable in children's motivation toward mathematics.

Should we ignore children's dispositions toward mathematics? Should we continually stress the importance of teacher-pleasing behavior when doing mathematics? Should we assume that young children fear mathematics and are as anxious as many adults when learning mathematics? Clearly, we should *not!*

Young children are motivated to do mathematics. Our job as teachers is to stress the importance of learning, model the joy of mastering tasks, and value errors as essential information to help us learn.

About this edition

In 2000, the National Council of Teachers of Mathematics published its landmark guide *Principles and Standards for School Mathematics*, setting mathematics education, prekindergarten through twelfth grade, on a path toward an exciting but "highly ambitious" new vision of "mathematics classrooms where students of varied backgrounds and abilities work with expert teachers, learning important mathematical ideas with understanding, in environments that are equitable, challenging, supportive, and technologically equipped for the 21st century" (NCTM 2000, 4).

I wrote the first edition of *The Young Child and Mathematics* that same year, aiming for a practical book for teachers that communicated the main ideas of NCTM's Standards within the context of effective, developmentally appropriate practice. My book followed the structure of the Standards, too—one chapter on what young children should know and be able to do with the five "processes" of mathematics (Problem Solving; Reasoning and Proof; Communication; Connections; and Representation) and a chapter each on the five mathematics "content areas" (Number and Operations; Algebra; Geometry; Measurement; and Data Analysis and Probability).

This second edition of *The Young Child and Mathematics* is very similar in purpose and structure to the first. What's different is that in the intervening ten years, there have been a number of important developments in the field of early childhood math education. In particular, the following new resources have influenced my thinking and teaching, and their insights are reflected in this second edition:

• researched, field-tested curricula specifically written for preschool children, funded by the National Science Foundation;

• two research volumes by the National Research Council—*Adding It Up: Helping Children Learn* (2001) and *Mathematics Learning in Early Childhood: Paths toward Excellence and Equity* (2009);

• the NAEYC/NCTM joint position statement, Early Childhood Mathematics: Promoting Good Beginnings, adopted in 2002;

• NCTM's *Curriculum Focal Points for Prekindergarten through Grade 8 Mathematics: A Quest for Coherence* (2006), which describes general mathematics expectations by grade level and outlines which objectives teachers should give the most attention; and

• *Learning and Teaching Early Math: The Learning Trajectories Approach* (Clements & Sarama 2009), which details children's learning paths, including developmental information by content area.

But for me, the most important developments over the last decade were the many new experiences I have had with young children in very diverse settings: Head Start centers, public prekindergarten programs, private and public school settings, children's museums, child care centers—and most exciting for me, discoveries with my four young grandsons!

The chapters at a glance

This first chapter has introduced you to young children and their characteristics as learners of mathematics—and as sources of learning for teachers, too! Let me restate the understandings expressed in this chapter, including their implications for teaching, in their most simplified form:

• Young children
   – possess a large amount of intuitive mathematical knowledge;

- continually construct mathematical ideas based on their experiences and observations; and
- are strongly motivated to do mathematics.

- Teachers of young children should
    - encourage investigation of and experimentation with mathematical concepts;
    - spend time observing, listening, and watching children; and
    - remember that *every* child is important.

Throughout the book these ideas will be illustrated through my descriptions of classroom situations, children's work products, and their interactions with one another and with adults.

Chapter 2 describes the framework that has guided me in my own work teaching and learning from young children. It consists of twelve guidelines for *curriculum, instruction,* and *assessment*—the three components of teaching. Further, the guidelines integrate what the National Association for the Education of Young Children suggested in its most recent statement on developmentally appropriate practice (NAEYC 2009) with NCTM's Focal Points (2006).

Like the first edition, the major portion of this book is six chapters that describe what young children should know about and be able to do with mathematics. Chapter 3 focuses on the five essential *processes* of mathematics. Chapters 4 through 8 focus on the five essential *content areas* of mathematics. In line with my belief about what makes for effective professional development (see the Question box opposite), the chapters on mathematics processes and content were written to connect teachers' knowledge and understanding with national curriculum standards and with children's learning paths.

Across my many, many conversations with teachers in classrooms and in trainings over the years, I often have been asked the same questions about teaching mathematics to young children. Some of these questions are answered in boxes sprinkled throughout the book. Other frequently asked questions, particularly those whose answers send readers elsewhere, I have collected in chapter 9.

This book contains two appendices. Appendix A provides instructions for accessing the accompanying DVD. Appendix B is a chart of learning trajectories for each of the content areas discussed in this book, originally from the NAEYC/NCTM joint position statement.

Finally, this 2010 book is accompanied by a DVD, on which NAEYC and I offer a menu of useful resources, including an expanded children's book list, the 2002 NAEYC/NCTM math position statement, and NCTM's Standards and Focal Points for prekindergarten through second grade. Most important, the DVD provides video clips from my own work in classrooms, demonstrating mathematics education in action and also giving a visual accompaniment to several of the activities I suggest in the content chapters.

*　　*　　*

I am constantly intrigued by young children, their characteristics, and their ways of learning mathematics. I hope as you read this book that my excitement is communicated and ignites your interest and efforts in educating the young child.

I'm a director of a preschool; what kind of mathematics professional development is best for my teachers?

Based on my experience teaching young children and my understanding of the research on adult learning, I believe the most effective professional development for teachers working with young children has seven critical elements:

The professional development fills any gaps in teachers' own *mathematics content knowledge* (Ma 1999; Ball & Bass 2000) and their *understanding of child development* or learning paths in specific mathematics areas. It helps teachers *make connections* between national standards (e.g., NCTM's Focal Points) and state/local learning outcome requirements. It describes *specific mathematics activities* for teachers to use in their classroom routines, small-group instruction, whole-group activities, and centers. It identifies which *instructional strategies* are particularly effective in mathematics. It *models activities* for teachers, as video clips and/or live in-class demonstrations. And it offers *coaching* that provides follow-up and specific goals.

This type of professional development is intensive and can be costly. But if mathematics is foundational to a young child's learning, and if we are to teach it with intentionality in early childhood classrooms, all these elements are necessary!

Chapter 2

A Framework for Teaching Mathematics to Young Children

It was the last day of the school year for me in my role as math consultant. The children had done well on their end-of-the-year tests and they were ready for second grade. As I was leaving the first grade classroom that I had shared with Ms. Frank each week during my instruction time, Brian came running up, bursting with some very important information. "Mrs. Copley, you always have lots of problems! Come by anytime next year and we will be happy to help. Have a good summer. . . . Oh, and remember, we will be in *second* grade!" Then, with a little wave, Brian ran off to play with his friends.

On that Friday afternoon, I traveled home elated by Brian's parting words. He was right; I always had a problem for them to solve. And I was glad he invited me to return next year. But those things weren't the cause of my elation. Why was I so excited? It was the idea that Brian *knew* that he and his classmates could solve problems! He felt powerful! I had taught them that they could solve problems and that they could help their teacher—because they had been doing it all year long. Yes! I had taught these first-graders to be powerful learners!

What made Brian's classroom a place where mathematical problems could be solved and children felt empowered? What was it about the curriculum that made solving problems the focus? What about my instruction gave ownership of the problem-solving process and solutions to the children? How had my weekly assessments during and after instruction affected my teaching and their learning? In other words, exactly what conditions are necessary for powerful mathematics to be learned and taught in early childhood classrooms?

This chapter discusses three components of teaching: (1) **curriculum**—*what* mathematics content and processes should be taught; (2) **instruction**—*how* children should be taught that curriculum; and (3) **assessment**—*finding out* what children know and can do and what more they need to learn. Further, from current research and resources (see the accompanying DVD for a detailed list), along with my own experience in teaching mathematics to young children, I have synthesized **guidelines** that I believe are critical in designing each component.

As valuable as I believe these insights are, they come with caveats: First, I offer these guidelines not as all-inclusive of *everything* you need to know to teach math well, but merely as a subset of ideas that I have found particularly useful in my own work with young children. Second, although I offer separate guidelines for each component, know that curriculum, instruction, and assessment are not distinct and separate areas. In fact, in a high-quality learning situation, they are interwoven and not easily teased apart. As Copple and Bredekamp (2009, 48) write in *Developmentally Appropriate Practice*, "Excellent teachers know that it's both what you teach [*curriculum*] AND how you teach [*instruction*]" that are important. To that statement I would add . . . AND how you know what to teach specific children [*assessment*].

Now let's look at each component.

My Guidelines for Curriculum	
1. Focus on important mathematics	Focus on the ideas, concepts, skills, and procedures that form the foundation for understanding and long-lasting learning.
2. Plan for connections	Intentionally plan for connections to guide the integration of the mathematics content with other content areas and with the child's world.
3. Emphasize the processes of mathematics	Emphasize the specific mathematics processes: problem solving, reasoning, communication, connections, and representation (all discussed in chapter 3).
4. Create a mathematics-rich environment	Create a setting that contains mathematics materials, ideas, books, visual models, and organization schemes and routines.

My Guidelines for Instruction	
1. Plan experiences	Plan experiences based on the curriculum and focusing on both child development generally and each child's specific development.
2. Orchestrate classroom activities	Orchestrate the environment and classroom events in which children engage in mathematical experiences.
3. Expect *all* children to learn mathematics	Challenge and support *all* children to learn mathematics.
4. Interact with children	Employ a variety of roles to promote interactions among the teacher, children, and their peers.

My Guidelines for Assessment	
1. Make child-centered choices	In making assessment decisions, take into account children's knowledge, abilities, and interests with the ultimate purpose of benefiting children's learning.
2. Observe and interact purposefully	Plan experiences for purposeful assessment and be prepared for unexpected opportunities.
3. Employ multiple sources of evidence	Collect multiple sources of evidence on a systematic basis over time.
4. Assess both children's learning and your teaching effectiveness	Be responsible; assess your own effectiveness in teaching each child, and also assess each child's learning.

Curriculum

- *What mathematics should we teach to young children?*
- *How could I possibly teach everything children need to know? Isn't there really too much to cover?*
- *What types of materials should I use to teach mathematics? Should I use a textbook or published curriculum?*
- *Is mathematics content or mathematics process more important?*
- *What about the center approach that is used in early childhood classrooms?*
- *How does mathematics curriculum fit into the environment of my early childhood setting? Where will I find the time to teach mathematics?*

The Curriculum Principle—one of six Principles that characterize high-quality mathematics education according to the National Council of Teachers of Mathematics—defines a high-quality mathematics curriculum as "more than a collection of activities: it must be coherent, focused on important mathematics, and well articulated across the grades" (2000, 14).

To teach mathematics effectively to young children, it is important that the teacher know the subject matter well. Yes, a teacher should be prepared and certainly have used many different sources to plan the curriculum she will teach. Yes, a teacher should carefully set up the environment to teach mathematics in the most effective manner. Yes, a teacher should be knowledgeable about the processes important in mathematics—such as reasoning and representation—and transfer that knowledge into her teaching practice.

But that said, classroom events that a teacher can link to mathematics learning occur hourly or even minute to minute—*if* she knows the content (the curriculum) well enough to make the jump away from what she had planned to teach. Young children especially will get excited or express special interest in a given center, a specific activity, or an intriguing problem—all of which present particularly good opportunities to extend children's mathematical thinking and learning—*if* their teacher recognizes and can capitalize on those occasions.

Curriculum guideline 1: *Focus on important mathematics.*

Mathematics for the young child is much more than arithmetic, counting, and learning to identify a square, rectangle, or triangle. That fact is evident in the very extensive lists of learning expectations detailed in NCTM's *Principles and Standards for School Mathematics* (2000). But at any point in children's math learning, some areas and concepts are more important than others.

NCTM's publication *Curriculum Focal Points for Prekindergarten through Grade 8 Mathematics: A Quest for Coherence* (2006) addresses this by synthesizing, from those many expectations, a set of "focal points"—ideas, concepts, skills, and procedures that need to be acquired at each grade level to form the foundation for understanding mathematics at various ages. Just three focal points are recommended for each grade level, prekindergarten through second grade, with the aim of helping teachers focus on the most important curriculum goals and expectations for an age group. Across the grades, *number and operations* is a focal point for all four grade levels; *geometry* and *measurement* are each a focal point for three of the four grade levels. (See the charts on the accompanying DVD.)

Identifying a limited number of focal points in mathematics content means that the curriculum can be coherent, articulated across each grade level, and relevant to children at each level. Most critical, when there is a focus on important mathematics, teachers can plan their curriculum to achieve important learning goals. The Focal Points identified by NCTM are based on what we know from research about the relationships and learning trajectories of important mathematical ideas, which build upon one another sequentially. The content of mathematics should be worthwhile for young children to learn, as accurate and clear as possible, and not oversimplified or presented with confusing or incorrect information (NAEYC & NCTM 2002).

Curriculum guideline 2: *Plan for connections.*

The three focal points for mathematics that NCTM identifies as the major emphases for a given grade level comprise only part of the mathematics that is useful and important for children at that age. There are also important connections to other curriculum areas, in math and in other content domains. These connections are critical to consider as teachers set up the classroom environment and learning experiences and plan integration activities across the curriculum.

Finally, understanding mathematics is an essential goal in any math classroom. By definition, a person "understands" something if she sees how it is related or connected to other things she knows (Hiebert & Carpenter 1992; Lambdin 2003). That a curriculum make such connections is especially important, and connecting should be intentionally planned to occur in a variety of classroom activities and places.

Curriculum guideline 3: *Emphasize the processes of mathematics.*

To *know* mathematics is to *do* mathematics. While mathematics content is very important, the mathematics *processes* (problem solving, reasoning, communication, connections, and representation) are equally significant for young children.

To incorporate these process skills, the curriculum must include: (1) the use of mathematics to solve problems, (2) an application of logical reasoning to justify procedures and solutions, (3) multiple ways to communicate about the ideas within and outside of mathematics, (4) connections between different mathematics content areas as well as connections across grade levels, and (5) an analysis of multiple representations. A good mathematics curriculum includes experiences in which children solve problems, reason and think, communicate in a variety of ways, make connections, and represent concepts with pictures and symbols (NCTM 2000).

Curriculum guideline 4: *Create a mathematics-rich environment.*

The physical environment is a key part of the mathematics program. In planning curriculum, teachers should consider the manipulatives, games, books, and other math materials that will help children acquire the skills and concepts in the curriculum, as well as how these materials should be organized and placed in the room. The goal of such planning is to provide a mathematics-rich environment. Math materials include concrete manipulatives (e.g., blocks, counters, base-10 blocks, pattern blocks, attribute blocks, two-color counters, a variety of containers, measuring tools, tangrams); symbolic materials (dice, dominoes, number lines, graphs, 10-frame, 100s chart, and other visual models); and more abstract representations (plastic numerals, diagrams, calculators, computers, store coupons).

The typical day in an early childhood classroom can and should be mathematics rich across the full schedule. Each of the day's activities—class projects, art, science, language arts, music, and physical exercise—should be conducive to mathematics and be adapted to a variety of settings (transitions, centers, small groups, circle time, outside and inside play, and at-home activities). In a mathematics-rich environment, mathematics can be found anywhere and everywhere!

The guidelines in action

To illustrate these four curriculum guidelines, let's listen in on a group of prekindergarten teachers in a program for children who have been identified as "high need" students. The teachers have just returned from a presentation on mathematics entitled, "Where's the Math? Intentionally and Appropriately Teaching Mathematics in the Early Childhood Classroom." They have been asked to make an action plan for mathematics for the next month in their classrooms, a plan that will be shared with the school director at the end of the week.

This teaching team consists of four teachers: Valerie, the team leader, with more than twenty-five years of experience; Samantha, a new teacher to prekindergarten, with ten years of first grade experience in a private, highly academic school; Craig, an experienced teacher strongly focused on literacy; and Dana, a teacher with less than five years of experience who has always loved mathematics. Three of them have a college degree, one in language arts and teaching, one in early childhood and child development, and the other in education, including certification for first through sixth grade. One teacher has a CDA and is working on an associate's degree in early childhood education at a local community college.

> **Valerie:** Well, what did you think of the presentation? You know I need to submit an action plan on Friday, so we will need to think of something that we will do from what she said.

> **Craig:** It wasn't bad considering it was math. . . . I have never liked math, and I really am not sure why we should spend so much time on it. As we all know, literacy is the primary focus of what we do with young children!

> **Samantha:** You're right, Craig, as long as you include social and emotional skills. You know how important those are to *our* students. They need those skills to compete with others when they go on to kindergarten. It's our responsibility to focus on the most important things for our kids, don't you think? I am not sure we have much time for the math that lady was talking about.

> **Dana:** Oh, I know I am new and everything, but I really like math and I think some of our children like it, too. I was listening to Jeremiah and Ellie yesterday and they were trying to count all the blocks in the block center. It was so cool! They spent a long time making sure everything was counted right and they didn't leave anything out. I thought it was really amazing how they worked at it. . . . Oh, they left out some numbers, and after they got to "forty-nine," they just said "one hundred" together! They just giggled and giggled and then tried it again, each time ending on "one hundred" regardless of how far they got! It was really neat.

> **Samantha:** Yes, counting is important. We can certainly stress that more. In fact, I really liked that pattern counting idea the presenter suggested for transitions. The kids would enjoy it *and* it would help with their physical development. *And,* as I have said, I think it is important for children to understand 100 because they will need to in first grade!

> **Valerie:** Okay, let me write down that idea . . . "Use pattern counting in daily transitions." That's one thing and it certainly won't take much time. What about other number ideas? She said they were important.

Dana: I loved all the number games she showed us! We could add those to the game center . . . I could do that! And I think we could do more number activities in the other centers, don't you? Like number sculptures in the art center or that tower game in the block center with the die? Those would be good for the kids *and* we would be focusing on the important number ideas!

Craig: Now that I think of it, I really liked the idea of the children publishing a math book every once in a while . . . I know that is not a surprise to you all! Let me work with that idea. I think some of the books we read every week could incorporate math sometimes, and then the children can make their own versions.

Valerie: Okay, I think I have the next idea for our plan: "Put number ideas in the game center, the art center, the block center, and the publishing center." Does that sound okay? Now, what else?

Samantha: Well, I think we are ignoring an important idea, but it's one that I am just not sure about. She talked about teaching math in small groups just like we do literacy and then having the children work in math stations. How will we have time for that?

Valerie: Yes, I thought about the same issue while she was talking. Let's investigate that idea next week at our regular meeting and meanwhile let's all think about the possibilities. I bet we can come up with some workable ideas . . . we are quite a team, you know! I will even put that in our action plan: "Investigate teaching math in small groups and possibly math stations." What else?

Craig: One more idea. What about doing some math things in our classroom environments? I know my classroom doesn't even have written numbers, and I certainly don't have any children's math projects or work displayed. I need to get those math shapes out of the closet, too. . . . I need you guys to help me!

Valerie: Great! That is one more point for our action plan: "Make suggestions to each other about how our classrooms can be more mathematical." Thanks. I will write this up and let you all look at it before I give it to Ms. Nevaras.

This vignette illustrates the importance of teachers understanding the mathematics curriculum that *should* be taught in the prekindergarten classroom. But because prekindergarten teachers often are not aware of the important mathematics they could be teaching, they don't allot a sufficient amount of time to try. These teachers focused on number and patterns as they began to plan for increased math studies with their students; however, although they didn't come up in this particular conversation, other math content areas, particularly geometry and measurement, are also very important for young children.

Q There is so much to do in an early childhood classroom. How do you fit in mathematics?

Mathematics belongs in any part of the day and connects with *all* the other curriculum areas such as literacy, social studies, social/emotional development, and the rest. The more you observe children doing mathematics and become aware of mathematics content and processes, the more connections you see and the more mathematics "fits into" your day. That said, there are some specific things that the teacher can do to find the math in each day.

First, identify the events in your classroom that typically occur each day: routines, small-group meetings, center time, circle time, guided reading, and so on. Now, consider how mathematics can fit into each event. For example, for the specific routines and transitions that you do every day, make some of those incorporate counting and pattern rhymes (see chapters 4 and 5), growing patterns (chapter 5), or graphing activities (chapter 8). Mathematics should be evident in centers and during small-group meetings when mathematics is the primary focus—for example, Exploring Pennies (see the Connections section in chapter 3) and "Where's the Bear?" (see the Activities section in chapter 4). Additionally, during your circle time activities that begin and end each day, you can involve mathematics by playing games that encourage mathematical reasoning—for example, Guess My Cage (see the Reasoning section in chapter 3), Domino Flash or Mystery Shapes (see the Activities section in chapter 6)—or by reflecting on math-focused activities that children did during center time.

We know that early mathematics is foundational to a young child's learning and a predictor of later school success, and math should be a pervasive and intentional part of every early childhood classroom.

Valerie, Samantha, Craig, and Dana, coming to their discussion with very different experiences, were able to take some small steps toward teaching important mathematics. Because they were required to construct an action plan, the professional development experience became more than just another presentation easily forgotten. Instead, it was an opportunity for the teachers to use some of the ideas presented and make those ideas their own.

Did you hear them plan for the mathematics process of connections? Dana's mention of centers helped Craig volunteer for some math ideas around his favorite subject, literacy; and Samantha was able to connect a number activity to transitions. The teachers did not explicitly consider how to promote children's use of the other mathematical processes, but those such as representing and communicating number are likely to arise in Craig's book publishing center, Dana's number sculptures, and other experiences they plan. And the teachers can give the processes more explicit attention in their subsequent planning sessions.

Finally, Craig's acknowledgment that he needs some help with his un-mathematical classroom was just the first step in creating a mathematics-rich environment. This team of teachers is just beginning to see a mathematics curriculum that can develop powerful learners. Ultimately, if all four of the curriculum guidelines I suggest in this chapter are implemented, children will benefit from relevant mathematics and gain an important foundation for understanding and learning.

Instruction

- *How does an effective teacher support children's learning in mathematics? What should I do to help young children develop their mathematical reasoning?*
- *What kinds of classroom interactions and other instructional strategies promote math learning?*
- *In what ways should classroom learning be child guided and in what ways should it be teacher guided?*
- *How do I interact with children? What about those children who have difficulty or who already seem to know the concept or skill I am focusing on?*
- *How can I expect everyone to learn the same mathematics?*

"Instruction" typically describes the *how* of the education process—the pedagogy. NCTM's Teaching Principle says, "Effective mathematics teaching requires understanding what students know and need to learn and then challenging and supporting them to learn it well" (2000, 16), which is an excellent summary of my instruction guidelines. Naturally, assessment of each child's strengths, needs, and interests along with a firm knowledge of child development are important prerequisites for effective instruction. Then, having methods and strategies at the ready to help challenge and support children's learning is critical. As you analyze the guidelines below, note that they all emphasize the teacher's intentionality. As early childhood teachers, we must be intentional and thoughtful as we plan experiences, orchestrate classroom activities, communicate high expectations, and interact with children in a variety of ways.

Instruction guideline 1: *Plan experiences.*

To plan experiences in mathematics, teachers must make decisions based on many considerations. Intentionally planned experiences are based on the curriculum goals; are often related to children's interests; and take into account child development, the cultural backgrounds of children and their families, and differences among children as individuals.

Teachers must teach mathematics with understanding, actively build new knowledge from experiences, and use a variety of modes (visual, auditory, physical, emotional, cognitive) to communicate. To introduce mathematical concepts as well as the language of mathematics, a range of appropriate experiences and teaching strategies should be employed.

Instruction guideline 2: *Orchestrate classroom activities.*

The effective early childhood teacher works to enable each child in the group to attain a number of learning goals in mathematics as well as in other areas. To do this, the teacher orchestrates the many learning activities, events, groups, and experiences typical in early childhood classrooms. This includes scheduling small- and whole-group times, indoor and outdoor play, projects, and centers during the day and across the weeks and months. Through the physical environment, schedule, learning contexts, and materials, the teacher can facilitate the learning of mathematics.

Across the many activities planned during the day, young children require and should expect consistency and equality modeled through schedules, plans, and general organization. Learning experiences should include opportunities to use mathematics processes—to problem solve, reason, communicate, connect, and represent. A variety of learning formats and materials should be used purposefully so that the needs of children may be met. All young children should be able to expect that they will have ample time to explore, materials to facilitate and support their learning, and teacher support.

As emphasized in the NAEYC/NCTM joint position statement, our instruction should "provide for children's deep and sustained interaction with key mathematical ideas" (2002, 9).

Instruction guideline 3: *Expect* all *children to learn mathematics.*

NCTM's Equity Principle states, "Excellence in mathematics education requires equity—high expectations and strong support for all students" (2000, 12). Differences in children's math knowledge are already evident when they begin kindergarten or even preschool (Denton & West 2002; Barbarin et al. 2006) as a result of differences in the learning opportunities they have had. And research shows that early math performance is a strong predictor of later achievement (Duncan et al. 2007). Yet some teachers think that mathematics is "too hard" or "inappropriate" for young children.

Nothing can be further from the truth. Teachers must understand that *all* children can learn mathematics—and the belief in each child's capability for mathematics learning must show in their instruction. What does that mean? It means that teachers need to provide learning opportunities for *all* children, so that each child can reach his or her potential. To that end, teachers must challenge and support children equitably; consider all domains of learning; and continue to base their

How can we put into action the philosophy that *all* children can learn mathematics successfully?

Through a combination of high expectations and strong support for all children, according to both NAEYC (1996b; 2009) and NCTM (2000).

To make equity a reality, certain things must happen. First, young children must have ample opportunity to learn mathematics. For the teacher, this imperative means constructing a solid curriculum based on what children should know and be able to do at a given grade level, providing the learning experiences to achieve these goals, and individualizing instruction to meet the needs of each child.

Second, high expectations for children must be conveyed by the adults in their lives, family members and teachers alike. But the nature of those expectations matters. We want children to understand it is through their *efforts* that they will be able to learn mathematics. This means we emphasize and reinforce effort ("Peter, you've been working on that puzzle for a long time, and now you've finished it . . . nice work!") rather than focus on some presumed math aptitude ("You have such a good math brain, Peter. You always get your addition problems right!"). Also, we model and emphasize positive dispositions toward math, such as persistence, flexibility, and effort, when children see us working through math problems ourselves.

Finally, access to mathematical resources is key to equity. That means being aware of manipulatives, technology, books, and other materials that help children develop mathematical understanding. Recognizing the value of such materials, we can advocate for adequate and equitable distribution of resources within the school, district, and community.

teaching practice on knowledge of mathematics content and processes, understanding of young children's mathematical development, and familiarity with what each individual child knows and is able to do.

Instruction guideline 4: *Interact with children.*

Research clearly documents the importance of the early childhood teacher in children's learning (see Anderson, Anderson, & Thauberger 2008; NRC 2009). But the nature of the teacher's role has been widely debated. To what extent should classroom learning be child guided or teacher guided? When should a teacher intervene? Which learning goals are best achieved in teacher-planned and -guided activities? When should an adult not interact with a child and encourage peer interactions instead?

There are many teaching strategies in a teacher's toolkit, and their effectiveness depends on the activity, the purpose, and the child or children involved. These strategies can fall anywhere along a continuum—from direct to indirect interactions, or from a largely teacher-guided to a highly child-guided approach. The teacher's interaction with a child can be simple acknowledgement ("You've picked the triangle") or modeling ("Hmm, I need to check my answer") or a direct demonstration (writing the number 6). At another point, the teacher may decide to add challenge to the activity; for example, she may cover three of five checkers and ask, "Remember there are five checkers in all. How many are under the napkin?" Or she may offer a hint or clue as scaffolding to allow a child to take on a challenging task. Whatever role the teacher plays in the interaction, the teacher should take it on *intentionally*.

Just as important as having strategies available is choosing which strategy to use and when. The effective early childhood teacher decides when to let a child struggle with a problem; when to give a direct or indirect clue or demonstrate a process; and when to pose a new, more challenging question. The teacher also needs to decide when to give a child feedback about a response and when to comment about a child's result or product.

The teacher also makes a set of decisions concerning interacting with children to promote math thinking and learning. For example, the teacher decides how to provide support when children are frustrated, how to pose problems in ways that engage children, and how to respond to children's answers or offer cues to encourage further thinking.

The guidelines in action

This fourth instruction guideline emphasizes that classroom discourse is an essential component in the learning of mathematics and that the teacher's decisions about those interactions are critical, as is evident in the vignette below.

> In a large elementary school in a culturally diverse, urban setting, Ms. Henekee teaches twenty-five second-graders, who show varying levels of ability. In her classroom, children often work on a variety of activities, independently and in learning centers, while Ms. Henekee works with one small group and then another. In order to help the children do this, Ms. Henekee prints clear, concise instructions on the chalkboard every morning.
>
> This morning she writes an estimation question: "How many times could you snap your fingers in a minute (if your fingers didn't get tired)?" The children get index cards from the middle of the table and practice snapping their fingers. As the children are talking to each other and recording numbers, she walks around answering questions, showing a child how to snap his or her fingers when asked for help, and encouraging them to record their estimates.
>
> **Ms. Henekee:** [stopping at Seth's table] Seth, what's your estimate?

Seth: [shrugs] I don't know.

Ms. Henekee: I don't know either, but I wonder . . . maybe one thousand? Do you think one thousand is too much? Or what about five—too little?

Seth: [gives a small smile] No, you're silly. It can't be that big or that little. Umm, maybe twenty? [doubtfully waits for a response]

Ms. Henekee: [smiles] Who knows? Could be. [She pats him on the shoulder and whispers an encouragement.] I'm glad you're trying!

When everyone has recorded an estimate, the children form a number line, arranging themselves in order from the smallest estimate to the largest, and holding up their estimates written on index cards.

Children: [talking to each other] I wrote 34. Is my number bigger? . . . No, you are smaller than me. . . . I wrote 28. . . . Hey, you are out of order! You belong over there! . . . Wow, I've got 100. I'm probably way over there.

In a few minutes the line gets quiet.

Ms. Henekee: We are ready to look at our data. Alicia, I think it is your turn to be Data Director. I will hold your place in the number line.

Alicia: [stepping out of position] Okay, everybody say your number. Listen for the number that's said the most, because I will ask you when you're done. [points to the beginning of the line] Start here!

One after another, the children say their numbers. Several children are out of order and change places as the errors are discovered.

Alicia: Okay, what number did we hear the most?

Sam: Twenty-five—there were three of those.

Alicia: That means 25 is the *mode*. Fernando, will you be the Recorder? [Fernando goes to the chalkboard and records the mode underneath the question Ms. Henekee had written earlier.] . . . Now, what about the *range*?

Paula: It starts with a 3 and goes to 200!

Some of the children start to giggle about the large guess of 200. Ms. Henekee gives a "teacher look" to those who appear to be making fun.

Ms. Henekee: So then, what would the range be? Remember, to find the range, it is 200 subtract 3. . . . What would it be?

Alicia: It's . . . uh . . . 197. Fernando, would you please write it? . . . I think we are done. Ms. Henekee, is that everything?

Ms. Henekee: Thank you, Alicia, but I think there is one more thing we need to know. What about the middle number, the *median*?

The class find the median by returning to their seats two at a time—one from each end of the line. When only one child, Chet, is left standing, he says his number. Ms. Henekee reminds the children that the number in the middle of data arranged in a number line is called a median. (If two children remain standing, the number halfway between their two estimates is the median.) Fernando records Chet's number on the chalkboard.

Ms. Henekee: Remember that we will work on getting a better estimate at the end of class today. Alicia, you were an excellent Data Director. Thank you. Everyone, think about what kind of sample we will need to make a better estimate. Our first estimation range was from 3 to 200, or 197! Remember, we will know we have a better estimate when our estimations have a smaller range of answers . . . something smaller than 197!

While the teacher meets with two groups of children for about twenty minutes each, the others continue to work independently or together in various centers or at their seats.

When Ms. Henekee returns to the finger-snapping activity later that morning, she asks the children to suggest how they might make a better estimate. The best suggestion (as determined by a class discussion) is to count finger snaps for half a minute and then double the number. Ms. Henekee times the thirty seconds, and the children record their counts then begin their calculations.

Conversation is lively as the children try to determine a better estimate, sharing methods and discussing calculations. Some children get calculators; others count on their fingers. Several get place-value blocks, while still others calculate on paper.

When the lunch bell rings, Ms. Henekee reminds her class that they can do more estimating at home. She asks them to time someone at home snapping his or her fingers for thirty seconds, record the number of times that person snaps, and add the number twice to get a better estimate. The next day they will share their results and make a new number line.

Ms. Henekee has thoughtfully planned the day's schedule, activities at the learning centers, small-group meetings, and the various strategies she used throughout the activity to contribute to a mathematics experience that meets each child's individual needs. Her expectation is that *all* children can participate in this activity and learn mathematics. Her interaction with Seth—providing boundaries for his first estimation—is an indication that she wants him to be a successful thinker.

Note that this teacher's interactions with the children are highly dependent on the context and the children's responses. While the children are talking, helping each other, and comparing numbers, Ms. Henekee appears to be very nondirective—answering questions, demonstrating, and encouraging. During Alicia's leading, she even participates in the activity with the children by holding Alicia's place in the number line. Throughout the activity, however, she encourages self-regulation and interactions among the children. Her role is that of facilitator when Alicia acts as the Data Director. Ms. Henekee briefly lends a hand when the children forget to find the median. The organization and structure provided by Ms. Henekee, although not obvious to the children, underlie all aspects of the math activities in her classroom.

This classroom vignette illustrates a well organized, intentionally planned classroom experience in which children are exploring statistical concepts. The teacher has planned experiences, orchestrated classroom activities, and interacted with children in a variety of ways. She knows the math content that is relevant and appropriate for children of this age and is able to translate it into a physical activity that allows them to visually see the data and connect it accurately to vocabulary. Most important, her interactions and the content of her lesson indicate that she expects all children to learn . . . *and* that they are motivated to do so!

Assessment

- *How does an effective teacher assess what young children know about mathematics? How can a child's reasoning or problem-solving skills be assessed?*
- *How can I know what is developmentally appropriate for young children in mathematics?*

- *What sequences of learning are there for the concepts and skills we want children to acquire?*
- *As busy as I am—organizing an inviting learning environment, planning and carrying out the curriculum, interacting with children to enhance their learning—how can I still find time to assess each child's understanding in mathematics and other learning domains?*

When people hear "assessment," they often think of testing; but the word has a much broader meaning. The Assessment Principle described in NCTM's *Principles and Standards* states, "Assessment should support the learning of important mathematics and furnish useful information to both teachers and students" (2000, 22).

Assessment includes observing children; gathering evidence about each child's knowledge, behaviors, and dispositions; documenting the work that children do and how they do it; and making inferences from that evidence for a variety of purposes. Certainly, many of those purposes are important: to report and inform parents, to identify a child who could benefit from early intervention, or to analyze the benefits of a particular program or curriculum. In this book, however, assessment for the purpose of informing instruction—thus directly benefiting the child—is the primary focus.

With practice and persistence as they continue to learn about children's mathematical thinking, teachers are able to make the processes of thoughtful observation and questioning that characterize good assessment part of their natural routine. To develop these important skills, teachers should plan daily observations that involve watching and listening as children interact, as well as talking with each child and carefully listening to the child's responses. Because different children show what they know and can do in different ways, assessment should include multiple approaches in order to give a well rounded picture and allow each child to show his or her strengths (NCTM 2000).

Assessment guideline 1: *Make child-centered choices.*

An instructional purpose of assessment is to identify children's progress toward goals that are developmentally and educationally significant. To do this, teachers must first focus on each child's knowledge, abilities, and interests and then assess the child's current status with regard to those goals. When curriculum outcomes and goals for each child's learning align, teachers can make child-centered decisions about their teaching that take into account each child's knowledge, abilities, and interests, with the ultimate purpose of benefiting children.

To be most effective, assessments should take place before, during, and after instruction. The teacher assesses before instruction to plan the children's learning experiences. During the learning experience, the teacher observes and asks questions, listens to children's responses, and watches their behaviors. After the experience the teacher observes, considers work samples, or otherwise assesses what the children have learned.

If aspects of a child's work or his responses indicate a misconception or lack of understanding, the teacher uses this information to make adjustments in the curriculum or her teaching practices as needed to enhance the child's learning and understanding. For example, if assessments show a particular mathematics program to be ineffective with a number of the children, with respect to either their learning or their development of positive dispositions toward math, the teacher may want to consider a new curriculum or new instructional methods. Most important, assessment of mathematical understanding should identify strengths and specific needs of young children.

Assessing children's understanding of mathematics in real, natural settings helps teachers to adapt their teaching styles and curricular materials to children's diverse learning styles. Moreover, when assessment becomes a routine part of the ongoing classroom activity, learning is not interrupted.

Assessment guideline 2: *Observe and interact purposefully.*

Observation of and interactions with children in purposeful ways can provide much assessment information. Young children often are not proficient in expressing themselves in writing or conversation; this is especially true when children's home language is not English. Thus, it is not always evident what children know and can do from just their written or verbal answers. Instead, the teacher also must plan experiences expressly to closely observe children's actions, behaviors, and interactions and carefully listen in on them as they talk. Observations that are systematic and planned, sometimes recorded on audio or video for later review, make for valid, objective assessments (Bergen 1997; Boehm & Weinberg 1997). Observations should be planned to relate directly to mathematics goals and outcomes. For example, a teacher might set up an observation of two children playing a game that involves the rolling of a number cube and moving a specified number of spaces to provide himself with data regarding each child's ability to subitize and use one-to-one correspondence to count (see chapter 4 for more number and operations examples). Or he might arrange to interact with a few children as they complete a square puzzle made up of triangle pieces; asking them to explain how the pieces should fit can provide evidence of each child's understanding of spatial vocabulary (see chapter 6 for more geometry and spatial sense examples).

Such planned occasions are a core part of being intentional, but the excellent teacher also is prepared when unexpected assessment opportunities arise. As a child talks about his "giant" dog, a teacher familiar with measurement content can ask specific questions using measurement vocabulary and note the child's understanding of such attributes (see chapter 7 for more measurement examples). Or when a child exclaims, "I see a pattern!" when looking at a 100s chart, the teacher can ask him to recreate the pattern by coloring the squares that are part of the pattern and using his words to tell about it (see chapter 5 for more pattern examples).

Effective questioning and careful listening are just the beginning of assessment. The teacher should also have ready a method of recording the specific observations, the context in which they occur, and which children are involved. By observing and interacting on both planned and spontaneous occasions, the teacher can get a good picture of each child's understanding and can use the information in planning instruction.

Assessment guideline 3: *Employ multiple sources of evidence.*

Evidence of various kinds from multiple sources should be collected and reviewed on a systematic basis over time. Assessments should gather evidence about all aspects of mathematics learning: the mathematics that children know (content), their ability to use it (processes), and their attitudes toward math (dispositions). That evidence could take many forms, including samples of children's mathematical work, audiotaped descriptions of their problem-solving discussions, and anecdotal records describing children's work at centers and on mathematical tasks.

One important source of evidence would be developmental checklists specific to mathematics. Such a checklist, or *learning trajectory*, describes the goals of learning and the thinking and learning processes typical of children at various levels of development. (Clements and Sarama's 2009 book *Learning and Teaching Early Math: The Learning Trajectories Approach* is an excellent, research-based source of information for mathematics goals and child development concepts.) Because each level provides a "natural developmental building block to the next level" (Clements & Sarama 2009, 5), assessments matched to the checklist would provide important information on what the children—as a group and individually—will be ready for next.

Assessment guideline 4: *Assess both children's learning and your teaching effectiveness.*

At its best, assessment supports the learning of important mathematics and furnishes useful information to both teachers and learners about their growth and progress (NCTM 2000). To assess children's growth in mathematical understanding, the teacher observes, listens, collects, and documents what they can do independently and with assistance. To assess his or her own teaching behavior and effectiveness, the teacher uses this evidence of children's learning to figure out what is working and what is not with regard to curriculum and instruction.

The guidelines in action

The activity described in the vignette below provides examples of the four assessment guidelines in a kindergarten classroom.

It is circle time, and the children are participating in a weekly activity involving a particular type of reasoning. The gathering provides many assessment opportunities for Mr. Garza, the teacher. The activity requires children to answer the question of the day by placing their vote (in the form of a wooden cube) in either the YES bag or the NO bag. The question of the day, "Do you have a dog?" is represented in rebus form on the YES/NO bags.

Mr. Garza: Can anyone tell me how many children are in our class?

Ian: Twenty-two. There always is, unless somebody's gone!

Mr. Garza: Is everybody here? Has everybody voted?

Antonio: Maria's gone and so is Lisa. So we just got . . . uh [looks at the numbers on the 100s chart, finds 22, and goes back two numbers] . . . twenty, I think.

Mr. Garza: Let's listen to Antonio as he tells us how he got his answer.

Antonio describes and demonstrates his procedure using the 100s chart, a representation with ten numbers per line, displayed as a 10-by-10 grid.

Mr. Garza: Does everyone agree with Antonio? Amy, what do you think?

Amy: Yeah! I just counted us and got twenty.

Everyone quickly counts the class members present and a consensus is reached. Mr. Garza circles the numeral 20 on the 100s chart.

Mr. Garza: Let's see, what is our question today? [He points to the question of the day: The YES bag has a picture of a dog; and the NO bag has the same picture, but with a large X over the dog.]

Children: "Do you have a dog?"

Mr. Garza: All right, let's empty the NO bag. [As the teacher empties out the NO cubes, he assigns Counters.] Hunter, Joanne, and Jorge, you are the Counters today. Remember that the three of you must get the same answer before you report it back to us.

Hunter, Joanne, and Jorge: [returning to report their findings after a quick count] We got five in the NO bag, so five people don't have a dog!

Mr. Garza: Okay, now comes the hard question. How many cubes are in the YES bag? Remember, twenty people voted and there are five NO votes. . . . I wonder how many cubes are in the YES bag? . . . Let's think about it for a while. Remember, good thinkers don't yell out answers; they put them in their heads and think about them.

The teacher observes the ensuing flurry of activity. Some children seem to be counting the class again and trying to eliminate five children, while others use their fingers and ask friends for help. Still others focus on the calendar board, counting backwards. A few children watch everyone else and seem totally confused. Patrick sits quietly, looking confident. Mr. Garza makes notes in a notebook, recording the children's behaviors.

Mr. Garza: Well, I think everyone is ready. Please share your answer with a partner. [The children are used to this request and quickly share their results.] Now, who would like to share their answer with the class?

One at a time, answers are shared, discussed, and demonstrated. As children tell their answers, Mr. Garza takes more notes.

Eleana: It's a lot. More than ten because I counted the five cubes in the NO bag on one hand, and I needed Terry's fingers *and* mine to figure out how many were in the YES bag.

Federico: It's twenty-two because I know it.

Patrick: It's fifteen! I know because we have done this one lots of times before. A 5 and a 10 always make 15!

Silvie: I think it's sixteen because I counted on that [points to the 100s chart].

Tatanene: It's five! . . . [Mr. Garza asks whether he thinks there are five cubes in both the YES and the NO bags.] Yeah, I guess so. That way it would be fair!

Dominique: Can I count the YES cubes?

Making anecdotal records, Mr. Garza jots down phrases to describe some of the children's responses: "Eleana has good number sense about the value of the cubes in the YES bag." . . . "Federico demonstrates no understanding of the problem and answers using the one piece of information he remembers." . . . "Patrick understands the part-part-whole relationship of 5, 10, and 15." . . . "Silvie has almost mastered the counting backward strategy." . . . "Tatanene has this concept confused with an equalization problem from last week." . . . "Dominique can solve the problem only by counting the cubes in the YES bag."

From his notes, Mr. Garza can plan further experiences that will address individual children's needs as well as continue the weekly YES/NO activity during circle time.

In this vignette Mr. Garza listens carefully to children's responses to his problem-solving activity so he can plan more activities to benefit their learning. To best accomplish this, teachers must spend a great deal of time observing and listening to children, a process detailed in the second assessment guideline. Note the many opportunities for Mr. Garza to listen and observe children's thinking throughout the lesson. Finally, because this is a weekly activity, the teacher has a regular opportunity to assess children's mathematical understanding as it develops. Based on his notes, he can examine the growth of individual children as well as analyze the effectiveness of his teaching across the whole class.

In this learning activity, all four guidelines of assessment are evident, as well as many of the instruction and curriculum guidelines. Good assessment benefits children. It involves observing and listening, collecting and documenting evidence, and assessing growth. Effective assessment enhances instruction, which in turn is grounded in a well designed curriculum.

All three sets of guidelines are essential and intertwined in good educational experiences. As we look at specific mathematical processes and content in the chapters that follow, remember the statement suggested at the beginning of this chapter: Excellent teachers know that what you teach (curriculum), how you teach (instruction), AND how you know what to teach (assessment) are all important.

As you read the vignettes throughout this book, you should see examples of the twelve guidelines of my framework for teaching, and then try to apply them to your own settings.

Organizing the classroom to maximize math

Questions I am asked about classroom organization are some of the most common and important . . . and ones I consider on a daily basis in my own work with children. To teach mathematics effectively, I know I must make good decisions about the size of groups that I teach (i.e., is a whole-group format best for the activity I want to do, or would it be better to break into small groups?), the centers I will use, and the organization of materials in my classroom. In addition, I need to be intentional and appropriate about how I make these decisions.

Should I teach the whole group, or should I work only with small groups and at learning centers?

Sometimes I work with all the children as a group; for example, doing graphing activities that require total class participation (see chapter 8) or very active and noisy experiences such as the launching of a balloon rocket or a race to the watering hole (see chapter 7). Teaching the whole group of children in these cases just makes sense. But in small groups, I see children really thinking and learning math particularly well, I can follow up more, and I see those experiences carrying over to children's play, their daily routines, and all areas of the curriculum. So I make sure to do lots of small-group work, and I hear other teachers say they find it helpful, too.

When making decisions about forming groups, I first focus on what the children will be doing and learning. Sometimes what we are going to be doing requires children to have learned certain concepts and yet not be well beyond for the activity at hand. In these cases, I group children with roughly similar knowledge and skills.

In other instances, having mixed groups of children can be a plus. For example, if children are creating quadrilaterals from pattern blocks, they might work with a mix of other children to create the shapes. The teacher would provide vocabulary or offer questions and remarks that cause children to notice, check, or describe aspects of what they are doing. In this activity, children with varying knowledge and experience are able to identify shapes together, pick up ideas from one another, and transform their creations into new ones.

Teachers often wonder how they can work with small groups and at the same time have ample opportunity to observe, orchestrate other children's activities around the classroom, and interact with them as they work and play. Many classrooms do not have an assistant teacher or other adult, or may have such help only on a limited basis. This is challenging, but teachers with too many children don't have to resort to only whole-group instruction or free play. This situation calls for creativity.

Dana is a case in point. She uses third grade "math buddies" to help the children in her prekindergarten class. Each 4-year-old is paired with a third-grader, and they meet twice a month to do special activities and then later work together in center activities. "There are so many great math activities that are much harder for me to do with twenty children by myself," Dana says. "The older kids help me tremendously, and my children love the interaction. And I really benefit from the third-graders' help in writing down what my children say about their math ideas."

Continued on page 28

How can mathematics be taught in centers?

Centers are a normal part of the typical early childhood classroom. Unfortunately, mathematics is a content area that is often ignored in centers, except in "the math center." But mathematics can and should be intentionally involved in *every* center! Here I want to suggest how to integrate mathematics into two types of centers common to the early childhood classroom: choice centers and "must do" centers.

Choice centers are the type typical in every early childhood center time or choice time. Standard offerings include the block center, computer center, sensory center (e.g., water and sand), puzzle and game center, dramatic play center, and library center. Mathematics can and should be part of every choice center. The tasks or experiences should be active, independent, and related to the child's interest and the class theme of study. Here are just a few examples:

• Blocks—Adding photos of neighborhood buildings can help children represent a two-dimensional picture with three-dimensional blocks, a geometry goal.

• Water and sand—Providing 1-cup and ½-cup measurers along with a variety of different containers can involve children in capacity experiments.

• Puzzles and games—Completing substitution puzzles (i.e., that require children to fill a specified space with different blocks) is an occasion for spatial thinking as well as recording numerical relationships (e.g., "I used six blue rhombi or two yellow hexagons to cover the space").

• Dramatic play—Supplying receipt pads, play money, and price lists, along with bouquets of plastic flowers, tissue paper, and plastic vases, provides endless opportunities for children to use mathematics skills in a flower shop.

"Must do" centers are assigned to children in connection with mathematics concepts being taught during a whole- or small-group meeting. Research tells us that children's learning increases significantly when the strategy of teacher-led small groups is used. But while the teacher is meeting with a small group, what are the other children to do? One solution is the "must do" center. The activity can be part of a standard center in the classroom or be something children set up from a tub containing the necessary materials. Either way, the task is an independent activity that reinforces a concept just taught. Here are some examples:

• Class book projects that focus on mathematics concepts can be part of a "must do" publishing center, where some or all children contribute pages for the class book. (See the Literature Connection sections in chapters 4–8.)

• A "must do" art center where children create a "number sculpture" (i.e., a creation that uses a particular number of shapes or objects) can reinforce number concepts.

• Cutting and pasting geometric shapes for a class poster entitled "Quadrilaterals and NOT Quadrilaterals" can be part of a "must do" center that reinforces geometry concepts.

Lots of manipulatives and math tools are used to teach mathematics. How do you organize them?

You are right! There are lots of tools, many of which are noisy, small in size, and easily misplaced. Here are several suggestions:

To help with the noise factor, I suggest using manipulatives made of heavy foam (Manipulite™ is one company's product) when possible. Strong and nontoxic, a variety of foam blocks and counters are available at about the same price as the plastic and wooden objects. The use of workmats (plastic placemats or cloths) can also alleviate noise and provide children with specific workspaces.

For the organization of materials, I recommend that items be sorted and stored so they are easy to count and accessible for all children. I use plastic ice cube trays to store small counting items. If two items are placed in each compartment, they can easily be counted and any missing ones identified. In addition, ice cube trays can be stacked for easy access. Other materials can be stored in labeled containers, with the number of each type of material listed on the outside.

Most important, manipulatives should be used by children to learn mathematics. One class job you might assign could be a "Counter"—a child who is in charge of particular containers of materials and who checks them on a regular basis. If children view the class materials as theirs and take ownership in the organization of the room, mathematics can be taught effectively with materials of all kinds.

Chapter 3

Mathematics Processes in the Early Childhood Curriculum

Young children learn by doing. That familiar adage is true, but it represents only part of the picture; in reality, children learn by doing, talking, reflecting, discussing, observing, investigating, listening, and reasoning. To learn mathematics, children must be actively involved with mathematics content (e.g., number and operations, geometry, measurement) and, importantly, with the processes of mathematics, defined by NCTM as: *problem solving*, *reasoning*, *communication*, *connections*, and *representation*. As NCTM makes clear through its Standards, mathematics content and process are "inextricably linked" (2000, 7). When taught and learned, the processes act as "vehicles for children to deepen, extend, elaborate, and refine their thinking" and "explore ideas and lines of reasoning" (NRC 2009, 42).

Do the processes of mathematics sound powerful? Yes! Do they sound essential to the learning of mathematics? They are! In fact, children cannot solve problems if they don't understand number concepts or identify and analyze patterns without reasoning. Similarly, children cannot begin to think algebraically if they haven't developed the abilities to represent relationships, connect the ideas represented, and then communicate those ideas.

The processes involved in learning mathematics are especially important to teachers of young children. Both NAEYC and NCTM emphasize mathematical processes in one of their recommendations from their joint position statement. "In high-quality mathematics education for 3- to 6-year-old children, teachers and other key professionals should use curriculum and teaching practices that strengthen children's problem-solving and reasoning processes as well as representing, communicating, and connecting mathematical ideas" (NAEYC & NCTM 2002, 3). To be good or proficient at mathematics, children must know more than the content. They must be able to communicate that knowledge, connect that knowledge to other mathematical ideas and to other subject areas, represent their understanding, use that knowledge as they solve problems and reason, and demonstrate a disposition to think flexibly and with persistence about mathematics to solve problems (NRC 2001; Lesh & Zawojewski 2007). Yes, children learn by doing, and if they don't use the processes to understand mathematics concepts, they really can't learn mathematics!

This chapter looks at each of the five processes in turn.

Problem solving

Mr. Ketner's second grade class enjoys frequent games of Hidden Tiles. Mr. Ketner hides different color square tiles and gives the children clues describing the tiles and their whereabouts. During the games he introduces math vocabulary. Here is an example of a Hidden Tiles game conducted early in the year that illustrates the process of problem solving.

Hidden Tiles

Look for the video clip of "Tile Clues" on the DVD!

Mr. Ketner: I have some color tiles hidden under the file folder. Your job is to be detectives and figure out which tiles are under the folder by using the word clues I give you. I've given each of you lots of tiles to use to show your guesses. . . . Now, I've just told you that I have some tiles. Using that clue, show me what I might have underneath the folder.

Children make various arrangements of color tiles on the table. Some children watch their friends and copy arrangements; others are clearly creating unique tile arrangements.

Clarice: Is this right?

Jonah: Is mine like yours?

Diego: Why don't you just show us?

Mr. Ketner: I want you to use your words and your brains to figure out the answer. Let's see [pointing to the arrangement of tiles on one child's desktop]. . . . Could this be right? Did you put some tiles on your desk? . . . Yes. In fact, everyone's design with tiles could be right! So I'll give you the next clue: I have more than three tiles and fewer than five tiles. Now show me what the hidden tiles might look like.

Children again become busy working on their answers. Some realize readily that there are four tiles in the solution. Others use only one part of the clue, creating a solution that has more than three but not fewer than five, or fewer than five but not more than three. In each case the teacher asks the children to share their solutions with a partner and decide whether the solutions could be correct. The teacher circulates, reviewing children's guesses by describing their tile configurations using the words in the clue.

Mr. Ketner: [points to Akim's guess] You have more than three tiles and fewer than five tiles. That could be right! . . . [pointing to Becky's guess] You have more than three tiles. Let's see, do you have fewer than five tiles?

Becky: No. . . . [changes her solution to show four tiles] Yes, now I do!

Mr. Ketner: Oh, what a good problem solver you are. You changed your answer when you remembered the second clue. A good problem solver changes her answer when she gets more information. . . . Everyone ready for another clue? Here it is: The four square tiles are put together in one large square. Now, try it!

Mr. Ketner continues to provide clues, reviewing children's guesses and reminding them to make sure their solutions fit all the clues. Finally, only two solutions are possible. With partners, children discuss and then share the possibilities with the class and give justifications for their solutions.

As children share their guesses, the teacher records notes about their guesses and behaviors on a checklist. He will use this information to plan follow-up experiences and questions for the group and for individual children.

This particular game of Hidden Tiles took longer than thirty minutes. The children were highly involved, asking questions that demonstrated their reasoning, discussing the meaning of the clues, and listening attentively to ideas and questions posed. The teacher gave clues that required negation (e.g., "I do not have any blue tiles") as well as clues that used mathematical terms ("My tiles form a large square" . . . "The yellow tiles are diagonal to each other" . . . "The red tile is on the top row"). After solving a few Hidden Tiles problems posed by the teacher, the children create their own problems and share them with their classmates.

Problem solving in the early childhood setting

All young children solve problems; yet even among preschoolers, differences can be seen in children's "approaches to learning," or *dispositions*, toward problem solving (NRC 2001; Lesh & Zawojewski 2007). One 3-year-old persists for ten minutes in building a graduated tower, while another quickly gives up in frustration. One 5-year-old keeps trying the same unsuccessful strategy again and again, while her friend seeks a fresh way to solve the challenge.

Dispositions relevant to math problem solving include more than having a positive attitude toward math. An effective problem solver perseveres, focuses his attention, tests his hypotheses, takes reasonable risks, remains flexible, tries alternatives, and exhibits self-regulation. Young children have far to go before their dispositions and self-regulation reach the level of mature problem solvers, but they are already learning (or failing to learn) key lessons. Just as so-called "math minds" are not distributed at birth, neither are children simply born with dispositions suited to problem solving. Instead, their accumulated learning experiences combine with their inherited characteristics to contribute significantly to their dispositions.

Letting children solve problems themselves. Informal opportunities for problem solving occur all the time in an early childhood classroom. For example, when distributing materials to their classmates, children may need to determine whether there are enough items to go around, and if not, figure out how their classmates can share fairly. Often teachers resolve classroom problems themselves, to model the "right way" and to keep their teaching day running smoothly. But when teachers solve all the routine problems, they are robbing children of the learning experiences that occur in authentic situations. In fact, problem solving very often *is* the lesson.

> Mrs. Nix is a prekindergarten teacher who is at the point of interrupting a child's problem-solving efforts when she catches herself. Four-year-old Steven has decided to build an upside-down volcano using the new beveled blocks in the block center. As he works at this difficult task, which requires him to balance and position blocks in an alternating pattern, Steven spends more than thirty minutes in deep concentration. Several times he watches his structure fall and then tries again.
>
> Just as Mrs. Nix is about to intervene, Steven discovers the position pattern required for the blocks to stand in an inverted volcano. Steven throws up his hands and shouts, "I got it! I got it!" The look of excitement on Steven's face testifies to his strong motivation in problem solving, and all the children can see his enthusiasm. During circle time Mrs. Nix asks Steven to share his discovery, emphasizing the hard work Steven put into solving the problem and the great satisfaction he felt when he succeeded. Later Steven sits in the block center explaining the solution to his peers and helping them with their projects.

Look for the video clip of "Baby and Blocks" on the DVD!

Teaching the problem-solving process. The approach most commonly taught for problem solving involves four steps: (1) understanding the problem, (2) planning how to solve it, (3) carrying out the plan, and (4) reviewing the solution (Polya 1957; Lesh & Zawojewski 2007).

For young children (or for adults), this process is seldom linear or automatic. In fact, taking time to explore the materials and possibilities in a problem situation, a natural inclination for children, is key to the first step. Having uninterrupted time to explore is critical in the problem-solving process, especially for young children. They gain understanding of the problem and have a much better chance of generating possible solutions when they have had the opportunity to play with materials and experiment.

Second, the problem solver needs to plan. Planning involves thinking ahead and considering alternatives—both of which are challenges for young children. Teachers can model the planning step and encourage children to plan by asking questions that scaffold children's learning and using other strategies to get children to think ahead. In the Hidden Tiles game, for example, children get time to consider the solutions they will put forth, and the teacher can ask them about their reasons, have them check clues, and so on, all before they find out whether their guesses are right. The teacher also acknowledges children's thinking, planning, and reflecting on solutions. Thinking ahead and considering alternatives are things children have to learn through engaging in mathematical experiences. As children see planning modeled, explore a variety of alternatives, and experience the positive results when planning occurs, their planning skills gradually develop.

The next problem-solving step is to carry out the plan—to try it out and see whether it works. If the plan does not work, the problem solver can modify it and try again. Young children, however, often get an idea and immediately put it into action, so there may be little or no separation between their second and third steps. Children tend to quickly try one solution, then another, and then another. Yet reflection is key to effective planning. To promote the development of good planning, teachers must get children to pause—not in every instance, of course, but at times—and to take time to think about what will happen before they try out their plan.

Finally, looking back is a critical but frequently neglected step in the problem-solving process. Mr. Ketner kept drawing the children's attention to the earlier clues and reminding them to check to see whether their guesses still fit all the clues. With young children, this reviewing step often occurs quickly, if at all. They need reminders: "Now see whether your answer works" . . . "Check back with your clues" . . . "Look back to see whether your answer makes sense."

Promoting children's mathematical problem solving

Being able to use what you know to solve problems is an essential component of being good at math (NRC 2001). A vital teaching role is to provide a setting rich in possibilities for solving problems. Early childhood teachers should design and stock the learning environment so that it offers interesting problems and an array of materials for children to use in solving them, such as counters, geometric shapes, blocks, and puzzles.

Another task for teachers is to help children identify and work on those problems. Children encounter problems every day in their lives at home (e.g., "Do you have enough money to buy the book?" . . . "How many different outfits can I make with my favorite shirt?" . . . "How many days until we see Grandma?") and at school ("If you share the markers, how many will each of you have?" . . . "Do I have enough blocks to build a tower as tall as George's?" . . . "How many cars do you think we need for our field trip?"). Often teachers (or parents) solve problems that could be solved by the children themselves given the time and opportunity. Instead of offering solutions, the teacher can help children to see themselves as problem solvers by clearly stating problems, providing class time to listen and talk about problems, and connecting some of the problems occurring in children's lives to mathematics learning.

Children gain a great deal when teachers model problem-solving strategies and dispositions. They learn a powerful lesson when the teacher conveys the joys of solving problems and acknowledges the frustrations, giving them encouragement and strategies to handle the taxing moments in problem solving.

By posing questions and making comments along the way, teachers help children learn to stand back and consider possibilities and evaluate various ideas before deciding what to try. Children become more reflective when they are encouraged to share their thinking with others, verbally or through other methods of representation and communication. As a further bonus, teachers find out what children are thinking. Knowing a child's interests and how she constructs and understands problems enables the teacher to present a new problem that extends the child's mathematical thinking and problem-solving skills—that is, it enables the teacher to tailor instruction to the child's individual needs.

Young children frequently solve problems using the guess-and-check strategy: "Take a guess, check it out, and try something else if that idea fails." Although this almost random method may eventually lead to success, children need to learn to consider *why* the first solution did not work in order to become better problem solvers. Further short-circuiting such reflective thinking is the unspoken stratagem, "Take a guess and then check out the teacher's reaction." Often a teacher is so quick to reinforce children's right answers and dismiss their wrong ones that she does not give them time or encouragement to rethink a problem.

Focusing on the teacher's reaction cuts off problem solving and reflection—not only for the one child giving the answer but also for all the children who hear the teacher's response or see the yes or no on her face. For this reason, teachers do well to cultivate an interested but noncommittal facial expression that conveys, "Hmmm, that's an interesting idea . . . " and leaves plenty of time and space for children's thinking to continue.

Reasoning

Reasoning opportunities are abundant in the life of the young child. In early childhood classrooms, children play games, classify and label sets of objects, solve problems, and observe and listen to others as they think. Guess My Cage is a game to promote reasoning and is played often in Ms. Lim's class during circle time.

Guess My Cage

Ms. Lim's class of 4-year-olds returns from a "creature hunt," during which they searched the playground for creatures of various sizes and shapes drawn on red and blue paper (hidden there by their teacher). Back in the classroom are six "cages," each labeled with a card to indicate a single characteristic: Red, Blue, Big, Little, Horns, and Hair. The children survey the cages then place each creature they captured in an appropriately labeled cage. Ms. Lim then launches the second part of the activity.

Ms. Lim: Wow, we have done a great job! All the creatures have a cage. Let's see if every creature is where it belongs. Myra, why did you put this creature in this cage?

Myra: [after a pause] Because it's blue, and the sign says "Blue."

Ms. Lim: Good. What about this one, Eli?

Eli: 'Cause it's big, like this one [points to another creature in the same cage].

Ms. Lim: Do you agree with Eli, Jackie?

Jackie: [nods yes] Uh-huh, and it's red.

Ms. Lim: So, could I put Eli's creature in this cage, too? [indicates the cage labeled "Red"] . . . Where else could it go? What else do you notice about this creature?

The discussion continues, with children discussing the distinguishing characteristics of various creatures and justifying their placement in the labeled cages. Ms. Lim introduces a new twist.

Ms. Lim: Would you like to play a game? It's called Guess My Cage. [Mr. Allen joins the group.] Let's see if we can fool Mr. Allen. . . . Mr. Allen, we are going to try to fool you. Look at our cages. In just a minute we are going to send you out of the room. Then we will choose one cage, take away the label, and see if you can figure out which cage it is from the children's clues. We are not going to tell you the answer. You'll have to figure it out by yourself!

Mr. Allen leaves the room, and Eli accompanies him to make sure he doesn't peek. Ms. Lim asks the children to choose a cage. They quickly decide on the Red cage, and Ms. Lim removes the creatures in that cage and removes its label. The children then put away the other cages, redistributing all the creatures amongst themselves.

Ms. Lim: Now we are almost ready. Let me show you again the card for the cage you chose; put it in your heads and remember. [She shows the card labeled "Red" and motions for the children to put the word in their heads and lock their lips.]

She asks Dick to sit on the Red card so Mr. Allen can't see it when he returns.

Ms. Lim: Evangelina, please tell Eli to bring Mr. Allen back into the room. Remember, don't tell Mr. Allen!

Eli brings Mr. Allen back. There is a great deal of giggling and excitement.

Mr. Allen: I wonder which cage that is. Will you tell me?

Children: No! . . . No way!

Ms. Lim: No, Mr. Allen, we won't tell you which cage it is, but we will give you some clues. Jo-Lin, will you be first? Pick one of your creatures, and tell Mr. Allen if it belongs in the cage.

Jo-Lin picks up a big, red, horned, hairy creature and places it in the unlabeled cage.

Mr. Allen: So, does your creature belong in the cage? [Jo-Lin nods yes.] . . . Pete, how about one of your creatures?

Pete nods yes and places his little, red, horned, hairy creature in the cage.

Mr. Allen: I have just learned something new! I see that both of these creatures are alike in some way [appears to be thinking and points to the creatures in the cages]. They are both red, they both have horns, and they both have hair. . . . How about one of your creatures, Evangelina?

Evangelina picks up a big, blue, horned, hairless creature and looks at Ms. Lim, who shakes her head no. Evangelina shakes her head no and holds her creature in her hand.

Mr. Allen: Oh, Evangelina, could you put your creature outside the cage so I can compare it with the others?

Evangelina places her creature just outside the cage.

Mr. Allen: Let me think about it. I think your creature can really teach me something important! [He pauses.] . . . I have just learned something the cage *cannot* be! It can't be Horns! If it were, Evangelina's creature would be in the cage. [Again he pauses and appears to be thinking about that idea.]

Mr. Allen continues questioning children, and the children place their creatures. Eventually, there are fifteen in the cage, while more than ten creatures, all blue, remain outside the cage.

Mr. Allen: [appears to be thinking] . . . Oh, I think I know which cage this is! At first I thought it was Big, but then I saw that this creature was little [points to one creature inside the cage]. . . . And then I thought it was Hair, but this creature has no hair [points inside again]. . . . And then I thought it was Red, and I checked, and every creature in the cage was red, and all the creatures outside were blue! [indicates all the blue creatures] . . . So I think your cage is Red!

Children: [groaning] He's so lucky. . . . Did you tell him? . . . Man, he guessed it!

Ms. Lim: Let's see if you are right, Mr. Allen. Dick, would you give me the card? Let's see. [She shows the "Red" card label to everyone.]

Eli: He got it right!

Ericka: He's so lucky!

Jo-Lin: Let's play again!

Jo-Lin's enthusiasm is shared by her classmates. They will play this game over and over for months. Each time they try to fool an adult, and each time the children express surprise that the adult "guessed it!" But over time the game changes dramatically as children learn to listen to the adult's reasoning and eventually discover that they, too, can find the solutions. After many experiences, children and teacher change roles and the children try to guess the teacher's cage. Later, children play the game as partners during choice time, challenging each other with new attributes or objects.

Reasoning in the early childhood setting

The children's reactions in playing Guess My Cage are typical of 4-year-olds. For example, they believe that someone who solves a problem correctly is lucky—that thinking has nothing to do with it! Preschool children tend not to understand that people use reasoning to solve a problem; they have even less understanding of how reasoning works.

Another example of 4-year-olds' thinking is that the children consider clues to be useful only if they concern the creatures *in* the cage. While Mr. Allen considers the creatures *not* in the cage, the children don't see those creatures as relevant. They do not comprehend that finding out about a creature not in the cage can be even more revealing than learning about creatures in it. Children typically need extensive experience with such problems before they see that eliminating possibilities is important in solving the problem.

Reasoning experiences with the concept of *not* can be emphasized during routine activities. For example, children learn important reasoning words when teachers give directions such as "Those people *not* wearing red may get their jackets to go outside" or "Those boys and girls who did *not* have a turn yesterday. . . ."

Preschool and kindergarten children tend to focus on only one property or attribute at a time. For example, picking up a blue fish, a child will say, "This is blue," and put the fish in the Blue pile; or she may say, "A fish!" and put it in the Fish pile. For a young child, this focus on one property may (and often does) change in the middle of a single sorting task. Young children find it difficult to focus consistently on only one attribute; additionally, they will be surprised when someone classifies an object differently than they do. By second grade, however, children recognize that an object has multiple properties, and they use classification schemes that take into account more than one property. Now the child might sort a collection of animals into sets of blue fish, green fish, blue crabs, and green crabs.

Young children reason, but their reasoning tends to be intuitive; they are not aware of how they arrive at an answer. They tend to respond to *why* questions with short, unrevealing answers. Shoulder shrugs and phrases such as "I just know it" or "Just because" are typical. One first-grader used a calculator to correctly answer a number pattern problem. When asked how he figured it out, he responded in a characteristic way: "I thunk and I thunk and I mashed and I mashed and out came the answer!" Although we chuckle over such explanations, teachers also need to keep in mind the value of persistently encouraging young children's justifications and reflections on reasoning.

Promoting children's mathematical reasoning

Being able to think logically and to reflect on, explain, and justify that thinking is another of the characteristics that indicates proficiency in math (NRC 2001). Even in their early years, children need to have experiences that help them begin to develop clarity and precision in their thinking (Tang & Ginsburg 1999). To give children familiarity with the language of logic and reasoning, teachers should get into the habit of using words such as *or*, *not*, *because*, *some*, *all*, *never*, and *probably*, and phrases such as *if...then*. For example, a teacher could say, "You may choose apple juice *or* grape juice to drink with your crackers," or "*All* of you have families, and *some* of you have sisters in your family."

Teachers should also encourage children to make guesses (or *conjectures*) and to investigate and justify them, as well. For example, when children make their own conjectures about natural phenomena, teachers should encourage them to investigate their notions, no matter how unlikely the premise. Armand in chapter 1 was certain that earthworms have eyes. Encouraged to investigate his idea, he created charts and graphs to justify his beliefs. Although he was wrong (earthworms do not have eyes), Armand used reasoning and other mathematical skills to support his conjectures—powerful mathematics! In another example, a young child demonstrates his reasoning behind a rule about numbers:

> Second-grader Gareth tells his teacher that an even number added to an odd number is always an odd number. He explains his reasoning by first showing the teacher examples using numbers: 1 + 2 = 3 (odd), 5 + 10 = 15 (odd), 7 + 2 = 9 (odd). Then he builds a model out of cubes: He builds an even number with paired cubes (6, for example, is made of two 3s stacked evenly beside each other), and he builds an odd number with paired cubes and one odd cube (11, made of two 5s and one 1). When he puts the cubes together (two 3s, two 5s, and one 1), he shows he still has one lone odd cube (the 1) and thus an odd-number sum.

The teacher's role in fostering children's reasoning processes is critical. Teachers should ask questions that require investigation and reasoning:

- *Are you sure?*
- *How do you know?*
- *Why do you think . . . ?*
- *What else can you find that works like this?*

- *What would happen if . . . ?*
- *I wonder how this could be changed?*
- *What would the pattern be?*
- *What if . . . ?*
- *I wonder why . . . ?*
- *Perhaps it's because . . .*

In addition, teachers should continually model reasoning language in everyday experiences, such as "If that is right, then . . ." or "I want to find out if . . . so I will try . . ." or "That can't be, because if it were, then. . . ."

Words and phrases are not the only way that a teacher models the process of reasoning. Pausing before responding, reorganizing data to search for patterns, and recording what happens after each trial in an experiment are just a few reasoning behaviors that teachers can model. The teacher should also model reasoning for young children by thinking out loud and expressing his or her own thoughts about problems, which will facilitate children's learning to think in similar ways.

Most important, to emphasize and develop children's reasoning abilities, a teacher must listen to their reasoning. Only when the teacher knows and understands a child's own justifications can that teacher effectively encourage more sophisticated and reasonable conjectures.

Communication

To communicate about mathematics ideas, children must be able to articulate, clarify, organize, and consolidate their math thinking. As they struggle to capture their ideas and reasoning in words or other modes of communication, children become more conscious of *what* they know and *how* they solve problems. At the same time, through children's communication efforts, their teacher finds out more about what they think and know. Their peers also listen, observe, and learn, becoming aware of perspectives and strategies other than their own and asking questions that push the speakers to be clearer and to consider their listeners' needs (i.e., to be less what Piaget called "egocentric") in their communicating.

In the vignette below, first-grader Ong creates a picture of fish and dogs during a classroom drawing activity. His teacher, Mrs. Wyman, uses questions to get Ong to describe how he calculates the total number of eyes belonging to the fish and dogs in his picture.

Animal Eyes

Mrs. Wyman: Ong, would you tell me about your picture?

Ong: My dogs and fish have lots of eyes. There are sixteen!

Mrs. Wyman: But I don't see sixteen eyes. How do you know how many there are?

Ong: [places two fingers on one fish] There are two eyes, but one is hiding. I will show you!

Ong takes his crayon and draws two dots in the middle of the page to represent that fish's eyes. He adds two more dots for each animal to represent the eyes of all eight creatures in his drawing.

Mrs. Wyman: Are you sure there are enough?

Ong: [holds two fingers over each animal's face and then points to the corresponding dots in his drawing] They all have two. This fish has two eyes, and this fish also has two eyes, and this dog has two. See, I was right! Sometimes you have to count stuff you only see in your brain.

When Mrs. Wyman asked Ong about his drawing, Ong responded by explaining the drawing, elaborating on his explanation by adding the dots for each animal's eyes, and then acting out the completed solution using his fingers. In this way, he articulated information about his drawing (and, therefore, about his thinking) that would not otherwise be clear.

Communication in the early childhood setting

In mathematics-rich classrooms, children have the materials to be able to use a variety of means, verbal and nonverbal, to communicate their mathematical ideas to others. They have reason and opportunity and the materials to manipulate objects, draw pictures, use fingers, and devise other ingenious ways to show what they mean. They also learn to explain their answers in writing, use diagrams and charts, and express ideas with mathematics symbols.

When children are deeply invested in an undertaking, they are often particularly keen to share their ideas and creations with others, even when doing so takes some hard work.

In the block center, 4-year-old Teddy creates an ornate pattern using curved blocks of various colors. He spends more than fifteen minutes describing his pattern to Andy and directing Andy to make his pattern "go the other way." Teddy names his pattern "The Wave" and describes each step in its construction using specific color, position, and size words.

In the end Teddy and Andy created a ten-foot-long symmetrical pattern of wooden blocks together. With a strong motivation to cooperate in making The Wave, the two boys eagerly strove to communicate with each other. Thus, the experience enhanced their mathematical understanding (e.g., as Teddy articulated the steps in his process) and their math vocabulary skills far more than an artificial communication task would.

Interactions involving math occur from child to teacher, from teacher to child, and among children (NCTM 2000). To learn to express themselves clearly, listen attentively, ask for clarification, and use other communication skills, young children need to observe these skills in action and have many opportunities to practice them. Young children are not adept at listening to others share ideas, nor are they skilled at stating their ideas with clarity and precision. However, with practice they can learn to listen to each other and describe their reasoning. As children strive to express their ideas, they organize and consolidate their mathematics thinking and concepts.

While young children have not yet acquired advanced writing skills, they can draw pictures, write simple words, or frame sentences that communicate their mathematics ideas. Samples of children's written work can reveal their intuitive (and often inaccurate) understandings as well as their emerging skills in written communication. What they write or draw is generally more comprehensible when they add a verbal explanation. All these expressions (visual, written, and verbal) help teachers to assess what the child does and does not understand about both math and mathematics communication, and to make instructional decisions accordingly.

Promoting children's mathematical communication

To help children develop in mathematics communication, teachers can verbalize and restate math concepts and processes as children work through a problem. Teachers can ask questions and describe what they see a child doing, and they should listen carefully to children's answers. When restating, it is important to use clear, age-appropriate mathematical language, and to ask questions that help children clarify or extend their ideas. But of the three strategies, the most important in promoting communication is attending carefully to what children say (Chapin, O'Connor, & Anderson 2009).

Children's direct responses to teachers' questions are not the only source of information about what they are focusing on, what they understand and misunderstand, and what they are struggling with. Their side comments and their questions can reveal much, too. Observing in early childhood classrooms, however, I frequently notice well-meaning but busy teachers ignoring important clues and information children are giving them. By listening well, teachers will gain an important window into the child's mind.

To foster math communication, teachers also should give children many opportunities to talk with and listen to their peers. Working in small groups or pairs on a reasoning game or task is particularly helpful. In such an activity, when children cannot follow a classmate's thinking, their questions and misinterpretations will provoke the speaker to restate her idea or try other ways to communicate it. At times, the teacher can provide extra encouragement and support, saying, for example, "Marina, can you find another way to help James understand how you figured that out?"

Connections

As described in the first chapter in this book, young children gain a vast amount of intuitive, informal mathematical knowledge through their own experiences. They naturally use mathematical terminology ("Mickey's got *more*, no fair!"), and they continually construct mathematical understandings from what they see, hear, and discover ("I get to go to Grandma's house in three sleeps!").

The teacher's primary role is to help children to make a connection between this informal, intuitive mathematics and formal, school mathematics—that is, to help "mathematize" the experiences they are having in their everyday lives (Clements & Sarama 2004). "Mathematizing happens when children can create a model of the situation by using mathematical objects (such as numbers or shapes), mathematical actions (such as counting or transforming shapes), and their structural relationships to solve problems about the situation" (NRC 2009, 44).

This bridge between informal and formal mathematics is the foundation that supports children in making other connections—connections between different mathematical concepts, between different mathematical topics, between mathematics and other subjects, and between mathematics and everyday life. NCTM's *Principles and Standards* elaborates on the value of children seeing connections:

> Students' abilities to experience mathematics as a meaningful endeavor that makes sense rests on these connections. . . . [Understanding connections helps children] realize the beauty of mathematics and its function as a means of more clearly observing, representing, and interpreting the world around them. (NCTM 2000, 132)

In the following vignette, the teacher had put out coins simply as objects for children to magnify, but she capitalizes on their interest and helps them see mathematical connections.

Exploring Pennies

Miss Hewitt is listening and observing during center time in her kindergarten classroom. Three children are in the science exploration center using magnifiers to explore a collection of shiny new coins she had put in a jar earlier. After having some fun using the magnifiers on each other and giggling at their magnified eyes and fingers, they begin looking at the pennies. Miss Hewitt overhears them talking.

Arun: I have numbers on my penny! I got a 2, a 0, a 0, and a 6.

Julie: Where? [briefly consults with Arun] . . . Oh, so do I! I got a 2, a 0, a 0, and a 1!

Roger: Me, too. I got a 2, a 0. . . . Man, this is weird!

After a few minutes, Miss Hewitt comes over and asks the children about their discoveries.

Julie: Well, every penny we look at has a 2 and a 0 on it. Roger says it's weird!

Miss Hewitt: I wonder if this is just true about pennies. Why don't you go check out the nickel collection?

The investigation continues for several days. To their amazement they find a 2 and a 0 on every coin! Rather than give the children the explanation (coins are always stamped with the year they were minted), Miss Hewitt encourages them to graph the results and engages them in discussing possible reasons for this weird phenomenon.

The children offer a variety of reasons, and Min mentions the calendar date. (If no one had thought of the calendar, Miss Hewitt would have brought it, along with other items, for the children to search for clues that might explain the many 20s.)

More discussion ensues as children make conjectures about this intriguing connection. Finally, comparing the years that the coins were "born" to their own birthdates, the children make a wonderful timeline.

Connections between mathematics content areas and other content areas often occur quite unexpectedly.

Mrs. John's kindergarten class has just finished reading *Where the Wild Things Are*, by Maurice Sendak. Each child is working to create a costume for his or her own Wild Thing. Having learned about patterns during recent math experiences, many of the children put color patterns in their costumes. When Mrs. John remarks about the patterns she sees, all the children immediately add other patterns to their costumes. A wide variety of patterns result, some made with geometric shapes, others with zig-zags and other design patterns, and still others with color patterns. Later, children make patterns with color dots on lined music paper and perform their music dressed in their costumes as "Wild Thing Rock Stars!" Lasting several weeks, this project has many connections between art, music, and reading and the mathematics content of pattern, geometry, and number.

Connections in the early childhood setting

Mathematical experiences and opportunities can occur in any classroom context, part of the curriculum, or mathematics content area.

Mrs. Bresselman's class of 3- and 4-year-olds is reading a familiar book aloud, *Chrysanthemum*, by Kevin Henkes. Dana, who has just learned to write his name, says, "Wow! Her name is stupid. It's too hard to write!"

Pointing to the Name Wall (on which each child's name appears along with his or her photo), Mrs. Bresselman asks the children whether they can find any names there that are long like Chrysanthemum.

The children become very excited about long names and short names and those in between. During the following week, children begin to count the letters in their names, and they construct a class graph showing short names, in-between names, and long names.

Although Mrs. Bresselman had not planned to teach mathematics during a reading activity, children's interest led naturally to the connection.

To the observant early childhood educator, many mathematics connections present themselves every day. Besides keeping an eye out for connections between mathematics and everyday contexts, teachers can link different mathematical ideas. For example, teachers can help children connect a geometric concept with a concept in number by asking children to count the number of square faces (sides) on a cube, which requires children to keep track of which faces they have counted.

Finally, mathematics connects to other subjects. Children tapping out patterns in the music center or creating patterns during a tie-dye project in the art center are making connections between the arts and mathematics. Children who collect data about the number of insects found in different areas of the playground are making connections between number, data analysis, and science concepts, as well as discovering something about the most conducive environment for insect life.

Although children sometimes find such connections themselves, they would miss many useful and interesting connections if teachers did not spotlight them.

Promoting children's awareness of mathematical connections

Of course we want children to truly understand mathematical concepts (NRC 2001). But what does *understanding* mean? Lambdin (2003) proposes that children understand something if they can see how it is related or connected to other things they know. The early childhood teacher plays an important role in helping young children notice connections and build understanding. Teachers commonly highlight connections between math and children's experiences or other parts of the curriculum using calendars and clocks, cooking, counting objects, and some aspects of science. But there are countless potential connections that are not so commonplace.

The teacher who incorporates number in a movement game by asking children to "stop and make five elbows" is making an explicit connection between movement and math. The teacher who enlists children's help in counting class materials by fives is illustrating the important uses of mathematics. The teacher who asks children to sketch their block creation before taking it down is fostering geometric awareness and visual representation. Many art projects and activities with sand and water help to develop children's measurement concepts and skills as well as spatial sense.

An infinite number of connections can be made quite easily between mathematics and literature, language, science, art, construction, physical movement, and music. For the early childhood educator, it is important that these connections be natural and not forced. Contrived experiences or stories are not necessary and can inhibit children's development of a meaningful understanding of mathematics.

Representation

When children represent ideas mathematically or connect representations to mathematics, their understanding of math is enhanced. Representation is also crucial for recording information, communicating solutions, and explaining reasoning. "Representations make mathematical ideas more concrete and available for reflection. Students can represent ideas with objects that can be moved and rearranged. Such concrete representations lay the foundation for later use of symbols" (NCTM 2000, 137).

Young children convey their mathematical ideas and methods in a great variety of ways. They make use of concrete objects of all sorts, including their own fingers. Children draw, produce diagrams, and make tallies, symbols, and markings of various kinds. They also use language, of course, sometimes on its own and often in conjunction with other representations.

Representation is very closely linked to the process of communication, each contributing to and supporting the other.

Hungry Ants

Mrs. Petri has taught kindergarten for ten years. She frequently uses literature to discuss mathematical concepts, and she constantly "talks mathematics" with her students. After reading *One Hundred Hungry Ants*, by Elinor J. Pinczes, the children line up for lunch, forming two equal lines at the door. Their discussion as they line up prompts the use of mathematical representation.

Mrs. Petri: Let's see, we have two lines that are exactly the same in number. How many are in each line?

Everyone gets busy pointing and counting.

Eunice: I think there are ten in mine.

LeRoi: Yeah, ten in my row, too.

Mrs. Petri: So, do we have even rows, rows like the marching ants? How can you tell?

Michelle: Well, it's like our bar problems when we do our graphs. Everyone has a partner to shake hands with. There's no extra!

Mrs. Petri: Let's check.

Children begin shaking hands with their partner across from them in the other line.

Mrs. Petri: Ten in each row. Hmmm. [sighs] . . . How can we remember how we are lined up? Who is our Recorder today? Bob, would you write on the board about our lines so we can remember?

Bob readily consents and goes to the chalkboard to record. He looks uncertain, counting but not knowing exactly what to write.

Mrs. Petri: Would you like someone to help you? How about Michelle?

Bob and Michelle work at the board. Bob begins to draw stick people in two rows, whereas Michelle makes tally marks for each person in the two lines. Michelle finishes first, shows Bob, and returns to her place in line.

Mrs. Petri: Bob and Michelle, that looks great. Now, I wonder if we could line up any other way and still have even lines? . . . Let's see, we have ten in this line [holds up her ten fingers so everyone can see] and we have ten in this line [holds up both hands again so everyone can see]. I wonder what we could do?

Keith: [standing in the middle of one of the lines] We could split the lines here maybe [points to the middle of the line in which he is standing], and then have fair lines . . . you know, like the ants!

Geraldo: I know! One line will have five, the next line will have five, and then five, and then five! That would work!

Mrs. Petri: Wow, let's check it out. Five here . . . five here . . . five here . . . five here [separating each line of ten into two segments of five children each]. Now shake hands. . . . It works! Five in every row! . . . How did you know that, Geraldo? What did you do?

Geraldo: Well, see, you had ten in this line, like this [holds up two hands] and ten in the other line, like this [holds up two hands again], so you take one hand for one line, one hand for another line, one hand for this line, and one hand for this line [places one hand at a time in front of each line] and it works!

Bob records the four lines of five children each using tally marks like Michelle's. When the class returns after lunch, the teacher suggests they use their math journals to see if they can find any other ways to line up like the hungry ants.

Representation in the early childhood setting

Representations for number, operations, patterns, and geometric and statistical concepts are all essential to the young child's mathematical understanding. Representations often help to make mathematical relationships more obvious. These include common mathematical representations introduced by teachers, as well as child-created representations.

In the Hungry Ants discussion, representations helped children solve a problem originally presented in a story. Bob's picture representation of stick people, Michelle's use of tally marks, and Geraldo's use of fingers helped children visualize and remember solutions, represent number quantities, solve problems, and explain their reasoning.

Teachers and parents often introduce children to common forms of numerical representation: tally marks, finger models, domino pips, pictures of objects, and dots used with 10-frames. Even very young children use fingers to show their age, not always understanding what the fingers stand for but gradually getting the idea. The use of fingers is a common representation, in part because the concept of *10* modeled by five fingers on each hand is easily learned and often serves as a useful benchmark.

During circle time in a prekindergarten classroom, 4-year-old Lucas tells his teacher that only six people can play a particular partner game because "you only got three boards!" When the teacher asks Lucas to explain his reasoning, he holds up two fingers three times, saying, "One game, two games, three games. See, six people!"

Lucas used his fingers to appropriately and purposefully represent the solution to a problem.

Promoting children's mathematical representation

To encourage flexibility in mathematical representation, early childhood teachers should introduce children to a wide range of representations—pictorial (drawings, maps); graphical (bar graphs made from stacked objects, timelines, pictographs); and symbolic (tables, prose descriptions) (Greenes 1999).

Providing meaningful contexts that encourage children to represent and communicate their understanding is part of the teacher's role. Children should also learn that representation helps them remember what they did (i.e., how they reached their answer) and explain their reasoning. In addition, teachers should often ask children to verbally or concretely represent a concept or number by showing it in another way or by using their words and objects to communicate their ideas.

When children see their teacher referring to representations they have created ("Let's check back to your diagram and see how many were in each group"), the usefulness of representing is reinforced for them. Teachers should also make it a point to connect children's informal mathematical representations with commonly accepted representations in mathematics; for example, children may initially just draw random sticks to represent "how many"; later, if their teacher helps them make the connection, they may begin using a tally mark system to show the count in sets of five.

*   *   *

The five processes of mathematics—*problem solving*, *reasoning*, *communication*, *connections*, and *representation*—are critical to the young child and his or her understanding of mathematics. It is impossible, and simply not practical, to describe all the ways these processes will be used in the different content areas. As you read the content chapters that follow, look for the processes that children use as they are learning about number, pattern, geometry, measurement, and data analysis. Because the relationship between processes and content is so important, the processes will be referenced frequently and emphasized as they relate to the specific focus of each content chapter.

Introduction to the Mathematics Content Areas

The teacher's role in the math curriculum is to provide a bridge between children's informal knowledge of mathematics and the more formal "school" mathematics. As described in chapter 1, young children enter school with many intuitive mathematical understandings. This is especially true in the area of number and operations, and to a lesser degree in the areas of patterns, measurement, geometry, and data analysis. Our job is, first, to gain insight into each child's interpretation of a mathematical concept and assess what that child knows and doesn't know. Then, through our subsequent teaching, we help the child move from intuitive concepts and constructions to more formal mathematical understandings.

How each child's mathematical understanding develops is individual, but research tells us that development generally follows predictable *learning paths* (or *trajectories*). Two recent publications, *Learning and Teaching Early Math: The Learning Trajectories Approach* (Clements & Sarama 2009) and *Early Childhood Mathematics Education Research: Learning Trajectories for Young Children* (Sarama & Clements 2009), outline specific goals and child development concepts for the important mathematics content areas. Both of these resources provide excellent detail and research support for the learning trajectories of many specific components of each content area. In general, mathematical skill development is governed not by children's specific ages but rather by a range of ages that typically indicates specific developmental benchmarks.

Five content areas

The following five chapters focus on the essential content areas of the early childhood mathematics curriculum—Number and Operations; Patterns, Functions, and Algebra; Geometry and Spatial Sense; Measurement; and Data Analysis and Probability.

Each chapter briefly describes the particular content area, as well as how deep and how central the learning in that area should be in children's early years. A classroom vignette from my own experiences follows, to show how math concepts can be incorporated into the classroom in an engaging and exciting way. I give examples of learning experiences that might occur within the content area—some spontaneously (in play, during routine events, while children are at centers) and others as part of teacher-planned activities. Next, I outline general learning paths across the important skills and concepts of the content area. Finally, I offer suggestions for a mathematics-rich classroom environment, a literature connection, and an assessment that can be completed during instructional time. At the end of each chapter are activity ideas for teachers to implement or adapt in their classrooms.

Scope and sequence

The mathematics presented in these chapters is varied and rich—and *all* of it can be very meaningful to young learners. Should the five content areas be taught in a particular sequence? Should some receive more emphasis in the early childhood curriculum than others? These are especially difficult questions.

For years researchers, curriculum experts, teachers, parents, and others have considered and debated issues of scope and sequence in mathematics education. As evidenced throughout the chapters in this book, the most authoritative voice among them has been the National Council of Teachers of Mathematics. Its 2006 publication *Curriculum Focal Points* helped identify the most important topics in mathematics for each grade level, prekindergarten through second grade. And back in 2000, its *Principles and Standards for School Mathematics* identified the "big ideas" in mathematics and described what young children should know and be able to do.

For young children *Curriculum Focal Points* strongly emphasizes two areas: number and geometry. About half as much emphasis is given to the area of measurement, and data analysis receives only minimal attention. Algebra receives the least weight of all; however, pattern awareness and pattern understanding, which are fundamental in algebraic thinking, are a strong thread throughout NCTM's early childhood standards.

In other words, for children prekindergarten through second grade, number and operations (chapter 4) should be the most important content area, with geometry (chapter 6) second, and measurement (chapter 7) third. Providing important connections to these three areas of primary focus would be the content areas of patterns (chapter 5) and data analysis (chapter 8). Because of the varying importance of the particular content areas, early childhood teachers should spend more focused time teaching concepts in number and operations and in geometry, and less time on measurement concepts. Also, rather than teaching lessons that focus solely on graphing or patterning, teachers should intentionally connect those two areas to number and operations and geometry, as well as to other, nonmathematical content areas. (For examples of possible connections, see the vignette "Graphing" with Blobs, Bars, and Circles in chapter 8 and the activity Quilts at the end of chapter 6.)

Of course, the five content areas of mathematics and the processes in mathematical thinking (chapter 3) are not isolated domains. Doing mathematics usually draws on concepts from several areas and uses at least two or three of the processes. Because I consider integration essential to an effective math program, I have given many examples of making such connections throughout this book.

Beyond this question of *what* mathematics to teach, there is also the question of *when*. Is there a natural sequence for introducing math content to young children? Decisions about order and timing need to take into account the needs, experiences, and interests of the particular children. But I can offer a few general guidelines and ideas:

• Some mathematics is naturally sequential. In these cases, children typically acquire one concept or skill before they acquire the next, which builds on the first. Throughout chapters 4–8, I have pointed out such sequences.

• In any discussion of sequence of instruction, we need to remember that math areas should not be taught as separate, discrete units (e.g., data analysis, then number, and so on). Rather, children should visit and revisit the content areas throughout the year.

• Learning and teaching follow a sequence—a *cycle*, actually—which is important to children's building of mathematical understanding. First, they become *aware* of a concept, and then they *explore* it. Then comes *inquiry*, and finally, they *use* the concept. (This sequence in young children's process of constructing knowledge, and their teachers' role in supporting that construction, is elaborated in the box Cycle of Learning and Teaching opposite.) This process of learning and teaching repeats as each new concept is introduced. It's a cycle because when a child begins *using* his new knowledge or skills, he becomes more *aware* of what he doesn't yet know or cannot yet do. Similarly, seeing others (adults, more competent peers) operating at the "utilization" level heightens the child's awareness (Bredekamp & Rosegrant 1992, 33).

*   *   *

In any early childhood classroom, the teacher is the primary decision maker in determining the scope and sequence of mathematics curriculum. Experienced teachers know that a year's worth of teaching and learning cannot be definitively mapped out in advance; however, they do have an overall understanding of what builds on what. As the year unfolds and teachers interact with children, they continually assess children's knowledge, interests, and learning needs, and they are very intentional in choosing, adapting, and anticipating what learning experiences should come next for each child.

Cycle of Learning and Teaching		
	What children do	**What teachers do**
Awareness	Experience Acquire an interest Recognize broad parameters Attend Perceive	Create the environment Provide opportunities by introducing new objects, events, people Invite interest by posing problem or question Respond to child's interest or shared experience Show interest, enthusiasm
Exploration	Observe Explore materials Collect information Discover Create Figure out components Construct own understanding Apply own rules Create personal meaning Represent own meaning	Facilitate Support and enhance exploration Provide opportunities for active exploration Extend play Describe child's activity Ask open-ended questions—"What else could you do?" Respect child's thinking and rule systems Allow for constructive error
Inquiry	Examine Investigate Propose explanations Focus Compare own thinking with that of others Generalize Relate to prior learning Adjust to conventional rule systems	Help children refine understanding Guide children, focus attention Ask more focused questions—"What else works like this?" "What happens if . . . ?" Provide information when requested—"How do you spell . . . ?" Help children make connections
Utilization	Use the learning in many ways; learning becomes functional Represent learning in various ways Apply learning to new situations Formulate new hypotheses and repeat cycle	Create vehicles for application in real world Help children apply learning to new situations Provide meaningful situations in which to use learning

Source: Reprinted from S. Bredekamp & T. Rosegrant, "Reaching potentials through appropriate curriculum: Conceptual frameworks for applying the guidelines," in *Reaching Potentials: Appropriate Curriculum and Assessment for Young Children, Volume 1,* eds. S. Bredekamp & T. Rosegrant (Washington, DC: NAEYC, 1992), 33.

Chapter 4

Number and Operations

in the Early Childhood Curriculum

Number and operations is a core content area to any early childhood mathematics curriculum. It is the one that is the most researched, the most taught, and the most important to a young child's mathematics learning. The development of number concepts and skills does not occur in one lesson, one unit, or even one year. It is a continuous process that provides the foundation for much of what is taught in mathematics.

Curriculum Focal Points (NCTM 2006) lists topics in number and operations as the first important mathematics focus at every grade level, and it even includes an additional number and operations focal point for first and second grade. This prominence of number advocated by NCTM and other sources (e.g., NRC 2009) confirms the importance and depth of number learning that children require at an early age.

Beginning at the prekindergarten level, NCTM suggests that children focus on counting and comparisons; at the kindergarten level, on representing, comparing, and ordering whole numbers. Simple addition (joining) and subtraction (separating) begins at the kindergarten level and should be developed throughout children's early years. NCTM further states that at the first grade level, children should be developing a more complex understanding of addition and subtraction and strategies for the basic addition and subtraction facts. In addition, first-graders should begin to group 10s and 1s, which leads to their fuller understanding in second grade of the base-10 numeration system. Second-graders should develop a quick recall of addition and subtraction facts, along with an understanding of the procedures necessary for multidigit addition and subtraction.

It is important to note that conceptual understanding is emphasized at each level, as well as fluency of important skills (counting in prekindergarten and kindergarten, basic fact strategies in first grade, and multidigit addition and subtraction in second grade).

Children engage with number and operations in a variety of contexts

The following vignette is from a kindergarten program. Most of the children are 5 years old, and their proficiency in English is limited. Notice the children's excitement as they successfully use math skills, such as problem solving and number understanding, in these activities, extending their math abilities across learning domains.

The Octopus Story

Children sit on the floor in a semicircle facing the story chair. Ms. Scott sits in the story chair, holding a covered basket. The children have just finished a project about "minibeasts"—all types of insects and spiders. Using magnifiers, they counted legs, created their own minibeasts, and collected lots of data about where the various minibeasts live. In addition, they used insect and spider puppets in the creative dramatics center. All of the puppets are realistically made, with the appropriate number of legs.

Look for the video clip of "How Many Are Hiding?" on the DVD!

Ms. Scott: Today I want to introduce to you a new puppet. But before I do, you must solve a riddle. Listen carefully. . . . First clue: The puppet I have in my basket has eight legs.

Ms. Scott pauses. Children are counting on their fingers, pointing to the spiders still on the project table, excitedly raising their hands, or shouting out, "Spiders!"

Ms. Scott: Oooh, listen to my second clue: My new puppet is not a spider.

Again the teacher pauses. Some children look disappointed; however, it is clear that others do not understand the use of the word *not* and still believe the puppet to be a spider. Still others seem confused and begin talking and looking around the room for more clues.

Ms. Scott: Talk to your neighbors and see if they can help you.

Children: [to each other and the teacher] It's a spider. . . . It can't be a bee, a bee has six legs. . . . No, it's not a spider, that was the other clue. . . . Hey, I heard about a weird dog that had eight legs. . . . Oh, you're silly. . . . That can't be. . . . What about those things that live at Galveston? . . . We saw one once, their legs sting and hurt. . . . Octopus. . . . *Pulpo.* . . .

Ms. Scott: Okay, I am hearing lots of ideas. Listen now as I give you one more clue: I have a special book, and the illustrator, Eric Carle, put this creature on the front cover of the book. See if you know what it is.

Ms. Scott shows the front cover of Eric Carle's *Animals, Animals.*

Children: Octopus! . . . *Pulpo!*

The teacher brings out the blue octopus puppet and shows its eight legs.

Ms. Scott: Now I have another tough question for you. Let's see, there are eight legs on this puppet . . . eight places for my fingers. If I put the fingers of my one hand in the legs, I wonder if there will be any legs that don't have a finger.

Ms. Scott begins to slowly put her fingers into the puppet. Some children count on their fingers, others watch the teacher, and others excitedly shout out an answer.

Rena: You have extra legs, I think.

Tomas: No, it will be just right.

Mario: I know, you will have three legs empty! Just like the spider puppets. 'Cause they have eight legs, too. The answer's not going to change!

Ms. Scott: Let's see if you are right. [She shows the puppet with her fingers in the legs, emphasizing the three empty legs.] Wow! Such good thinking! Now tell me what you know about an octopus.

A lively discussion ensues, with interesting stories and myths and partially correct facts. The teacher decides to focus on a mathematical concept for the rest of the lesson, and she makes a note that octopi would provide an interesting focus for a project on the ocean.

Ms. Scott: I wish I had a puppet like this for each of you. This one will be in our creative dramatics center later if you want to play with it. But for now, I have

a different kind of octopus puppet for you. The only thing is that you will have to make the legs.

She brings out a small paper plate with two large "googly eyes" glued on the bottom. Holding the plate between the palms of both hands, she wiggles her fingers. After questioning Ms. Scott about the number of legs, the children seem satisfied that her new puppet has eight of them.

The teacher distributes a plate to each member of the class. Children experiment with ways to hold their octopi and create exactly eight legs with their own fingers.

Ms. Scott: We are going to do a play. Everyone will get a chance to be an octopus. Half of the class will be the octopus actors, and half of the class will be the audience. Then we will switch places. Okay, first group, over here, you will be the actors. Audience, over there.

Such spontaneous dramas are a common occurrence in Ms. Scott's classroom. Children often work in two groups. While *dividing in half* is not a concept that they have been explicitly taught, children are very aware that it is a fair way to take turns acting out stories. They know that everyone will get a chance to be actors and audience members.

Ms. Scott: First, let's read the play lines [reads from a poem she has written]:

1 octopus, 2 octopi, 3 octopi, 4 octopi, 5,

6 octopi, 7 octopi, 8 octopi, 9 octopi, 10 . . .

10 octopi swimming in the sea,

Everyone's swimming, happy as can be.

Oh, no! Black ink's a'coming . . .

Some run hiding . . . everyone's a'running.

How many octopi do you see?

[The teacher continues.] Now, before we practice our lines, our actors must practice being octopi. Let's see, do you have eight legs? [observes children holding plates and creating eight-legged octopi] . . . All right, let's see you swim happily. [Children wear large smiles as their octopi swim happily.] Can you show your octopi running? How about hiding and being very still? . . . Good! Okay, we're ready! Audience, let me introduce our characters: Octopus number one, Yodit! [The audience claps as Yodit steps forward, wiggles her octopus's legs, and smiles.] . . . Octopus number two . . .

After the teacher introduces all the octopi, octopus actors go through the actions as the audience reads the verses. There are ten octopi standing at the front of the room. When the words "Oh, no!" are read, an assistant teacher brings over a large piece of black butcher paper—the black ink—and covers four actors and their octopi. Children in the audience can still see the eight feet of the four hidden children showing below the black paper.

Ms. Scott: So, how many octopi do you see?

Chere: Six.

Ms. Scott: Are you sure? Show me with your fingers.

Most children easily show six fingers, five on one hand and one on the other; others look at their neighbors and model responses after theirs.

Ms. Scott: Can you show me another way to make six?

The children are familiar with this question. Some immediately show three fingers on one hand and three on the other. Others try different configurations. Still others, satisfied with their first way, only observe their friends' fingers.

Ms. Scott: Now, here's the tough question. How many octopi are hiding in the black ink? They are being very still so you can't see them. I wonder how many are hiding. Listen as I think out loud. . . . "Let's see, we started out with ten octopi, and now we see six."

There is a flurry of activity as children count using their fingers, look at the black ink covering and count legs underneath, or talk to their friends about possible answers. Ms. Scott ignores children who respond verbally and seems to be thinking about the problem herself. After a long pause, she asks the children for their ideas and explanations of their thinking.

Jimmy: I think there's six hiding because I see six.

Chris: Me too!

Rachelle: No, there's four because a 4 and a 6 make 10 octopi [shows fingers]. . . . See?

Phillippe: I counted the feet. There's eight!

Huong: No, people gots two feet. See?

Huong models by placing two fingers in front of each person hiding under the black paper. Then he turns to Phillippe and smiles expectantly, as if he is sure Phillippe will understand. Phillippe shrugs.

Juanita: No, there's three because Hernando, Eduardo, and Phong are back there. I remember!

Ms. Scott: Oh, I like your thinking. I can tell you are all working very hard. Now I want everyone to show me with your fingers what you think, and then we will see. Show me!

When everyone has shown their finger answers, the assistant teacher removes the black paper and the children count the four octopi that were hidden. The actors and audience then change places, and the play is performed again, but with a different number of octopi hidden by the ink.

Ms. Scott: I liked seeing how hard you worked to think about this problem. Now I would like you to make up your own stories. [shows a half strip of large manila paper] Make your ocean on this piece of paper. Then make as many octopi as you want in your ocean. Fold one end of your paper over . . . it's the black ink! When you finish, tell your story to a friend. See if your friend can tell how many octopi are hidden!

Children excitedly begin creating their octopus stories. Their pictures will later become permanent fixtures in the classroom. Months afterward children will still be trying to guess how many octopi are hidden in Mario's or Susie's picture.

Opportunities to emphasize number and operations concepts abound in early childhood settings. For example, Mrs. Nielson observed four prekindergartners at play in the housekeeping center:

Brother (Allen) is setting the table for his pretend family and company. Joshua, as Daddy, is reading the newspaper upside down, and Mommy (Amanda) is cooking the meal. Jennifer is watching but is not involved in the dramatic play. There is one place setting each for the mommy, daddy, brother, and company; however, the company place setting includes all of the extra dishes, stacked in a pile.

Mrs. Nielson asks, "Could I please be the company? And what about Jennifer?" After Allen and Amanda agree, Mrs. Nielson says to Jennifer, "Oooh, this meal looks great. I hope they have enough dishes and spoons and cups for both of us."

Immediately Allen and Amanda begin to match dishes with spoons and cups and make two places for the company. They quickly notice that there are more than enough plates for the company but not enough cups. They send Daddy (Joshua) to the store to buy more—"Just one more cup." When Joshua returns with one paper cup from the classroom sink, the imaginary meal is served and enjoyed by all.

Beginning literacy activities often provide opportunities for number and operations exploration. Kindergartners learning to use a computer software program in Ms. Tank's class selected pictures and wrote words to tell about their pictures. When children discovered the COPY command, they began to make many pictures of the same thing. Ms. Tank decided to ask children to write a number story to tell how many they created. Children loved the activity, and their pictures soon became number stories, complete with number equations.

5 lit ing a en 4 ubg = 9

"5 lightnings and 4 umbrellas equal 9 pictures"

2 fr ad 3 elefhs = 5

"2 flowers and 3 elephants equal 5 pictures"

18 curs + 7 elphets = 25

"18 cars plus 7 elephants equal 25 pictures"

Shared reading experiences are common to early childhood classrooms. While teachers often read stories with a literacy focus, there are many stories that can generate number experiences, as well.

As part of an ecology project, Mr. Lathan reads *The Messy Monster*, by J. Pellowski, to his class of kindergartners. Children retell the story and count all of the items the monster threw away. Then Mr. Lathan asks them to write their own word problems about the animals of the forest.

The children's stories include their own invented spellings, a question involving quantities, and number equations.

"Sam Skunk was eating popcorn in the trees. He ate up five boxes. He didn't know where to put it, so he threw it on the ground. How many now?"

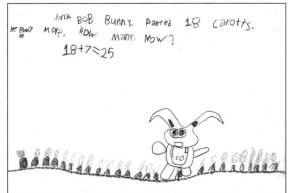

"Bob Bunny planted 18 carrots.
He planted 7 more. How many now?"

Number and operation concepts can be emphasized when children are working in various centers in the classroom.

Abigail and Samantha are arguing in the block area about who has more blocks. The assistant, Ms. Lazarow, asks each girl how many she has. Abigail says she has only 14: "See . . . 1, 2, 3, 4, 5, 6, 7, 8, 9, 10, 12, 16, 18, 14." Samantha says, "That's not right. Let me show you . . . 1, 2, 3, 4, 5, 6, 7, 8, 9, 10, 12, 13, 14, 15, 20, 22, 20, 26, 28, 40, 41, 42, 43, 20, 21, 22. Abigail has 22 blocks!"

Rather than count the blocks correctly herself, Ms. Lazarow suggests a method for comparing quantities: "Let's match Abigail's blocks with Samantha's blocks to see who has more." Having some familiarity with this strategy, the girls make two long rows, matching each of Abigail's blocks to each of Samantha's. When Samantha ends up with two extra blocks, she gives one to Abigail, and they continue their play.

General learning paths and development

Learning paths (or trajectories) in number and operations are detailed in *Learning and Teaching Early Math* (Clements & Sarama 2009). Children's skill development is not governed by their specific age but rather by a range of ages that typically indicates specific developmental benchmarks. Below, general age ranges are defined with the caveat that they are approximate, because skill development is largely dependent on children's experiences. Some general learning paths for number and operations are described below within five specific areas: (1) subitizing; (2) counting (verbal and object); (3) comparing and ordering; (4) early addition and subtraction; and (5) composing number and place value.

Subitizing. Defined as recognizing the numerosity of a group quickly, subitizing is a skill that young children should develop. Looking at a quantity for a short time and then being able to tell how many are in the group(s) without counting each object in the group begins to develop from small sets of two, three, four, and five objects, to parts of sets of six up to twenty. Generally, this development begins between ages 2 and 6. Later, the subitizer sees objects as groups of 10s and 1s and, combined with an understanding of place value, is able to see the numerosity of a large group of numbers quickly. Subitizing relates directly to each of the focal points, prekindergarten through second grade, on understanding and representing whole numbers.

Counting. As early as age 1, children repeat some counting words, although with little meaning or sequence. From ages 2 to 5, children continue learning the verbal sequence and the process of one-to-one correspondence as they count small numbers of objects to 10 and beyond, produce small groups of objects by counting out objects to 10 and beyond, and count backward from 10. Around age 6, they count on or back from any number, develop skip counting, and count to 100 using patterns. Then, using their understanding of place value, children count to 200, and count forward and back with multidigit numbers. Clearly, counting is an especially important focus in prekindergarten and continues to develop through second grade.

Comparing and ordering. Children begin comparing by matching objects one-to-one with other objects. Typically, by age 4 they can compare two small sets of one to five objects, nonverbally and by counting, and they can mentally order number quantities of 1 to 5. At around ages 5 and 6, children count to compare sets to 10, use the ordinal terms *first* through *tenth*, mentally order number quantities from 1 to 10, and estimate sets of objects from ten to twenty. With the development of place value concepts around ages 7 to 8, children compare and order numbers to the thousands. Specifically mentioned in NCTM's prekindergarten and kindergarten Focal Points, comparison of small numbers is an important precursor to the place value concepts that are focal points for first and second grade.

Early addition and subtraction. Children as young as 2 and 3 add and subtract by nonverbally matching the result of an operation with small numbers. Beginning at age 4, they can find the result of joining, separating, and part-part-whole relationships of numbers using direct modeling and counting all to find the sum or difference. As children develop, they begin to count on, find the missing addend, and develop specific counting strategies to find sums or differences. Around age 7, their addition and subtraction strategies become more flexible and they are able to solve problems using known combinations. Although addition and subtraction are a focus primarily in first and second grade, the emphasis on relationships and understanding at the prekindergarten and kindergarten levels is a necessary precursor.

Composing number and place value. Generally, children at age 3 inaccurately recognize part-part-whole relationships. Beginning at age 4, they know the number combinations for 4 and 5, then 6 and 7, and on to 10 and can name the parts of the whole or the whole given the parts. Around age 7, they compose with 10s and 1s and solve problems by composing and decomposing multidigit numbers. The Focal Points for second grade emphasize the importance of the development of place value concepts for the addition and subtraction of multidigit numerals and the fluency that develops with experience and understanding.

Promoting development of key skills and concepts

A great many young children will have learned to count to 10 or higher before reaching kindergarten (Van de Walle & Watkins 1993; Baroody 2004; Fuson 2004). When introducing their child to the kindergarten teacher, the parents may proudly assert, "This is Suzanne. She can read her name, and she knows most of her letters, and she can count to 100!" Counting is indeed an important component of number and operations. However, it is only one small part of that mathematical understanding.

Development of *Number* Knowledge

It has often been said that young children cannot "conserve" number—that is, they think that the amount changes when items are spread out or put closer together. In Piaget's (1965) classic *conservation* task, a child is first shown two lines of items exactly the same in number and length. When the child is asked whether the lines have the same number, the child readily answers yes. Then the items in one of the lines are spread out. Again, the child is asked whether the lines have the same number. Young children typically respond that the longer line has more items.

Ginsburg (1977) describes this behavior as phase 1, *direct perception,* in a three-phase model. Stated differently, the child's judgment is based primarily on the appearance of the lines—their length—rather than on the number of items in the lines.

Line 1   ■ ■ ■ ■ ■ ■

Line 2   ■   ■   ■   ■   ■   ■

In phase 2, children begin to develop their understanding of number and quantity by counting items in different arrangements. Ginsburg labels this *informal knowledge.* In this phase of development, children's concrete knowledge is based on everyday experiences, which help them determine their answers to this Piagetian task. The young child looks at the different spacing in the lines and either counts the items to check the answer or immediately answers the question correctly without needing to count, knowing that merely stretching out the line leaves the quantity unchanged.

As children learn mathematics in more formal settings, they progress to Ginsburg's phase 3, *formal knowledge.* At this stage, children learn the meaning of symbols (=, ≠, <, >) and numerals (6, 4, 20) and their uses in representing relationships between quantities.

Research over the last three decades suggests that with changes in the wording of questions posed to children, they show earlier understanding of *number* than was demonstrated in Piaget's research. Researchers have shown that young children possess considerable informal knowledge (phase 2) even before entering school.

Number sense is defined as "good intuition about numbers and their relationships. It develops gradually as a result of exploring numbers, visualizing them in a variety of contexts, and relating them in ways that are not limited by traditional algorithms" (Howden 1989, 11). Understanding of number and operations and sense about number do not just naturally occur. Number sense cannot be taught in one month-long series of lessons, nor does having number sense mean a child always responds correctly and with certainty. It is complex and develops gradually over time. It can and should be promoted through teaching.

Let's start our exploration of young children and number sense with subitizing, a key number skill that we begin to see in early childhood and that generally receives little adult attention.

Subitizing

Having children observe small quantities of objects organized in specific patterns is a first step in teaching them the skill of subitizing. Teachers can make dot cards with sets of one to five dots (using the typical patterns shown on dominoes or dice) and then "flash" the cards to children for quick identification. With practice, this becomes an enjoyable game, and they begin to see quantities by looking at groups of dots and identifying their quantity without counting. Later, teachers can show patterns that are more disorganized and teach children to view the objects in groups to identify the total quantity without counting. Lydia, age 4, demonstrated this skill to me while she played a game with a hoop:

> When I ask how many of the five pom-poms she had thrown landed inside the hoop if just one had landed outside, Lydia quickly says, "Four." When I ask how she knew without counting, she shows me her hand, folds down one finger, and then says, "See, it's four!" She does not count her fingers, yet she has a visual model to tell how many there are inside the hoop.

The 10-frame is another excellent model for subitizing. When taught with understanding, children can quickly identify sets of 10 and parts that make up 10. A favorite game of first-graders is what one teacher calls "Make 21." Using counters on a 10-frame, children place either one or two counters one row at a time on two 10-frames. When the final counter is placed, children know the game is over and they know exactly how many counters they placed without counting them. They can see it! (For more classroom ideas, see Make Four Elbows, Make Eight, and other similar activity suggestions at the end of this chapter.)

Finger Counting and Patterns

Fingers are an important tool for numerical problem solving. Using fingers to count, compare, and perform simple operations can provide children with a basis for understanding relationships between numbers up to 10. Because most children learn a method of finger counting from their families before entering school, there are cultural differences in the method of finger counting: In some cultures children begin with the thumb; in others, the index finger; and in still others, the little finger. Whatever the case, it is important for teachers to be aware and accepting of these differences.

A natural way of working with numbers, finger patterns give children the opportunity to represent a particular quantity with their fingers using different models. For example, children asked to show 5 with their fingers can show all the fingers on one hand, two fingers on one hand and three fingers on the other, or four fingers on one hand and one finger on the other (Baroody 1987; McClain & Cobb 1999; NRC 2009).

Counting

Many teachers and parents have had the experience of listening to a young child count aloud to 100 with no actual items to count. Taking a deep breath, the child begins counting with "one," continues with an unintelligible stream of numbers, and ends with "one hundred!" When asked to tell the number that, for example, comes after 20 or comes before 5, the young child may begin the long counting sequence again ("one, two, . . ."), demonstrating little or no understanding of the question or a possible answer.

Counting is a skill requiring several abilities. Reciting the sequence of number names—*one, two, three,* and so on—is a memory task, like reciting the alphabet. Many children can do this before they are 3. Children who have not learned this verbal sequence are clearly not able to count, at least in the usual sense of the word. Yet learning the sequence of words does not ensure that children actually can count with accuracy and understanding.

To progress in counting, children must recognize the patterns involved in counting numbers greater than 9—for example, after a number ending in 9, a new decade (10, 20, 30 . . .) begins; or after a new decade number (20), subsequent numbers require the addition of the numbers 1 through 9 (21, 22, 23 . . .). Researchers have discovered that many children beginning kindergarten can count to 12 or higher (Payne & Huinker 1993; Van de Walle & Watkins 1993; Baroody & Wilkins 1999; Baroody 2004; Fuson 2004).

The teen numbers are often the most difficult for children, at least in English. If the teen numbers followed a strictly logical pattern, as in some languages, then number 11 would be called "ten-one" or perhaps "oneteen," and the number 15 would be called "ten-five" or perhaps "fiveteen." However, the English words for the numbers 11 through 15 must simply be memorized, and teachers can use a variety of materials and strategies to make the meaning clear.

The names for the decade numbers (*ten, twenty, thirty* . . .) also deviate from the pattern of number names and need to be learned as distinct items within the counting sequence. Anyone who has listened to children count is familiar with the long pause before they change decades, whether correctly or incorrectly ("25, 26, 27, 28, 29 . . . 50!").

After children have become comfortable with the verbal sequence for counting by 1s, they go on to learn counting in groups; that is, by 2s, by 5s, or by 10s. Children's

---

Development of Number and Counting Skills

Many researchers have investigated young children's understanding of number and counting. Here are some of their discoveries, with the ages/grades stated that indicate the achievable content for children as cited by the National Research Council (2009):

Ages 2 and 3: can count orally the numbers 1 to 10; can count one to six items accurately, especially if they are in a row; can tell how many objects (1 to 5) are in a set without counting (i.e., subitizing).

Age 4 (prekindergarten): can count orally from 1 to 39; can count one to fifteen items in a row accurately; can decompose and compose numbers (6 to 10) and relate these numbers to fingers on two hands.

Age 5 (kindergarten): can count orally to 100 by 10s or by 1s; can count with effort twenty-five things in a row; can see the teen numbers (11 to 19) as sums that include 10 as an addend (e.g., 17 = 10 + 7).

Age 6 (grade 1): can arrange objects in groups of 10; can count by 10s using the decade numbers and then count the leftovers by 1s.

---

familiarity with the counting sequences increases when they join in songs, fingerplays, and rhymes that include counting ("One, two, buckle my shoe").

One-to-one correspondence. Beyond knowing the number words in sequence, counting requires linking a single number name with one and only one object at a time; that is, *one-to-one correspondence.* Many young children simply recite the counting sequence as they touch items, with no awareness that each item corresponds with one word in the counting sequence.

Often during center time or outdoor play periods, children look and sound as though they are counting—counting out grocery items at the cash register, distributing toys to others in their play group, or telling a friend how many pretzels each child has for snack. When we listen closely, however, we may find that children do not grasp the concept of counting, at least not entirely. They sometimes touch more than one item when they say one number, or conversely they say several numbers and touch only one item. In fact, children's verbal counting often seems to have no relation to the objects they are trying to count. A child counting six items may run through the verbal sequence very quickly and declare she has twenty. Or a child who produces the number words very slowly may only reach *three* instead of *six!* One-to-one correspondence for the counting sequence is a skill that must be modeled and often directly taught.

> Khan is a first-grader in my class who has great difficulty with the idea of matching one number to one item in counting. After many attempts, I invite him to stand on my feet and we walk around the room counting every footstep. After he feels, hears, and sees the counting skill, he better understands the process and is able to count accurately with other objects. Although my feet are sore, Khan has experienced the meaning of one-to-one correspondence in a way that he can grasp.

Keeping track while counting. To count correctly, the child also has to keep track of those items she has already counted, making sure not to count any twice. Young children often count an object several times and get an inaccurate result, despite having consistently used the correct verbal sequence and one-to-one correspondence. Moreover, at some point in their mathematical understanding, some children may not see a contradiction if they count their marbles and get *five* one time and *six* the next time. Other children are puzzled when this happens but do not know how to keep this error from happening.

Teachers can give children strategies to help them keep track of items they have already counted. For example, children can count objects into sections of an ice cube tray, making sure only one object is in a section. Or teachers can introduce a keeping-track strategy by placing a line down the center of a paper or workspace and instructing children to slide each object over the line as they count it. In a first-grader's words, "Put the balls you have counted into piles—one pile for counted ones and one pile for the others—then you won't forget."

In mastering counting, children benefit from exposure to a range of strategies and examples and lots of practice. Recall the varied counting experiences in The Octopus Story vignette. Children joined in reciting a songlike poem that emphasized the verbal counting sequence *one* to *ten.* They had occasion to count by 2s when only the feet of the other children were showing. At several points children used their fingers to count

The Young Child and Mathematics

out amounts. And the teacher asked "how many" questions various times, eliciting a variety of answers.

Another example in which a counting issue came up was the block argument between Abigail and Samantha. Neither child had mastered the decade pattern in counting; therefore, they could not do an accurate comparison using only counting strategies. The conflict was resolved when the teacher proposed a comparison method using concrete objects—the blocks themselves.

Quantity

Enumerating the objects in a set is central to the understanding of number and operations. When children realize that they can tell how many objects are in a set of items by saying the last number in a counting sequence ("1, 2, 3, 4, 5, 6—there are six cups"), they have begun to understand number quantity. To develop the concept of *number*, children should have experiences with representing quantity in a variety of ways. Domino and dice pips, 10-frames, tally marks, and finger patterns are all representations that help young children understand quantity.

Part-part-whole relationships. Fundamental in developing number sense are experiences that help children recognize part-part-whole relationships. For example, a whole of 7 can be represented as a 4 and a 3, a 5 and a 2, or a 6 and a 1. Any whole number can be represented in parts. A precursor to *change operations,* the part-part-whole representation helps children develop an understanding of the relationship between addition and subtraction.

> Three-year-old Rodney shows me how old he is using two fingers on the left hand and one finger on the right. He then changes hands, showing two fingers on the right hand and one finger on the left. His words indicate that he is beginning to understand part-part-whole relationships: "See, Miss Nita, I can make 3 like this. But I can't make all the fingers on one hand, like Mommy!"

> Five-year-old Rebecca looks at bug counters on the table and says very confidently without counting, "There are five bugs there. I know because, see, you have two there and three there. A 2 and a 3 always make 5, you know." Rebecca has not learned this as an addition fact; indeed, she is unaware that addition is involved. Rather, she is stating a part-part-whole relationship that is part of her mathematical construction of 5.

> When two bug counters are hidden, however, Rebecca's incomplete understanding is evident. Asked how many bugs are hidden when only three of the five counters are visible, Rebecca says, "Well, three . . . or maybe two." Her belief that a 2 and a 3 always make 5 is not quite strong or versatile enough to help her with the basic subtraction relationship of 5 – 3 = 2.

Three- and 4-year-olds are often able to describe the parts of small numbers (2–5). Understanding of the relationships for larger numbers (6–10) typically does not develop until a year or two later. When the teacher makes a point of providing many experiences with part-part-whole relationships, including hiding tasks (e.g., the Bears in a Cave game in the box on the next page), children's understanding is enhanced and solidified. Regardless of their age, a wealth of experiences should precede children's introduction to the more formal meaning of addition and subtraction.

In exploring octopi and number, Ms. Scott asked children to represent numbers using finger models. She also asked children to think of other ways to show the numbers using their fingers. Confronted with the challenges of the hidden octopi, the children gained experience with part-part-whole relationships. If children understand 10 as a quantity

made up of a 4 and a 6, they are beginning to see the relationship between a whole (10) and its parts (4 and 6). The independent work that children completed as they drew their own problems and story models of octopi swimming in the ocean gave them further opportunity to work with part-part-whole in various contexts.

Using representations. Multiple representations are essential for understanding number and developing number sense. Representations for 11 include the following:

Tally method

"Eleven is two 5s and 1 extra."

Finger method

"Eleven is two hands and a finger."

Ten-frame method

"Eleven is one 10-frame and one more."

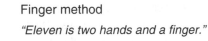

Domino method

"Eleven is 4 on each side and 3 in the middle."

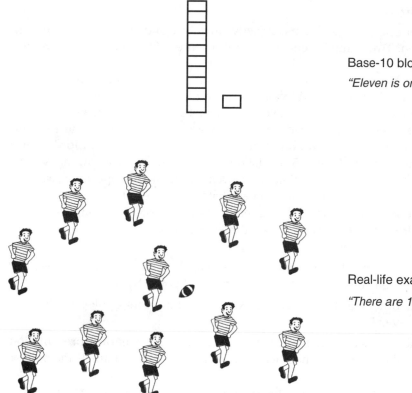

Base-10 blocks method

"Eleven is one 10 and one 1."

Real-life example

"There are 11 players on a football team."

Children represent number quantities in a variety of ways. The sample below shows three different representations by 5-year-olds:

This real-life picture was drawn by Chad in response to the teacher saying, "There were nine baseball players on the team. Four got sick and had to go home. How many were left to play the game?"

Stephanie used a modified tally method to express the number of pennies she had.

Juan used a 10-frame representation to show the number 8. He said he crossed out one box because "I got too many in the top line. There's supposed to be only five."

Change operations

The easiest number operation problems are active in nature and often can be solved by very young children. Two common change operations are *add to* (join) and *take away from* (separate).

Teachers can best ask a question or pose a problem by relating it to children's real-life experiences. When 3-year-old Ryan was given three pieces of candy and asked how many he would have if his brother gave him one more, he readily answered, "Four!" Adding more was something he valued—it meant more candy for him—and he could tell how many he would have if he got one more. Likewise, when 6-year-old Jordana was discussing the trade of some of her 105 special rocks, she knew exactly how many rocks she would have left if she gave Christina fifteen. Again, this active operation was one whose answer was important to Jordana, and she calculated it easily.

Research (Baroody & Standifer 1993; Carpenter et al. 1999; Baroody, Lai, & Mix 2006) suggests that children in all cultures follow a three-step developmental progression in solving such operation problems:

1. They count all the objects. For example, when adding 3 apples to 4 apples, they first count the four apples one by one and then the three apples one by one.

2. They count on. In other words, they already know they have four apples, so they say, "Four . . . five, six, seven."

3. They perform the necessary arithmetic in their heads through mental representation. Perhaps they manipulate objects in their heads or perhaps they have actually memorized the operation.

In the vignette The Octopus Story, the operation used was a part-part-whole relationship, a more static one than the active change stories. The children were later given other octopus stories that used change operations.

Comparison

Comparison terms such as *more than, bigger than, greater than, less than, smaller than, fewer than,* and *the same as* are invaluable to children when relating two or more number values. Children tend to have difficulty with the language of comparison.

> When waiting at a bus stop with an assistant teacher one day, 4-year-old Aston asked her if she was "bigger than his real teacher." Surprised that the child thought her heavier than the teacher, the assistant responded, "I am taller. Is that what you mean?" Aston said, "No, I mean more numbers." Realizing that he meant older, she laughingly responded, "Oh, yes!" and Aston was satisfied with the answer.

Comparing numbers is more than knowing the right words; the child must understand number quantities. A child may describe 100 as "more than 10," "much bigger than 10," or "more than twice as big as 10." In each case, the child uses comparative language to discuss the numbers. In the last two examples, however, the child uses greater comparative knowledge to describe somewhat more specifically the relationship between the two numbers. When children state that "ten 10s make one 100" or "100 is 90 more than 10," they are describing a numerical relationship and using the operations of addition and multiplication. An understanding of number quantity is necessary both to compare quantities in general and to assess specific number relationships.

Using ice cube trays or some other system in which children can sort and place objects of one type in one row and objects of a different type in the other row can help young children compare two number quantities.

Number lines are a good visual strategy for showing children increasing numbers and thus allowing them to compare different numbers. For example, the teacher can begin a number line to show the number of teeth lost by children in the class or the number of school days that have passed. Using tally marks on a roll of paper (such as adding-machine tape) gives children a visual model of number quantities growing progressively larger. As the number line progresses, the tape must be unwound from the roll so the visual model gets longer. Tally marks can be used to represent each number. Then when children compare numbers on the number line, they can see that the numbers at the beginning represent fewer items (teeth, days, etc.) than the numbers farther down the number line. The *before* or *after* position of a number in relation to another number also can be used to determine which number is larger or smaller. This visualization is often referred to as the *mental number line*. Children may make use of their mental representation of number order as well as partial visual models as they compare numbers.

Later, when children are ready to work with 10s and 1s, the adding-machine tape can be cut into strips of ten numbers and the strips arranged to make a 100s chart. Using the 100s chart, children can see the numbers in rows at the bottom being larger than the numbers in the top rows. Both visual models (number line, 100s chart) can be helpful in the comparing process.

Beginning number line

Two strips put together to begin a 100s chart

The comparing operation occurs frequently in daily situations and everyday language. For example, teachers ask when passing out individual cartons of milk, "Do we have enough for everyone? How many more milks do we need so that everyone can have one?"

In The Octopus Story, Ms. Scott asked a comparison question that engaged the children's interest. She gave a very precise comparison question, wondering aloud if the fingers on her hand would fill in all the legs of the puppet. Some of the children were able to grasp the concept, while others needed to watch Ms. Scott demonstrate the action so that they could see the legs before and after Ms. Scott tried on the puppet. Also, in Abigail and Samantha's disagreement over the number of blocks each had, when the girls matched the two sets block-for-block, they were able to easily see that one set had two extra blocks. Again, direct visual information was necessary.

The comparing and equalizing question is a difficult one, because it cannot be visualized as easily as the change operations of *take away from* and *add to*. However, teachers' comments and questions in a variety of contexts help children think about questions of the "how many more?" variety.

Recognizing and writing numerals

To progress in mathematics, children need to be able to use the standard written numerals of their society. In the United States and many other nations, this means becoming familiar with the Arabic numerals: 1, 2, 3, and so on.

There is a parallel in literacy. During the early childhood years, children are learning to recognize letters of the alphabet and over the same period are constructing their understanding of key skills and concepts that are basic to literacy, such as the *alphabetic principle*, phonological knowledge, and structures and patterns in language, among others. Similarly, during the same months and years when they are building an understanding of *number*, young children should be learning to identify and use numerals.

Moreover, just as effective early childhood teachers create literacy-rich classroom environments to promote children's recognition of letters and words, they need to make sure children encounter written numerals and number names in a range of meaningful classroom contexts. In The Octopus story, Ms. Scott pointed to each word and numeral as she read the poem. Although many children could not read the words or the numbers, she wanted to help them learn to recognize the numerals as representing quantity. The numbers were presented in context as the children acted out the poem.

Children first recognize the symbol for a number, connect it to the meaning, and then learn to write it. Describing the numeral 8 as a snowman without a hat, the numeral 1 as a stick, and the numeral 6 as a ball at the bottom attached to the side of the stick, for example, the teacher provides word pictures that help children recognize and later write numerals. Numerals can be classified into groups, such as those that have curves and those that don't, or those that have straight lines and those that don't.

The teacher can provide numerous opportunities, formal and informal, for children to become familiar with numerals. Children can go on scavenger hunts looking for particular numerals, identify the numerals in their phone numbers, cut out numerals from magazines, or find page numbers in their books. The numerals they find can be listed on butcher paper under titles like "Look Where We Found a 3!" or "Can You Help Us Find 9?"

Researchers (e.g., Payne & Huinker 1993; Goldin & Shteingold 2001) propose that whenever possible the number symbol be accompanied by some representation for that quantity (as shown earlier in the number line). The particular representation is not important; the fact that there *is* a representation is the critical part.

Writing numerals is also a fine-motor skill requiring muscle control and copying skills. Just as in early literacy activities, children need to practice writing numerals with many different media. Children can trace numerals in shaving cream, sand, salt, hair gel in a plastic bag, sandpaper, or cornstarch and water. They can create numerals with rolled clay, pipe cleaners, or Popsicle sticks. Children can also practice their writing skills with different writing implements (felt-tip pens, paints, chalk, crayons, pencils) and on a variety of writing surfaces (sidewalk, color paper, posters, easels, journal pages).

When children are learning to recognize and write numerals, it is important that teachers constantly describe the meaning of the numerals. Equally important, teachers should listen to children as they use words to describe what the symbols they write mean to them.

> Veronica, a 5-year-old kindergartner in a bilingual class, records the results of a
> buried treasure activity. When asked about the numerals she has written on one
> side of her paper and the numerals she has written upside down on the other side,

she responds, pointing to the numbers on the first side: "Oh, these numbers are for my teacher. She only speaks English. See, they say *one, two, three, four, five*. These other ones [turns the sheet over] are for my mother. She only speaks Spanish. They say [pointing to each one] *uno, dos, tres, cuatro, cinco.*" Although the symbols are written exactly the same, in Veronica's mind, one set is Spanish and the other is English. For her, the symbols represent two distinctly different counting sequences, yet the same quantities.

Place value

Understanding our decimal system requires the child to recognize that the place of a digit matters—12 is not the same as 21; 56 is not the same as 65. At the heart of the decimal system is the exchange principle: ten 1s for a 10, ten 10s for 100, and so on.

In their early years, children are in the process of learning the number names for two-digit and even three-digit numbers. But the number names are only the tip of the understanding iceberg. To fully comprehend the number 25, for example, children must grasp that it means two 10s and five 1s.

Children need easily identifiable benchmarks for 10 and 100 if they are to understand and confidently use our decimal system. Real-quantity representations that fit in their world can help children develop these benchmarks. For example, there are ten fingers on two hands, there are 100 pennies in a dollar, there are about twenty children in their class, and so on. Visual models are critical if children are to identify benchmarks for these numbers. The 10-frame for 10, the 100s chart for 100, and a large cube to show 1,000 centimeter cubes put together as 10 sets of 100 are all visual models that help children understand place value.

Beginning around age 6, children can respond to estimation questions with understanding (e.g., "Are there more than 20 in this bag or less than 20 in this bag?" . . . "Are there more than 100 or less than 100?"). Relating estimates to benchmarks or visual models helps children give more realistic estimates and provides many opportunities to develop the meaning of larger numbers, as well.

First-grader Tish illustrates the importance of benchmarks in her journal entry when she describes her solution to the problem of the day: "How many hours are there in four days?" Although Tish has never learned the formal algorithm for adding 24 four times, she often uses the 10-blocks and 1-blocks to represent numbers greater than 10. Her journal response illustrates her solution using the blocks. It says, "20 + 20 + 20 + 20 + 4 + 4 + 4 + 4. I did it by using 20s and 4s, which equals 96."

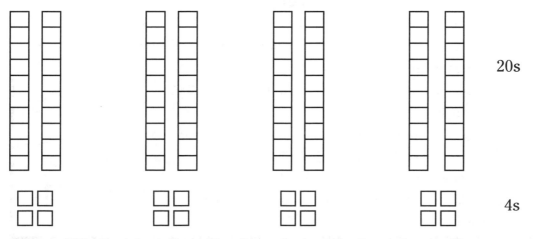

Six-year-old Tish's solution to the problem, "How many hours are there in four days?"

Providing a mathematics-rich environment

Many signs, labels, and papers contain numbers and mathematical symbols. Children often recognize numbers because they have seen them in restaurant menus or advertisements. Children growing up in the 1950s recognized the numerals 5 and 10 easily because five-and-ten stores were common. Today dollar stores and "under $5" stores are more prominent, and children have as a benchmark items that can be purchased for $1 or less than $5. Prices of a favorite treat or collectible, brand-name tennis shoes, or other popular items are familiar numbers and also become a reference point for children. Knowing a favorite item costs $5, the child has a rough idea what $5 is worth—far less than the cost of a bicycle or computer, but more than a candy bar.

Teachers should place labels and advertisements with prominent numerals in the creative dramatics center and change them often. In addition to familiarizing children with numbers and their everyday uses, such real-life items can also be used in presenting children with simple mathematics problems.

Calendar

Most teachers engage children in a daily activity with the calendar, perhaps centering on the day of the week, the date, and the weather, but they may fail to take full advantage of many of the calendar's mathematical possibilities. Calendars can convey information important to the children about schedules, such as the weekly visit to the neighborhood public library. Children can calculate the number of days until an eagerly anticipated

---

Getting Children Thinking about Number Concepts

Teachers provoke children's thinking about number and numeration when they use certain kinds of questions or suggestions. Excellent teachers ask variations of these questions during large- and small-group times, when children are engaged in the various centers, and during routines such as snack or getting ready to go outside. Some questions that facilitate thinking about number and operations:

How many more are in this group?

Is there any other way to show____?

Can you show me another way to make____?

What number comes after____? Before____?

How is this number different from____?

What would happen if I put ten more with these? Ten less?

What if I cover some of these____? How many are hidden?

You have told me that 5 and 6 are parts of 11. Are there different numbers that are parts of 11?

Do you think there are more than 10 in this set, less than 10, or about 10?

Do you think there are more than 100 in this set, less than 100, or about 100?

Estimate how many there are in____.

Count backward from____. Count forward from____.

How many different ways can I make the number____?

How can I make this number with as few place-value blocks as possible?

Tell me about the number 25 using as many different words as possible.

About how many are there in my hand?

---

event—a field trip to a firehouse or a visit from a storyteller—or the days elapsed since the beginning of the school year.

The 100th day of school is a time for celebration in many classrooms, and children participate in a variety of activities emphasizing sets of 100. Children can keep track of the number of days that have passed with numerals placed on a blank calendar shell, or teachers can use adding-machine tape to make a number line, adding a numeral each day. Children's finger representations can indicate sets of 5 or sets of 10 when counting by 5s or 10s on the number line.

Teachers can also introduce tallies as a way of recording days elapsed or days when something happens, such as all the rainy days in a month. Of course, tallies or other representations can record other events, such as someone losing a tooth, that can be kept as a total for each child and for all the children together.

Manipulatives

Using concrete materials known as *manipulatives* can help children develop a sense of number and operations. One basic kind of manipulative for math experiences is a counter. Counters should be uniform in size so that children can focus on number without the distraction of size variations. For example, dominos that use a large dot to represent a value of 1 but six *smaller* dots to represent the value of 6 can erroneously convey to children that 1 is bigger than 6.

School supply stores and catalogs offer a wide variety of counters, including Unifix cubes, connecting cubes, base-10 blocks, and plastic counters in a variety of animal shapes. Teachers can also find at discount stores an array of counters, such as little pom-poms (the fluffy balls that dangle from sew-on fringe edging), "squashed" marbles or smooth glass beads, and Popsicle sticks. Materials such as beans, small stones, or straws from children's daily environments also make good counters.

Another useful kind of material for exploring number is strings of colored plastic beads. A particular color strand can be cut up into sections of a particular number. For example, a string of blue beads can all be cut so that all the beads are separate. A string of green beads can be cut into sections of two beads each, orange into sections of three, yellow into fours, and red beads into fives. With these beads, children can make sets of 6, 7, 8, 9, or 10; or, using the beads as another way to emphasize the part-part-whole model, children can describe their sets of 6 as "2 greens and 4 yellows" or "1 blue and 5 reds."

Literature connection

Five Creatures, written by Emily Jenkins and illustrated by Tomek Bogacki, is an excellent book to emphasize number concepts. The book describes and pictures five creatures that live in a house: a dad, a mom, a daughter, and two cats. On each page spread, the five creatures are described in parts. For example, "Three short, and two tall" . . . "Four grownups, and one child" . . . "Three with orange hair, and two with gray" . . . "Two with long hair, three with short." This book can be used many times in a variety of ways.

For prekindergarten or kindergarten children, the book can be used at the beginning of the year to emphasize the concept of comparison. Each child can illustrate a picture of all the "creatures" that live in his or her home. Naturally, these pictures can contain any person and/or any animals children want to include. Then, using stacking cubes, they can match one cube to each creature drawn. When these matches are completed, they can then stack their cubes and compare their stack with their friends' stacks. Their excitement as they share the size of their stacks is obvious, and comparison vocabulary (*more*, *fewer*, *about the same*) can be introduced quite naturally.

Their pictures can be placed in number notebooks; for example, a class book entitled "Six Creatures" would contain all the pictures that matched a six-cube stack, "Four Creatures" would contain all the pictures that matched a four-cube stack, and so on. Then, throughout the year, as creatures are added to families, children would need to add to their pictures and the pages would need to be moved to the appropriate book. (I recommend that regardless of life circumstances, no creatures should ever be erased from a page, because as one 5-year-old told me, "CoCo is always in my heart!")

Five Creatures could also be used in first or second grade as a model of a part-part-whole relationship. I have used it to write a class book about the students in our class. It was entitled "24 Creatures" and contained information and illustrations about our class members. Some sample pages were, "12 people liked sausage pizza, and 12 people did not like sausage pizza," "5 people had older brothers, and 19 people didn't have older brothers," and "10 people preferred the art center the most, and 14 people liked other centers more." We added to the book weekly in connection to a class graph that we made. The title of the book was changed as new students arrived, but it became a favorite source for classroom discussion and was reread and rewritten many times.

In-class assessments

The Snake Game is an excellent assessment tool for beginning number concepts and skills. Adapted from a game played in South America using large seed pods, this version requires the creation of a game board in the shape of a snake, consisting of approximately twenty spaces, from the snake head to the snake tail.

The Snake Game

Look for the video clip of "The Snake Game" on the DVD!

Two players progress from the head of the snake to the tail of the snake by moving their counters from space to space, one turn at a time. In each round of play, one child is the guesser and the other child is the hider, and then the roles switch so both children get a turn. During a turn, the hider selects zero, one, two, or three objects to hide in her hand. The guesser then guesses how many objects she is hiding. If the guesser is correct, he moves that number of spaces. But if the guesser is incorrect, the hider moves that number of spaces.

Children quickly learn that as the hider, if they put three objects in their hand, they can move quite quickly if their partner guesses incorrectly. They then begin to "fool" their partner, by changing the number hidden. Eventually, they try to "really fool" their partner by placing zero objects in their hand, and they are quite excited when they surprise their partner with this. Their excitement does not last long, however, because they soon realize they get to move zero spaces, and that doesn't get them anywhere!

Observing children as they play The Snake Game, or even playing this game with a child, results in some interesting assessments of children's number skills and understanding of number concepts. As children move their counters across the board, their skill in counting can be observed by their use of one-to-one correspondence on each turn. As children look at the objects hidden by their partner, their ability to subitize small numbers can be observed quite easily. Finally, their understanding of quantity, especially the quantity zero, can be observed and noted. Realizing that the quantity of three is more than two or one is important. More important, this game emphasizes that zero means they do not move any spaces, an important understanding of quantity.

*   *   *

To write an exhaustive list of mathematics activities for young children would be impossible. This is especially true for number and operations; this content area is the one most often addressed in books, texts, or curriculum documents for young children. The examples presented in the section that follows should be used only if appropriate or if they can be adapted to your particular situation. While they are organized roughly in order of difficulty, many can be expanded or simplified to be more or less challenging.

Make Four Elbows!

Children form a circle and begin slowly walking in one direction. At a signal from the leader, they stop and listen to instructions. When the leader states, "Make four elbows," the children touch one or both of their elbows to other children's elbows to make a total of four connected elbows. After everyone shares their methods for accomplishing this task, new directions, such as "Make twelve fingers," are given. Some favorites: Make three ankles, make nine shoulders, and make seven feet.

Children delight in working together to make the required number of body parts. Their solutions are often creative and unusual. Two 4-year-olds, Rudi and Elise, made five shoulders by standing back-to-back, shoulders touching, with one other friend touching one shoulder to their shoulders. When asked how they made five, they responded, "We each got two. That makes four, and one more is five!"

Asked to make twelve fingers, three kindergartners touched four fingers each, stating that they wanted to "be fair." For seven feet, four 4-year-olds put their feet together, one child holding one foot off the ground. They explained that they had eight feet and they had to get rid of one, "so John held one up."

Tees and Tees and More

Children create sculptures using pieces of plastic foam, plastic stirring straws, pipe cleaners, and golf tees. Although the golf tees can be pushed quite easily into the foam, children often like to use plastic hammers and other workshop tools to make their sculptures. This is a good activity for the classroom's constructing center.

When they are finished, children describe their works of art using numbers and position words. For example, Charles and Kendall each used four tees in their constructions. In Charles's sculpture all of the tees were at the top of the foam piece, while in Kendall's, two tees were at the top and two at the bottom. The language the boys used to describe their constructions was delightful and included position words as well as number words.

More/Less Concentration

Sixteen number cards with representations of numbers (using 10-frames, numerals, tally marks, or pips like those found on a domino) are placed face down in a 4-by-4 grid. A More/Less spinner (half of the spinner is labeled More, the other half, Less) is spun to determine if the More game or the Less game will be played.

The first child turns over two cards. In the More game, if the numerical value of the second card is *greater than* that of the first card, that pair of cards now belongs to the child, and she takes them from the grid. If the value of the second card is less than that of the first card, the cards are turned face down again and the next player takes his turn.

Remembering the value of the cards previously turned over helps. The game is over when all sixteen cards have been collected by the players, but there is no need to compare which child has the most cards or to declare a winner.

The Less game is played in a similar way, but for a player to claim a pair of cards, the value of the second card turned over must be *less than* that of the first. Children 5 years and older generally find *more* an easy concept; *less* is harder for them to grasp, and they may need some assistance from the teacher when playing the Less game.

Children love to play the More and Less games in small groups and with partners during center time. Some children need to count the representations on the cards and look at a number line to help them determine which value is greater. Others compare both numbers using a visual one-to-one correspondence. Some players clearly do not know which number is larger or smaller, so their partners can help them find the solution.

How Many Legs?

Children make playbills or advertisements for a puppet show to be presented in the creative dramatics center, featuring insects, animals, and other creatures. Each puppet character needs to be accurately drawn in the advertisements and playbills!

Children's pictures often illustrate their understanding of number. In many of the pictures, the creatures initially may not have enough legs or antennas or spots. A few key questions ("Did you draw enough legs?" or "Does your ladybug have the same number of spots as our puppet?") help the children to correct their pictures so that the numbers of legs, spots, or antennae in their drawings match the puppets.

Block Towers

A die with two 1s, two 2s, and two 3s is added to the block center. The teacher may want to explain that this die is special, and that a regular die has pips for 1 to 6. The children throw the die and build towers with the indicated number of blocks. The towers are then compared by height. Number cards representing 1, 2, and 3 in a variety of different ways can also be used instead of a die.

Children's thinking is very evident in this activity, which is excellent for prekindergartners. Often, children change the activity by throwing the die a number of times and building many towers before comparing. They also figure out that the way the blocks are stacked affects how tall the towers are. Two blocks stacked "the tall way" are taller than three blocks stacked "the wide way."

Priscilla's Bows

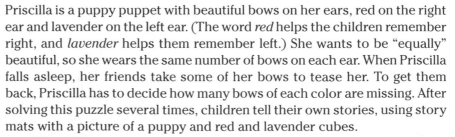

Priscilla is a puppy puppet with beautiful bows on her ears, red on the right ear and lavender on the left ear. (The word *red* helps the children remember right, and *lavender* helps them remember left.) She wants to be "equally" beautiful, so she wears the same number of bows on each ear. When Priscilla falls asleep, her friends take some of her bows to tease her. To get them back, Priscilla has to decide how many bows of each color are missing. After solving this puzzle several times, children tell their own stories, using story mats with a picture of a puppy and red and lavender cubes.

The children often tell the same exact story as the one modeled with the puppet. They pretend to be Priscilla and employ interesting strategies for finding out how many bows are missing. Shawna, a 4-year-old, said, "You just look real hard and when you close your eyes, you keep trying to remember how many were there until you open your eyes again." Amelia, another 4-year-old, said, "You just count how many are on one ear and then you know that's how many you need when you wake up. If you 'member, it works!"

Make Eight

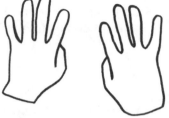

Children use a variety of materials, such as cubes, pennies, or fingers, to construct the number 8 (or any other number) as many ways as possible. They then record this process by drawing pictures (which may also include written numerals) illustrating their methods for constructing 8. For example, a child who uses red and blue connecting cubes might draw a train of three red cubes and five blue cubes. A child who uses pennies might draw two heads and six tails. Another drawing might show four fingers on one hand and four fingers on another hand. Many children know only a few ways to express 8. By modeling or asking questions, the teacher can encourage children to see and make 8 in other ways.

10-Frame Cookie Sheet

The teacher constructs a 10-frame by dividing a metal cookie sheet with colored tape. He then represents a number on the 10-frame using magnets and asks the children to look quickly and tell the number by showing the same number of fingers. The procedure can be repeated over and over representing different numbers as the teacher removes or adds magnets. The sound of the magnets being added to or removed from the metal cookie sheet helps children keep count.

Children learn to tell the number of magnets by simply looking. When asked how he knew so quickly there were five magnets on the cookie sheet without counting, Troy answered, "I just know. It filled up all the top line and that's always five!" When Crissy was asked how she knew there were seven magnets on the cookie sheet, she said, "Because there's two more than five—a row and two more!"

Number Necklaces

Children make number representations on paper plates or index cards using a 10-frame format, domino pips, tally marks, and/or numerals. The plates or cards are made into necklaces using yarn, and each child wears one.

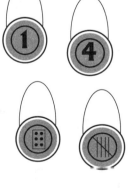

Many games can be played outside with the necklaces. Holding hands, children can run or skip in a circle until a whistle is blown. The teacher then calls out the name of a game. Find a Match requires children to find someone with the same number represented on his or her necklace. In Make a Train, the children make the number sequence 1–10 by joining hands to make a train.

Kindergartners love to play games with number necklaces. When children need physical activity, the teacher can take them outside to play Make a Sum. The children run or skip clockwise in a large circle until the teacher blows the whistle twice. Children then stop and listen as the teacher announces, for example, "Make 10."

> Timmy, whose necklace shows six tally marks, and Bill, who has seven shown on a 10-frame, are best friends and check each other's number first. Timmy says, "Uh-oh! We make too much. I need something littler." He then runs and finds Corinne, who has a 4 on her number necklace. After a careful check, Timmy and Corinne decide they make 10 and stand together.

When everyone has shared their solutions, the children go back to their circle and skip again until the whistle blows and the teacher calls a new sum.

Number and Operations

Guidelines in Action

The classroom examples and activities throughout this chapter reflect some of the curriculum, instruction, and assessment guidelines from chapter 2 that form the basis for teaching mathematics effectively to young children. To clarify how specific guidelines look in practice, this chart highlights five instances in which they are evident.

Curriculum Guideline 1—Focus on important mathematics	Each of the classroom experiences described in the chapter addresses one of the focal points for number and operations. In addition, the connections made to a children's everyday lives, as well as to their prior knowledge, contribute to their understanding of number concepts.
Curriculum Guideline 4—Create a mathematics-rich environment	There are many examples of materials that should be used. The visual models for number (dominoes, dice, 10-frames, 100s charts, and place-value blocks) are most important and contribute greatly to children's understanding and their skill with both single- and multidigit numbers. The activity Estimation & Quick Look was specifically designed to use visual models for evaluating quantity.
Instruction Guideline 1—Plan experiences	This guideline is especially evident in the chapter sections General Learning Paths and Development and Promoting Development of Key Skills and Concepts. The classroom experiences outlined in these sections illustrate the focus on both child and individual development. The Octopus Story is developmentally appropriate for kindergartners, and the teacher is quite intentional with the tasks, as the tasks connect to the focal points for number and operations.
Instruction Guideline 2—Orchestrate classroom activities	Deciding how and when to intervene is important. In the housekeeping center, the teacher intervened by acting as a player, drawing in an onlooking child (Jennifer), and asking a simple number question that might be posed in a real-life situation. In the block center, the assistant teacher did not step in to resolve Abigail and Samantha's dispute about who had more blocks. Instead, she proposed a comparing strategy the children could use without relying on the counting sequence. This strategy helped to consolidate their understanding of number, counting, and perhaps measurement.
Assessment Guideline 2—Observe and interact purposefully	Children's different levels of understanding can be noted during The Octopus Story. Jimmy's response to the "how many are hiding?" question reflected his preoccupation with only what he sees. In contrast, Rachelle's response suggested that she understands the consistency of the number 10 because it always is "a 4 and a 6." During the activity The Snake Game, the assessment occurs during a class activity and intentionally identifies specific criteria for assessment: counting, subitizing, and understanding of small quantities.

Twinkle Music

"Sheet music" (musical staffs with numerals instead of music notes) is added to the music center and corresponding numerals are written on a xylophone, with 1 written on C, 2 on D, 3 on E, and so on. Children play the xylophone following the numerals written in the music: 1, 1, 5, 5, 6, 6, 5; 4, 4, 3, 3, 2, 2, 1 represents the beginning of "Twinkle, Twinkle, Little Star," a song familiar to most young children.

Children constantly return to the music center to play Twinkle Music. Once they understand the procedure, they quickly memorize "Twinkle, Twinkle, Little Star," and the tune is frequently heard in the center. Children can create their own music by writing numbers on the music paper and asking their friends to perform concerts.

Music can also be made with large plastic bottles. Six 2-liter plastic soda bottles are taped together in a row and labeled 1 through 6. A small amount of water is poured into the first bottle, and each subsequent bottle is filled with more water than the previous one. The children make music by blowing across the tops of the bottles. The notes are not exactly those of a regular musical scale, but they make wonderful music nonetheless. Adding water to plastic bottles to make musical instruments is also a great way to connect mathematics with music and science.

Counting Books

The most identifiable mathematics books in the library are counting books. The variations are fascinating and applicable to almost every subject or theme. Children can read them, add more pages, or create their own type of counting book. Asking, "What page comes next?" provides a lesson in prediction.

One Tortoise, Ten Wallabies: A Wildlife Counting Book, by Jakki Wood, illustrates counting baby and adult animals. It pictures only the numbers 1 through 12, 15, 20, 25, 50, and 101, giving children a reason to add pages. *Mouse Count*, by Ellen Stoll Walsh, and *Bat Jamboree*, by Kathi Appelt, provide good beginnings for children's number stories. After reading and acting out the stories, children select new characters and a new setting for their stories. They create, write, and read their own stories to the class, asking questions in the form of "How many . . . ?"

If resources are available, these amazing stories by children can be captured on video. At the end of each story, the child can pose a question. An image of a large question mark indicates that viewers should give the answer. The question mark can be inserted using special effects, but simply filming a question mark drawn on a piece of poster board works just as well. Videos can be exchanged between classes. Children not only enjoy the dramatized stories, they work hard to solve their classmates' puzzles.

Children love books that can be acted out, but they are sometimes so familiar with a story that they become "functionally fixed" on an event or a number. For example, whenever a 4-year-old English language learner was asked to show three fingers, she always said, "Cha-Cha-Cha!" because the three bats in *Bat Jamboree* always say "Cha-Cha-Cha!" She needed to be introduced to a broader range of stories and a broader experience of the number 3.

How Many Windows?

After counting the number of windows, doors, or lights in the school as a class project, children are asked to count the windows, doors, or lights in their homes. Using tally marks is an important part of the assignment. Helping children record and accurately report the count also involves family members in schoolwork. The results can later be used for classroom discussions.

This activity can accompany a social studies unit on community helpers and responsibility. Using the results, the class discusses the jobs of glaziers, carpenters, and electricians. The teacher poses questions about work and time and asks children to make predictions: What would happen if someone broke all the windows in the school? If the glazier took five minutes to fix every window, how many minutes would it take to fix all the windows? How many hours? If we made our school twice as big, how many doors, windows, and lights would be needed?

After engaging in this activity, one class saw a large skyscraper from the bus window while on a field trip. When the children saw a window washer near the top, they spent ten minutes trying to figure out how many windows were in the skyscraper and wondering how much a window washer would charge for cleaning the windows. Because there wasn't time to count all the windows while on the bus, when the children returned to the classroom they discussed possible solutions to the problem by arraying colored tiles on their desks in rows, like the windows of the building. The children compared different ways to array the tiles and, as a group, decided which setup most closely resembled the skyscraper. They then counted the number of tiles to determine how many windows there were.

I Spy

I Spy Two Eyes: Numbers in Art, by Lucy Micklethwait, shows twenty famous works of art. Each picture contains a particular number of some objects. For example, "The New Year," by Picasso, contains seventeen birds.

Children can create their own art gallery, modeled after Micklethwait's examples. Each child selects a specific item and a number from 1 to 25, then paints or draws the item that number of times. The children's pictures are framed and displayed to create an art gallery; the exhibition is titled "I Spy." Children from other classes enjoy the art and have fun hunting for and counting the special items in each picture.

Where's the Bear?

Upside down plastic cups are labeled with a number from 1 to 20 and displayed in order on a chalk tray. A child hides a small plastic bear under one of the cups. The other children take turns asking questions—referring to the cups by their numbers—to determine which cup hides the plastic bear.

They may ask, "Is the bear under cup 4?" . . . "Is the bear in a cup before cup 16?" . . . "Is the bear in a cup after cup 6?" . . . "Is the bear in a cup between cups 7 and 10?" The child who hid the bear can respond, giving as many clues (visual and verbal) as he wants until the children find the bear.

Children love this game, and the position words they learn (*between, before, after, in front of, behind*) are helpful, as are the problem-solving strategies they discover. For example, when one child finds out that the bear is hidden in a cup after cup 6, another child may guess cup 7, another guess cup 8, and so on. After one such case in which the children finally discovered the bear hidden in one of the last cups, Amy said, "Hey! We shouldn't guess the numbers right in a row. Next time let's skip around and we can find out faster!"

Look for the video clip of "Where's the Bear?" on the DVD!

How Many Pips Are Hidden?

Children learn that a die has six sides (or faces) and that the dots on the die are called pips. Each side has a different amount of pips, ranging from one to six. By investigating, they learn that adding the numbers on opposite faces equals 7. For example, 5 is opposite 2, and 6 is opposite 1.

To play the game, children sit in a circle and one of them throws a large foam die into the middle. Children try to determine the number of pips hidden on the bottom side of the die. They typically solve this dilemma by counting the pips on each side and locating the side that is missing in the sequence 1–6. However, if they know that opposite sides add up to 7, then the task is much easier. If the top of the die shows one pip, then six pips are hidden; if three pips are on top, then four are on the bottom; and so on.

A similar but more challenging activity involves making dice towers. For example, if three dice are made into a tower, the bottom die will have seven pips hidden, the second die will also have seven pips hidden, and the top die will have 7 minus [the number of pips on the very top] hidden.

Where Are the Minibeasts?

In a search for "minibeasts," mathematics skills can be easily linked to science investigations. Minibeasts are any creatures smaller than the length of a child's pinkie finger. Children predict different places in which they will find minibeasts, such as in the air, on a tree, on the sidewalk, in the grass, or in the bushes. Predictions are recorded indoors, and then the expedition begins. Children work with partners, select a likely mini-beast environment, and tally the number of creatures they find. Upon returning to the classroom, the results are graphed and discussed.

Tallying and recording the numbers counted are important skills for young children. Teachers also gain insight from watching children count and tally moving minibeasts. Children are often stumped upon encountering a large group of squirming creatures. As one child remarked when investigating an ant colony, "How can we count this many? We don't have any more numbers!" A problem like this naturally leads to a discussion of really big numbers and sampling strategies.

And One Good Friendship

This activity helps the teacher recognize and assess social development as well as children's understanding of number. Using as a model the poem "two friends," by Nikki Giovanni, children can draw pictures of their own friends. The pictures are then described using number words similar to those in the poem.

two friends
lydia and shirley have
two pierced ears and
two bare ones
five pigtails
two pairs of sneakers
two berets
two smiles
one necklace
one bracelet
lots of stripes and
one good friendship

Look for the video clip of "Estimating Quantity" on the DVD!

Estimation & Quick Look

Children estimate the quantity of items in bags of materials, such as erasers and markers, by selecting from the following ranges: fewer than or equal to 50, more than 50 but fewer than or equal to 100, more than 100 but fewer than or equal to 150, or more than 150. After estimating, groups of children then empty the bags of materials and organize the objects into groups of 10, 20, 50, or 100 using 10-frames or 100s charts. When the organization is complete, children review the accuracy of their estimations by taking a "Quick Look" at the objects that had been in each of the bags and recording exactly how many objects were in the bags.

Pom-Pom Jacks

Place colorful pom-poms on the floor inside a yarn circle twenty inches in diameter. Use enough pom-poms to almost fill the circle. As a class, select a special "Number" to use in the activity. Children estimate how many sets of the Number of pom-poms can be collected during the time it takes the teacher to bounce the ball the Number of times. As the teacher bounces the ball, children place the sets they collect outside the circle.

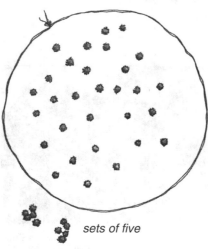

sets of five

After conducting the activity, children compare their results with their estimations. The selected number is changed often, and new experiments are tried. Note that this activity requires estimating a measurement (e.g., children estimate that the time it takes to bounce a ball three times is less than the time it takes to bounce a ball seven times) as well as estimating how many sets of that number of items can be made within their estimated time frame.

Observing children's comments during this activity provides insight into their learning processes. For example, after doing the activity with the number 8, one group of second-graders was asked to estimate what would happen if the number 4 were chosen. Ron said that it "would be half, because 4 is half of 8." Jackie disagreed. She said it would be much more than half because four pom-poms are easier to grab, and "We're a lot better at doing this 'cause we've practiced!"

The Number Dance

Physical experiences can help children understand big numbers and place value. Greenes (1999) suggests that children can "feel" large numbers by using large, circling arm movements for 100s, forearm movements for 10s, and finger flicking movements for 1s. For example, children can model the number 431 by making four large, circling arm movements, three forearm movements, and one finger movement. Similarly, children can model the number 134 by making one large circling arm movement, three forearm movements, and four finger movements. In this way children understand that 431 and 134 are very different numbers—because they "feel" different.

Because children are very interested in large numbers, an understanding of place value should be taught at an early age. Children love to do The Number Dance, and they often create even larger motions (such as jumping) for the 1,000s place.

Build the Numbers!

Wooden or plastic place-value blocks are common mathematics manipulatives. Small unit cubes represent 1s; long 10-unit rods represent 10s; 10-by-10 flat blocks represent 100s; and large, 10-by-10-by-10 cubes represent 1,000s. Given the rods and unit cubes, children try to build 100 as many different ways as possible. Similarly, given the flat blocks, rods, and unit cubes, children can build 1,000 a number of different ways.

Children often discover patterns in their solutions. For example, to make 100, one 100 block could be used, or one 10s rod and 90 unit blocks, two 10s rods and 80 unit blocks, three 10s rods and 70 unit blocks, and so on.

The children record their solutions by pasting cutouts of shapes representing the blocks to pieces of paper. A small square represents a unit cube; a long, thin rectangle represents a 10s rod; a large rectangle represents the 100s block; and a very large square represents a 1,000s cube. By second grade the children are also usually able to draw the different ways they construct the numbers.

All the Ways to Make . . . 222

After children learn the Build the Numbers! activity, they are ready for this one, which is more complex. Children find all the ways to make 222 using place-value blocks or all the ways to make $2.22 using coins. The number 222 (or 333, 444, etc.) is a good number to use because the same numeral is in each place value; children must have a real understanding of the difference between two units, two 10s, and two 100s.

After the children construct the number with blocks, the next step is to write equations or phrases illustrating all the possible ways to make or describe 222. This list can be added to throughout the year, emphasizing unique and creative solutions. Some possible solutions include "half of 444," "111 + 111," "a palindrome," and "more days than we are in school." One class came up with more than a hundred different ways to describe 222!

In My Bag!

The teacher or second grade child places some place-value blocks in a bag and tells the class how many. Children work as partners to figure out which place-value blocks are in the bag. To do so, they ask questions about the blocks' total value that can be answered yes or no. This game can also be played with coins.

> Mr. Emilio told his class that he had five coins in his bag. He asked the class to guess what the coins were. Mary Ann asked, "Is your bag more than a dollar?" Mr. Emilio responded, "No!" Willy whispered to his partner, "Well, they can't be all quarters!" Cameron asked, "Is it less than 50 cents?" Mr. Emilio said yes. Questions continued and children discovered with little trouble that Mr. Emilio had five nickels in his bag.

While the children in this example seemed to solve the puzzle easily, children often find the game very difficult when first learned. Over time, the teacher should observe that children refine their reasoning strategies by asking questions and listening closely to the answers.

Scavenger Hunt

At home, children hunt for numbers larger than 100. They record them by copying them and drawing a picture of where they found them, cutting them out (if possible) and pasting them on note paper, or photographing them. When the children bring the numbers to class, they can be classified by size (e.g., numbers greater than 100 but less than 200, or numbers greater than 1,000) or by their use. The discovery of special types of numbers, such as zip codes and phone numbers, leads to discussions of number meaning and the fact that some numbers are used only as locators.

Number and Operations

Roll and Make a Dollar

In this game for two players, two dice are used, one die featuring a picture of a coin on each face (one quarter, two dimes, two nickels, and one penny) and the other die featuring the numerals 1 through 6. Each player rolls both dice on his or her turn. The player then gets the number of coins shown. For example, if 3 is rolled on the number die, and a quarter is rolled on the coin die, the player gets three quarters. A player can stop at any time, but if she rolls the dice, she must take the indicated number of coins. After one or both players have rolled the dice ten times or both players decide to stop, the coins are totaled to learn which player has an amount closer to $1 without going over.

This activity provides useful experience in estimation and reasoning, which occur as children decide whether to stop rolling or to continue. It is an excellent learning center game for first- and second-graders. If the sum is changed to 50¢ and the quarter is eliminated, kindergartners enjoy it as well.

A Million?

Children love to say large numbers, and children and adults frequently say "a million" to indicate a very large amount. When asked to guess or estimate "how many," children often respond by saying the largest number they know, and *million* is often used with little understanding or meaning. Many library books use the word *million* in their titles or as part of their text.

The book *A Million Fish—More or Less*, written by Patricia C. McKissack and illustrated by Dena Schutzer, includes a picture of "a million" fish, which provides an interesting investigation of a million. After inspecting the picture, children count only sixty-five fish. Children pick up their calculators, and the teacher explains that they are to key in "65" and then "+65=" over and over to see if they can add 65 until they reach 1 million.

As children work, the teacher observes, saying, "Just tell me when you reach 1 million. . . . Are you there yet?" After a few minutes, as children get used to the keystrokes, they begin adding very rapidly and soon realize that it will take a long time to reach 1 million. Most children soon stop, put their calculators away, and go on to some other activity. However, there is often at least one child who carries the calculator with him throughout the day. After about three to four hours, he shouts, "I got 1 million!"

Ice Cream Shop

A creative dramatics center provides a wonderful opportunity for projects involving the use of number. An ice cream shop can be set up by converting the housekeeping or store center: bins filled with Unifix cubes represent scoops of ice cream; coins and cash registers (real or pretend) are used for monetary transactions; and paper hats and aprons are uniforms for the employees.

Ice cream prices, lists of flavors, store bills, and advertisements are written and illustrated. Customers are given numbers indicating the order in which they will be served. Making ice cream from recipes involving measurement is a great final event for the Ice Cream Shop project. This project takes some time, but the results are often quite beneficial to young children's understanding of mathematics and its use in everyday life.

Patterns, Functions, and Algebra
in the Early Childhood Curriculum

Children's first encounters with patterns are not in school but in nature, at home, at play, and in stories. Children watch the sun setting at the end of every day; listen to stories, songs, and verses that follow patterns; notice how a puppy plays and sleeps on a schedule; jump rope to patterned chants; and skip over sidewalk bricks laid in patterns. Preschoolers entering the world of schooling can already recognize patterns in their environment. Although they cannot always verbalize or represent the patterns with symbols, they are frequently able to predict what will happen next. A parent or teacher who changes a pattern gets a quick reaction from the child. Skipping a page in a story, forgetting the treat at the end of a meal, or not following the bedtime ritual to the letter brings a prompt protest.

Mathematics is the science and language of patterns. Thinking about patterns helps children make sense of mathematics. They learn that mathematics is not a collection of unrelated facts and procedures. Instead, recognizing and working with patterns helps young children to predict what will happen, talk about relationships, and see the connections between mathematics concepts and their world. Algebra is the fundamental language of mathematics, linking numerals and symbols together to represent the relationship between quantities and allowing us to use models to solve problems. An understanding of *function*—which at this age means being able to recognize a relationship between two sets of objects—will help children build a connection between patterns and algebraic thinking.

Though primary grade children are not ready to formally learn algebra, some algebraic concepts and ideas can be introduced to children in the early elementary grades because they enhance students' arithmetic ability (Carpenter, Franke, & Levi 2003; Mason 2008). Not all algebraic concepts are appropriate for young children, but at an early age they are ready to get a taste of symbols, representation, patterns, graphing, equations, and functions, to build a foundation for later mathematics learning.

Because the study of patterns is basic to all mathematical thinking, it has a close natural connection to the other math content areas. Patterns in number, geometry, measurement, and data analysis all belong in the math curriculum for young children.

NCTM's *Curriculum Focal Points* (2006) appropriately lists aspects of pattern as a topic with connections to number and geometry for prekindergarten through second grade. Explicitly, the teacher should provide a link between young children's informal observations of patterns in daily life and the more formal, mathematical descriptions of patterns, changes, and relationships. Initially, she encourages children to use their own language, representations, and symbols—that is, forms they find meaningful. Subsequent teaching helps to move children toward more formal school mathematics and conventional symbolic notations.

In addition, at the first and second grade levels, the basic facts for addition and subtraction are taught by writing equations, analyzing patterns and relationships between numbers, and employing a variety of strategies so children learn those number facts fluently by the end of second grade. For young children who can think algebraically, the learning of number facts is more than a skill drill activity. Rather, it is something they learn from using patterns, number properties, and the relationships between numbers. The ideas and concepts of algebra are powerful!

Children engage with patterns in a variety of contexts

The idea of patterns (with its later connection to functions and algebra) can be emphasized throughout the young child's day; opportunities to identify patterns occur frequently during spontaneous play with friends, routine activities, outdoor trips, literacy lessons, circle time, snack and lunch, shared reading, and travel in a car. With young children, helping them to understand patterns, functions, and algebra is a continual process of connecting what they are noticing in the outside world with what they are discovering in teacher-planned pattern activities in the classroom.

The following series of kindergarten activities and routines illustrates an ongoing investigation of number and pattern. The events described here took place over several months in varied settings, including a learning center, a small-group lesson, transition time, and even at home. The children are 5 and 6 years old, and many have limited proficiency in English.

Number Hangers

First event (early January)

Ms. Tinsley has set up a variety of number stations in her kindergarten classroom. Each station has a particular type of manipulative: Unifix cubes, color tiles, plastic chain links, strands of plastic beads, toothpicks and glue, golf tees and foam sheets, foam cubes, pattern blocks, or "squashed" marbles. The children, in groups of two or three, choose a station and create models of a given number.

At the links station, three children use red and blue plastic links to make chains for the number 5. The teacher challenges them each to make as many different combinations as possible, grouping red and blue links together in chains of five links each.

Amanda: I got a 5 chain! [holds up a chain of five links: one red at the end and then four blues]

Jorge: I got one! [holds up a chain of four links]

Amanda: Here's another one, two reds and three blues. And another one, one blue and four reds.

Mark: Mine is different [holding up a chain with alternating blue and red links]. . . . See? It's a pattern.

The children continue to work, creating a pile of chains in the center of the table. Some chains have six links and a few have four, but most of the chains conform to the rules. After about ten minutes, the teacher comes over to the links station.

Ms. Tinsley: You three have certainly made a lot of chains. What number are you working on?

Amanda: The number 5. See, here's one! [holds up a chain and counts the links] . . . 1, 2, 3, 4, 5.

Ms. Tinsley: You have all made so many chains; it would take a long time to count the links in every one. I wonder if we could tell, by just looking, if all the chains have exactly five links?

She lays out a few chains so that those with five links can be seen to match in length. Amanda, Jorge, and Mark soon begin matching chains and adding or subtracting links as necessary.

As they work, the teacher picks up Mark's chain with the alternating colors. She remarks on the pattern but also reminds Mark that in the activity that day, she wanted him to keep colors together. The aim of the activity is for children to see and work with patterns that show basic number facts—in this case, working with the number 5 (e.g., 2 + 3 = 5, 1 + 4 = 5, 3 + 2 = 5, 5 + 0 = 5). Children create and examine representations of these facts by staying within the teacher's constraint of "keeping colors together," as in a chain of two reds and then three blues—red, red, blue, blue, blue.

Ms. Tinsley: Well, keep working. I wonder how you'll be able to tell whether you have made chains showing *all* the different ways? I wonder how many ways there are?

Second event (later in January)

Ms. Tinsley and seven children are sitting on the floor around a bucket full of chains with five links each, which the children made the week before. Ms. Tinsley has a wire clothes hanger, some index cards, scissors, a hole-punch, and paste.

Ms. Tinsley: Here is the bucket of chains we made last week. Can anyone remind me what type of chain was supposed to go in the bucket?

Dana: Five links.

Ms. Tinsley: Yes, that's right. Five links on every chain. Show me 5 with your fingers. . . . Great, now can you do 5 another way?

Ms. Tinsley watches as the children show various configurations of 5: two fingers on one hand and three on the other, four on one hand and one on the other, and so on. She describes each child's response in words and numbers.

Ms. Tinsley: Well, clearly you are ready to help me sort these chains [empties the bucket]. Everyone, take a few chains and check them. Remember, five links in every chain, colors need to be together, and each chain should be different. Here's one with five links. I'll put it in the center of our circle so you can compare its length with the others'.

Children begin to sort chains. Some children can tell simply by looking at a chain that it is not five links long; they put those chains aside. Other children count individual links, often counting incorrectly as the links bunch together. Still others check the number of links by matching their chains with the one in the circle.

Amanda: Ms. Tinsley, I know this one is right. It's got five, the reds are together, and it's different from the one you got.

Ms. Tinsley: Oh, Amanda, show that one to Jorge and let him check it, too. I'm going to arrange these chains in a very special way, and I want them all to have five links. Use your words to tell Jorge why you think that one fits.

Children share their "good" chains with each other, sometimes using words to talk about them. Soon Ms. Tinsley asks the children for their attention.

Ms. Tinsley: You are doing a great job checking these chains, but I'm worried that we won't be able to tell whether we have all the different ways a 5 chain could be made with our keep-the-colors-together rule. I brought a hanger that I think will help us see the chains better. We can attach them here on the bottom wire.

Ms. Tinsley shows the children the hanger and then writes a 5 on two index cards. She pastes the cards back to back, punches a hole at the top, and slips this sign over the neck of the hanger, making a "5 hanger." She then sorts through the pile of chains and begins attaching particular ones to the hanger. Index cards cut in strips, folded over, and pasted at both ends of the hanger keep the links from sliding. As she places each chain on the hanger, Ms. Tinsley asks a child to describe it using numbers and color words.

Soon a color pattern becomes evident. Once five or six chains are arranged on the 5 hanger, Ms. Tinsley asks children to find places in the pattern where chains are missing, using interruptions in the color pattern as a clue. Before adding a missing chain, a child must describe it and tell where he believes it should go and why (e.g., "This has two reds and then three blues. It goes after the one with one red and four blues"). When the children declare the 5 hanger complete, she hangs it from a large pushpin on the bulletin board by the door.

In later lessons the children will make hangers for 6, 7, 8, 9, and 10. A hanger model is easily moved to small-group settings for discussion or hung on a bulletin board for display.

Third event (several times in February and March)

Children are lined up for lunch, standing next to the bulletin board where four number hangers now are displayed up all in a row—a 5 hanger, a 6 hanger, a 7 hanger, and an 8 hanger. Ms. Tinsley is notified that lunch is running late, so she decides to talk about the patterns seen on the hangers.

Ms. Tinsley: While we're waiting, let's look at our hangers. I think we have found all the ways to make 5, 6, 7, and 8. Does anyone notice anything about our board that is special? Do you see any patterns?

Ms. Tinsley pauses a minute while children talk to one another about possible answers to her questions (a common occurrence in this classroom). Many children feel more comfortable discussing answers with a friend before sharing them with the whole class.

Ms. Tinsley: I would love to hear some of your discoveries. Who would like to be first?

Scott: Chains on the 8 hanger are longer.

Amanda: The red color goes down like this [models a diagonal].

Jorge: The chains are on hangers.

William: It starts with a lot of red and then goes to a little red and then back again to a lot of red. Lots, little, lots.

Francis: You add on blue each time, and then you start taking it away.

Sheila: It's pretty because it looks like my belt.

Several weeks later a child initiates another discussion while the class is lining up for lunch.

Jorge: [excited] Ms. Tinsley, Ms. Tinsley! There's a pattern on the board. Look at the colors. It's got the same on each hanger, just more!

Amanda: I already said that, Jorge! You copied!

Ms. Tinsley: I think both of your discoveries are important and slightly different. Jorge, can you show us what you mean?

Jorge points out the repeating diagonal pattern he has just noticed across the four hangers. When asked for further clarification, Jorge goes to the housekeeping center and brings back a small quilt with a similar diagonal pattern.

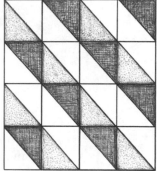

Fourth event (March and April)

In Ms. Tinsley's kindergarten, many small-group meetings occur like the following one. Included in the group are children who are writing numerals for number quantities with understanding. Ms. Tinsley selects the 5 hanger and brings it to the small-group meeting. She also has red and blue markers and a stack of index cards cut in half lengthwise.

Ms. Tinsley: I know that the year is almost over, and I want you to remember months from now what we made on our 5 hanger. I think we need to write it down so you won't forget. Jos, why not pick one of your favorite chains and tell me about it?

Jos: [takes a long time to select one] This one.

When Ms. Tinsley asks Jos how many red links the chain has, he shows two fingers; for blue links he shows three. Ms. Tinsley records a red 2 at the top of one of the skinny cards and a blue 3 at the bottom of the same card. She places it on the desk. She continues to make the cards as the children describe the chains, placing the cards on the desk in the same order as the chains with which they correspond.

   While the two cards in the center indicate the same combination of links (5,0 and 0,5), the order of the numerals on the cards reflects their placement in the pattern.

Ms. Tinsley: [replaces the 5 hanger on the bulletin board] Does anyone see any patterns on the number cards?

Freddie: Yeah. On the bottom row, the numbers go high to low and high to low again . . . high, low, high, low.

Christie: See [pointing to the top row], it goes 0 . . . one more . . . one more . . . one more . . . one more . . . one more. And then back to 0 and starts all over again.

John: Look, there are some matches: a 1 and a 4 here and a 1 and a 4 there. They are different 'cause they are different colors. . . . That's cool. And there's a 4 and a 1 and another 4 and a 1. They all are on the 5 hanger. Cool.

Ms. Tinsley: Can anyone find any other patterns like the ones John found?

Discussion continues. At this point, no one has noticed the relationship between the two numbers on a card: On any card, as its top number gets larger, its bottom number

0	1	2	3	4	5	0	1	2	3	4	5
5	4	3	2	1	0	5	4	3	2	1	0

gets smaller, and vice versa. (That recognition comes later, after the cards have hung at the bottom of the chains on the bulletin board for a while.)

   When the discussion concludes, Ms. Tinsley punches a hole at the top of each card and asks children to hang the cards on the last link of the corresponding chains.

Fifth event (April and May)

By now, six number hangers—for 5, 6, 7, 8, 9, and 10—are displayed on the bulletin board, with a matching number card dangling from the bottom of each of their chains. Children work in various centers making things to take home so they won't forget over the summer what they have learned in kindergarten.

At one center children make number hangers to take home, pasting construction-paper strips into chain links. Each child uses two colors of paper to make all the possible chains for a given number, plus number cards pasted at the bottom of the corresponding chains.

This activity helps to strengthen the connection between school and home. Children will have the hangers at home to refer to, perhaps making further observations and discoveries. Parents and children may decide to make additional number hangers. Further, when parents see this representation of pattern and number relationships, they become more aware of the math connections children explore in class and are more likely to continue such conversations at home.

The children's work with the number chains over many months illustrates how ideas and knowledge develop over time. Thoughtful teacher planning creates this developmental sequence and makes in-depth learning possible.

Calendars also present excellent opportunities for children to become familiar with patterns in the days of the week, the dates, and even the number of days in a month. In the next vignette, Tommy, a first-grader in Mrs. Brown's class, discovered a new calendar pattern when he remembered a game activity from the day before.

In preparation for a game called Trump Seven, Mrs. Brown had asked Tommy and Jonathan to collect the manipulatives in sets of seven. As the boys collected the materials, Mrs. Brown counted by 7s: "Here's seven; seven more is fourteen; seven more is twenty-one. . . ." This process was repeated many times until the boys began saying, "seven, fourteen, twenty-one, twenty-eight . . ." as they placed the manipulatives in plastic bags. Mrs. Brown wrote the corresponding numbers on the bags.

A day later, January 28, during calendar time, Tommy was the calendar leader. Suddenly he interrupted the normal routine and exclaimed, "Hey, look! The 7 pattern! It goes 7 . . . 14 . . . 21 . . . 28," he said, pointing to the numbers in the Thursday column. "It goes down!"

At first, many children did not understand Tommy's observation, but as he shared the 7 pattern eagerly with his classmates, recognition showed on their faces. Mrs. Brown said, "I wonder if any other months have that same pattern." She located an old picture calendar and, using a red crayon, circled the same 7 pattern on every month.

The children were very excited about their discovery, and other questions arose: "Will there be 7 patterns next year?" . . . "What about when our parents were children a long time ago, were there 7 patterns then?" . . . "Why does the pattern stop? Does it ever go to 35?" . . . "Why not? Why do the days of the month stop at 30 or 31?"

While Mrs. Brown had not anticipated Tommy's pattern discovery, she built on it to extend all the children's learning by asking questions, getting out another calendar, and conveying an infectious spirit of wonder.

Another pattern discovery occurred quite spontaneously during circle time in Mr. Willis's 4-year-olds class:

Seated on the floor, children play a counting game that emphasizes the number 4. A child counts "1, 2, 3, 4" over and over again as she points to children one at a time, clockwise around the circle. Each time she says the number 4, the child she is pointing to stands up.

Gabrielle suddenly becomes excited: "I know who is going to stand! I know!" Mr. Willis asks, "How do you know?" Gabrielle answers, "Look, it's a pattern: three sitting, one standing, three sitting, one standing. It happens every time!" The class continues the game and Gabrielle smiles as her predictions prove accurate. At the teacher's suggestion, she later draws a picture of the pattern in her journal. Thinking about how to represent the pattern is a further challenge that extends Gabrielle's understanding.

Even very young children can explore simple patterns, using concrete materials or charts and other graphics that highlight the relationship. In the previous example, Gabrielle discovered the sitting and standing pattern and the 3-to-1 relationship between its units.

General learning paths and development

An understanding of patterns develops over time, following general paths (or trajectories), and this learning progression is highlighted by some specific developmental benchmarks. Similar to the domain of number and operations, children's development is not governed by their specific ages but rather by a range of ages that represent these developmental benchmarks. Research indicates that children begin recognizing patterns as early as age 2 and can begin to fix, duplicate, and extend simple repeating patterns around the ages of 4 and 5. By ages 6 and 7, children can recognize the unit that is repeated and later can express growing patterns numerically (Clements & Sarama 2009).

Promoting development of key skills and concepts

Research has shown that learning experiences focusing on the concept of patterns effectively facilitate children's ability to make generalizations about number combinations, counting strategies, and problem solving (Nummela & Rosengren 1986; Payne & Huinker 1993; Caine & Caine 1994; Carpenter et al. 1999; McClain & Cobb 1999). If children see patterns in their world and connect them to mathematics, they are better able to remember what they have learned and transfer the knowledge to new situations or problems.

What do the words *patterns*, *functions*, and *algebra* in the chapter title mean, and why is it important to teach these concepts to young children? A pattern is a regular arrangement of objects, numbers, or shapes. Many early childhood programs incorporate activities relating patterns, particularly simple repeating patterns such as *aab-aab-aab* or *ab-ab-ab*. In the content area of patterns, functions, and algebra, the primary objective with respect to patterns is for young children to be able to identify and analyze simple patterns, extend them, and make predictions about them (NCTM 2000).

Function, a key idea in higher-level mathematics, builds on the understanding of pattern that begins in early childhood. A function is a special relationship between the items in two sets. Here, for example, each number in Set B (cost in cents) is 10 times the corresponding number in Set A (number of lollipops). In other words, *cost* is a function of *number of lollipops*. Knowing this function allows us to figure out that four lollipops would cost 40 cents. However, although it is important for teachers to explore the idea of function with children, using this terminology is not necessary. Between ages 3 and 8, children should be learning, at most, to recognize when patterns and relationships among groups of items exist.

Set A	Set B
1 lollipop	10¢
2 lollipops	20¢
3 lollipops	30¢
4 lollipops	?

Algebra is a branch of mathematics in which symbols are used to express general rules about numbers, number relationships, and operations. Is including it in this chapter meant to suggest that early childhood teachers actually include algebra in their curriculum? They certainly should not attempt to teach algebra at the level it is taught in high school. Rather, it is *algebraic thinking*, informally taught, that belongs in the early grades.

Algebraic thinking is being taught when teachers help children recognize patterns, make generalizations, and then use symbols to represent problems and their solutions. In the early years, children construct their own symbols to represent their ideas. Then, as they are introduced to more formal mathematics in school, children grow familiar with the standard symbols used to express quantities and relationships. The box Early "Equations" later in this chapter and the progression of specific skills in the sections that follow below illustrate this path from concrete to symbolic representation and help demonstrate algebraic thinking.

Repeating patterns

In a *repeating pattern*, a certain sequence of colors, shapes, sounds, or other elements is repeated again and again; for example, red-red-blue or loud-soft-soft. Young children most readily grasp concepts and vocabulary relating to patterns when teachers introduce these concretely and in context. Instead of talking about a pattern, the teacher "reads" the pattern using simple vocabulary ("Circle-square, circle-square, circle-square . . . ") and engages the children in doing so, as well.

Children often identify color patterns that repeat. Jenny, a 3-year-old, discovered that the caterpillar living in a tree by her house had an *ab* pattern of gold-brown, gold-brown. Rui Chen was quite excited one day to discover that his "bestest shirt" had a repeating *abc* pattern: red–light blue–dark blue, red–light blue–dark blue. He was also able to see that the pattern could be stated another way as red-blue-blue, red-blue-blue, which is an *abb* pattern. Children found repeating color patterns in the Number Hanger vignette. During the counting circle game, Gabrielle identified a repeating *ab* position pattern of three sitting–one standing, three sitting–one standing.

Although young children initially do not perceive the mathematical significance of visual patterns, such discoveries often bring them to greater awareness of number relationships and patterns. For example, Gabrielle may see that the pattern repeats itself in every group of four children and become more aware of the part-part-whole relationship of 3 and 1 as parts of 4.

Growing patterns

Patterns that change from one value to another in a predictable manner are *growing patterns*. The growth of a tree, adding one ring for each year, and the rapid (exponential!) growth of the class gerbil population are both examples of growing patterns. While a bit more complex than repeating patterns, growing patterns are also useful and intriguing for young children to analyze. They often are not linear. A child can readily find them in natural settings.

Young children can generate growing patterns with beads, blocks, marbles, or other items. They start with a certain number of objects, which is the first "term" of the pattern. Then a certain number of objects is added to the first term, yielding the second term. To establish the pattern, more objects are systematically added to

the previous term. For example, the configurations of squashed marbles shown here—based on a growing pattern—were created by 7-year-old Montie. He described the process he used to make his pattern: "I started with five marbles, and I added four marbles each time, one on each end." His teacher helped him record descriptions of his terms using numerals by writing them on a chart. The chart looked something like the one shown.

Using squashed marbles, Montie and one of his friends correctly figured out term six (25 marbles) and term seven (29 marbles). When they finished, their teacher asked,

1. 5 marbles
2. 9 Marbles
3. 13 Marbles
4. 17 marbles
5. 21 marbles

"I wonder if anyone could figure out how many marbles would be in the next step, or the next one, or even the one after that?" The boys began making more marble pictures and quickly ran out of squashed marbles. When they asked for more, the teacher responded, "Sorry, we are all out. Is there any way you could figure it out without the marbles?" Using their fingers, the boys quickly calculated the eighth and ninth terms and announced the correct numbers—"It's 33 and 37!"

In the creation of the number hangers, children also encountered growing patterns from one chain to the next. On the 5 hanger, the number of blue links per chain starts at zero, increases until the middle of the hanger, and then decreases after the middle, ending again at zero. Another growing pattern was the one Tommy discovered on the calendar (7, 14, 21, 28). If extended, this pattern can go on indefinitely in multiples of seven (35, 42, 49, 56, 63, 70 . . .).

Finding, copying, extending, and creating patterns

While children can find patterns easily, they may have difficulty copying or extending them. When they create their own patterns, they may not use a consistent rule throughout the pattern.

> Louis describes a pattern he created on the sidewalk with sidewalk chalk as "blue squiggly line, blue squiggly line, pink straight; blue squiggly line, blue squiggly line, pink straight; orange fire, red fire, yellow fire. . . ." When asked about his pattern and specifically why he shifted to orange, red, and yellow fire, he declares, "I was tired of making blue squiggly lines, and the fire was more fun!"

In this example, it sounds like Louis chose not to continue the pattern. Often, however, when young children begin extending patterns, they add a new color, start completely new patterns, or leave out a part.

> Three-year-old Hardy is making a yellow-orange pattern with blocks, repeating to himself, "Yellow, orange, yellow, orange, yellow, orange." When he begins adding blue blocks to the end of his own pattern, the teacher asks him why. Surprised, Hardy answers, "Because blue's my favorite color!"

Teachers can provide children with familiar materials and then they can create their own original pattern or copy existing patterns. For example, children can use cutouts that match the color and shape of pattern blocks to replicate or extend a pattern. When children have used all the cutouts, they can cut or draw more shapes to extend the pattern further.

Remember Jorge and the number hangers? When the 5 hanger was first displayed, he was focused on its individual chains ("The chains are on hangers"); he did not initially notice the diagonal, color, or number patterns. Later, after more experiences, he was able to discover a rather intricate pattern and share his discovery with his class. In part, he was able to do this because he had encountered that same diagonal pattern in different places, sometimes with the teacher pointing it out, and was able to make the mathematical connection. Jorge's classroom encounters with diagonal patterns laid the foundation for his discovery. These encounters included experiences in cooking (e.g., cutting square sandwiches into triangles) and in art (see, e.g., the activity Triangle Quilts later in this chapter).

Experiencing and representing patterns in various modalities

Patterns are everywhere in the curriculum. They may be seen in various modalities—auditory, tactile, and kinesthetic as well as visual. Inviting young children to create a pattern musically (loud-soft-soft-soft, loud-soft-soft-soft) or physically (jump-jump-clap, jump-jump-clap) especially helps them tune in to and understand patterns. Identifying a pattern on an area rug as "rough-smooth, rough-smooth" may encourage children to explore tactile patterns on other types of surfaces, as well. Children can represent a sound or movement pattern in a concrete medium such as Unifix cubes or tiles. Children can draw or string beads to model the pattern, and they can describe it verbally. Sound or movement patterns also can be represented with simple symbols. One dot might represent a hop on one foot, for example, and two dots, a jump with two feet. Children delight in interpreting the symbols as telling them to hop, jump, hop, jump!

The use of *all* the modalities facilitates the young child's understanding of pattern.

Dante, who has just turned 4, approaches many learning tasks in a very physical way. Unless number or pattern is presented as a physical activity that involves his entire body, Dante has trouble understanding it. When his teacher models an *ab* pattern by moving her whole body in an up-down, up-down, up-down pattern, Dante copies her enthusiastically. His entire body shakes, with his arms, legs, and head bobbing up and down. Doing this, he grasps the concept of *pattern* and is thrilled with his discovery!

Not every classroom has a Dante, for whom one learning mode is so dominant. But many children (and adults) learn more readily through one modality over others—that is, individuals vary in which of Gardner's (1983) "multiple intelligences" they demonstrate.

Because children learn best when several different modalities are involved, it is important for teachers to incorporate different kinds of learning experiences into activities about pattern. For example, in the Number Hanger vignette, many different modalities and representations were used: finger representations for 5, chain links for 5, numeral representations of number combinations for 5, and many verbal discussions and descriptions for the quantity 5 were used. In the counting circle game example, Gabrielle described a counting pattern using the terms "sitting, sitting, sitting, standing."

Skip counting can easily be done by using a physical pattern and an auditory pattern at the same time. Children in one second grade class frequently counted using a prescribed routine. For example, when counting by 3s, the children said one number at a time as they first touched their head, then their shoulders, then their waist, and back again to their head. The numbers they said when touching their heads and shoulders were whispered, while the numbers said at their waists were shouted. The chant that resulted was "one, two, THREE, four, five, SIX, seven, eight, NINE, ten, eleven, TWELVE! . . ." Children then recorded on a 100s chart the numbers they shouted. Working with partners, one child colored the shouted numbers, while the other child did the chanting and gesturing.

New counting routines can be created by extending the physical pattern: *head, shoulders, waist, knees* for skip counting by 4s; and *head, shoulders, waist, knees, feet* for skip counting by 5s. The figure at left is an example of a 100s chart completed when counting by 3s.

Physical, musical, concrete (three-dimensional), pictorial, and verbal representations are all methods that can be used to help children recognize and represent patterns. When such a multimodal approach to pattern—one involving "the whole child"—is used, the explicit connections made between the child's world and the world of mathematics are more effective.

1	2	3	4	5	6	7	8	9	10
11	12	13	14	15	16	17	18	19	20
21	22	23	24	25	26	27	28	29	30
31	32	33	34	35	36	37	38	39	40
41	42	43	44	45	46	47	48	49	50
51	52	53	54	55	56	57	58	59	60
61	62	63	64	65	66	67	68	69	70
71	72	73	74	75	76	77	78	79	80
81	82	83	84	85	86	87	88	89	90
91	92	93	94	95	96	97	98	99	100

Counting by 3s

The Young Child and Mathematics

Use of symbols to describe mathematics

Symbols provide a way to condense mathematical sentences into a logical depiction of relationships between numbers (e.g., the sentence "two blocks and four more make six blocks all together" can be depicted more concisely using symbols: $2 + 4 = 6$). For young children, the use of symbols is one tool for thinking algebraically. As described in *Principles and Standards for School Mathematics* in the Algebra Standard, children in prekindergarten through second grade are expected to "use concrete, pictorial, and verbal representations to develop an understanding of invented and conventional symbolic notations" (NCTM 2000, 90).

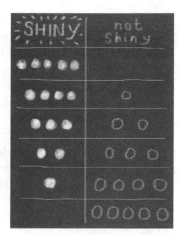

In one class, children spontaneously sorted a collection of pennies into groups of five and further divided them into those that were shiny and those that were not. As children verbally described their pennies ("Hey, I have two that are shiny" . . . "All mine are not shiny"), their teacher decided to record their descriptions on a chart that looked something like the one opposite. The first row shows there are five shiny pennies and zero that are not shiny. The second row shows four shiny pennies and one that is not shiny, and so on. Each row represents a possible combination.

Later, the teacher transcribed the chart into descriptive sentences: The first row could be described as, "Three pennies plus two pennies make five pennies" or "Five pennies can be three shiny pennies and two not-shiny pennies." Still later, the teacher wrote symbolic equations on the chart for each row: $3 + 2 = 5$ or $5 = 3 + 2$.

The *equal* sign (=) is probably one of the most commonly introduced symbols in early childhood classrooms. Yet to most young children, the symbol means "this is the answer." In fact, when given these three mathematical statements,

$$3 + 4 = 7$$
$$7 = 3 + 4$$
$$7 = 7$$

children usually say that the second and third equations are incorrect because "they are not written right."

Early "Equations"

Working with a pan balance and objects that weigh the same (such as Unifix cubes or counters), children get a wealth of concrete experience with the concept of an *equation*. For example, a child may place two counters on the left side of the scale and then one counter on the right side. Finding the left side heavier, she balances the scale by adding another counter to the right side. Now she has an equation, that is, a physical demonstration where one side is "the same as" the other side.

If children don't start such play themselves, the teacher may ask, "How can I make the scale balance, Michael?" or "I have a four-cube unit on this side. Can we make it balance using these two-cube pieces?" Note that the word *balance* will need to be modeled for children at first, until they understand *balance* to mean that the bar of the scale is exactly horizontal.

After children have had extensive concrete experiences balancing sets of physical objects, the teacher can encourage them to explore various ways of representing their "equations" and at some point acquaint them with the conventional representations of those equations using numbers as well as words:

$$2 + 2 = 4 \text{ or } 4 = 2 + 2$$

"2 and 2 more is the same as 4" or "4 counters is the same as 2 counters added to 2 counters"

The teacher's role is to give meaning to symbols by introducing them in context and sometimes providing a simple explanation. In the case of the equal sign, for example, teachers would introduce it as meaning "the same as" and make a point of illustrating it in a variety of equation forms:

$$7 = 3 + 4$$
$$2 + 5 = 3 + 4$$
$$7 = 7$$

Concrete representations help, too—such as a scale in balance (like the one that appears in the box Early "Equations" on the previous page).

Another example of gradually introducing mathematical symbols occurs in the sequence of the Number Hangers experiences. When representing the blue and red links in the chains, Ms. Tinsley first wrote the numerals by themselves on a card to help the kindergartners to see patterns and relationships, the initial focus. Later, when children could verbalize the patterns and relationships involved, she laid each chain horizontally and wrote the number of each color of link underneath, adding the *plus* (+) and *the same as* (=) symbols between the numerals to express an equation. For example, on a chain with three reds and two blues, the index card would read "3 + 2 = 5."

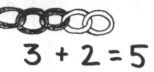

Making generalizations about number properties

Young children do not need to learn in a formal way about the properties of numbers; for example, in *addition*, the order of numbers does not affect the sum (the *commutative property*). With time and experience, children may begin to recognize these properties in various ways. In the shiny penny activity, for example, seeing on the chart 2 + 3 = 5 and also 3 + 2 = 5 helps them understand that the order in which the numbers are added does not affect the total.

The teacher can even more directly promote children's recognition of this property by using strategies that make the principle concrete. For example, he might ask them to hold the pennies on their palms (e.g., two on the right and three on the left) and then cross their hands, so the order is different (two on the left, three on the right). This way, children can literally see that the order does not change the total number of pennies they are holding. With this and other examples, children can begin to see that the sum of 3 + 2 is *the same as* the sum of 2 + 3.

> While learning the concept of *multiplication*, the teacher asked her second grade class to solve a problem about chickens and eggs: "There were twelve chickens and they each laid seven eggs. How many eggs did the farmer collect that day?" Most of the children solve the problem by drawing a picture and then counting their representations of the eggs. However, counting by 10s and ticking off seven fingers, Melani calculates that ten chickens would lay seventy eggs (ten chickens lay one egg each to make ten eggs, two eggs each to make twenty, and so forth) and two more chickens would mean seven plus seven more eggs, or fourteen. "So, altogether, there would be eighty-four eggs!" she announces.

Melani generalized a number property from her experiences with algebraic thinking, which is one of the understandings that teacher want children to attain in this content area of the curriculum.

Describing change and thinking algebraically

When children explore patterns and generalize relationships between numbers, they are beginning to develop algebraic reasoning. The concept of *change* is one that young

Getting Children Thinking about Patterns, Functions, and Algebra

Many of the questions below connect to other mathematics content areas and can also be asked about stories, science, or experiences in other content areas. To facilitate children's thinking about patterns, functions, and algebra, you might ask:

How are these alike? How are they different?

Do you see a pattern? Tell me about it.

What comes next? How could we make this pattern with these different materials?

Could you tell a friend about this pattern and see if he can pick out which one you mean?

How can we remember this pattern? How can we make a picture that will help us? Could we use numbers? How?

Can you dance your pattern? What would you do first? Second?

What do you think will happen next? Why do you think so?

How did ___ change? Did something happen that made it change? Do you think it will change again?

Tell me about these two things: Which one is bigger [heavier, smaller, lighter, more, less]?

What happens over and over again with these [beads]?

How can you read this pattern? Can you think of another way?

What would happen to the pattern if I changed ___?

children encounter in many areas of their lives, and it provides another opportunity to think algebraically. Change can be described qualitatively (e.g., "He's taller than last year") or quantitatively ("He's two inches taller than last year"). Change is an important idea: "The understanding that most things change over time, that many such changes can be described mathematically, and that many changes are predictable helps lay a foundation for applying mathematics to other fields and for understanding the world" (NCTM 2000, 95).

Describing changes that occur in science investigations and demonstrations is one of the easiest ways to introduce the idea of *function* to young children. Using comparison words (e.g., *bigger, smaller, more, less; heavier, lighter, colder, warmer*), children can describe what happens during a given event or activity.

> In an extended-day program, 4-year-olds each held tightly sealed plastic bags filled with varying amounts of baking soda and vinegar. Shaking the bags mixed the vinegar with the baking soda, and the bags filled with carbon dioxide—they "puffed up" and felt cold. The more soda and vinegar, the bigger and colder the bag (i.e., the change was a *function* of the quantity of the mixture). Children described what they discovered using their own words. This became a popular at-home activity.

Children can also describe changes quantitatively using numbers. Growing bean plants from seeds and periodically recording their height, children can tell how much their plants have grown after one week, two weeks, or three weeks. Counting the number of cars passing the front of the school before and after new road construction, children could describe how the construction affected traffic in the school zone. Describing and analyzing changes in various contexts helps children develop their algebraic thinking.

Providing a mathematics-rich environment

Many of the materials mentioned in chapter 4 (focusing on number and operations) also help children learn about pattern, and recognizing and working with patterns help children understand more about numbers.

Even the youngest children begin to notice the patterns in routines that are repeated—put coats on, go outside, come inside, take coats off—and anticipate the next action. Stories and poetry for young children are filled with patterns. Songs, of course, follow a pattern. Toys, furnishings, and children's own clothing often display bright, colorful patterns. Pattern scavenger hunts help children become more aware of patterns in their own classroom. Searching for patterns at home and bringing in information about these discoveries serves to connect home and school.

Many of the manipulatives used for number and geometry are useful also for considering pattern. In addition, pattern blocks (the colorful geometric shapes) are especially helpful. Children love to use them to cover large spaces. Because they fit together nicely and because of their regular shapes, the blocks create growing patterns almost naturally as children play. Other useful manipulatives include shape cutouts, Unifix cubes, base-10 blocks, plastic counters in a variety of animal shapes, and large beads.

The calendar is one staple in the early childhood environment that offers many opportunities to consider pattern. In addition to the 7 pattern that Tommy noticed in the Thursday column of the class calendar, other natural calendar patterns include days of the week and months of the year. Even weather conditions and holidays can be described in terms of patterns. Creating a linear number line (like the one in chapter 4) to count the days of school makes visible many place-value patterns.

Literature connection

There are many books that illustrate growing patterns. For example, *Hippos Go Berserk!*, by Sandra Boynton, is a humorous story of hippos attending a party and then going home again. First, only one hippo is present, then two more come, then three more, then four more . . . until there are a total of 45 hippos at the party! After "all the hippos go berserk!" they leave the party, beginning with nine hippos leaving, then eight hippos, then seven hippos, and so on. The growing pattern illustrated in the story generates a triangular display of numbers. The hippos that come to the party can and should be visually drawn that way.

Second-graders wondered how big the party would get if ten more hippos came, eleven more hippos came, and so on. The teacher added to their questions and wondered what would happen if the growing pattern continued to fifteen more hippos! The children quickly grew tired of counting from the beginning to solve the problems, and instead identified the addition pattern at each step. As one child said, "Wow, 120 hippos would be more than berserk. It would be crazy!"

In-class assessments

Children make connections to their understanding of patterns throughout the day. Pre-kindergartners notice patterns as they walk down the hall, put on their striped t-shirt, or play on a patterned rug. As children get older, they should use number patterns to

make discoveries about the properties of number that they can use to develop addition and subtraction strategies.

Children's errors often tell us what they understand about pattern. The child who predicts that 39 is the number following 35 shows he has little understanding of the pattern established with the order of the numbers 1 through 9. In contrast, the child who says that "ninety-ten" comes after 99 seems to understand the pattern of counting and simply needs help with the conventional symbolic form.

Because children make such connections during a variety of experiences, their understanding of patterns is best assessed using a checklist of some type. The following criteria should be included on the checklist: A child must be able to (1) recognize patterns, (2) extend patterns, (3) describe patterns, (4) represent patterns, and (5) translate patterns. Then, depending on the level of the child's development, the checklist could also include specific types of patterns (e.g., repeating, growing, number) along with what specific connections the child made.

*   *   *

Activities for exploring pattern and function and laying the foundations for algebra are described below. They are roughly in order of difficulty, but many can be extended or simplified to be more or less challenging.

Activities

Pattern People

Half of a group of children stands in a line, while the other half observes. The child leading the activity whispers instructions that follow a pattern to each person in line—for example, the first person in line is told to smile, the second to frown, the third to smile, and the fourth to frown. At the leader's signal, the children in the line carry out the whispered instructions while the observers guess the pattern. Roles are then reversed, and the game is played again.

Several days after playing this activity, 4-year-old Erica drew a picture of four children, frowning, smiling, frowning, smiling, and declared, "I made a pattern!"

My Aunt Came Back

The echo song "My Aunt Came Back" is familiar in many early childhood settings. As the children repeat each phrase, they add one more action to illustrate a growing pattern. Then each repeating action can be illustrated by adding a card to the previous set. The staircase visualization, shown here, helps children connect a pattern in a song to a mathematical plus-one pattern.

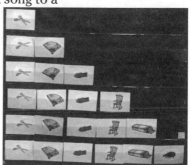

> *My aunt came back . . . and brought me back . . .*
> *From old Algiers . . . a pair of shears*
> *From old Japan . . . a waving fan*
> *From Timbuktu . . . a tapping shoe*
> *From the county fair . . . a rocking chair*
> *From old Belgium . . . some bubble gum*
> *From old Chile . . . an itchy flea*
> *From the county zoo . . . some nuts like you!*

Guidelines in Action: Patterns, Functions, and Algebra

The classroom examples and activities throughout this chapter reflect some of the curriculum, instruction, and assessment guidelines from chapter 2 that form the basis for teaching mathematics effectively to young children. To clarify how specific guidelines look in practice, this chart highlights four instances in which they are evident.

Curriculum Guideline 2—Plan for connections	The connections between number and pattern have been modeled, discussed, and represented in a variety of ways during the Number Hanger experiences, which involved index cards with number patterns written on them. Using the written cards to represent the patterns in the chains is important in helping children begin to understand the connection between number symbols and quantity. In another example, the visual patterns illustrated in both the book *Hippos Go Berserk!* and the song "My Aunt Came Back" were methods used to help children make connections.
Curriculum Guideline 3—Emphasize the processes of mathematics	The many different ways that patterns are represented in this chapter illustrate representation strategies as well as the process of communication. Patterns are physically demonstrated, visually outlined, and described by children in their own words.
Instruction Guideline 2—Orchestrate classroom activities	As the patterns in number combinations featured in the second Number Hanger event can be very complex and represented many ways, the teacher orchestrates this activity so the patterns can be viewed over a long period of time.
Assessment Guideline 3—Employ multiple sources of evidence	The assessment checklist could be used on a systematic basis to assess a child's developing understanding of patterns and relationship. It could also be used in a variety of contexts and by both teachers and parents.

Sidewalk Patterns

After studying patterns with two repeating parts—for example, red, blue, red, blue—children create their own patterns on the sidewalk with chalk. With a partner, each child draws one part of a repeating pattern. Patterns are copied onto black paper to share with the rest of the class when the children return inside.

Children often demonstrate understanding of position when describing patterns. As one kindergartner explained, "Our pattern starts with a purple squiggly line, then has a straight red line, then there is another purple squiggly line, and next there's a straight red line again."

Spin and Match

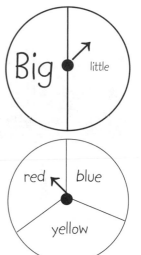

This activity requires game pieces of varying colors and features (attribute pieces work well) and spinners made by the teacher or children. The spinners are designed to reflect the features of the pieces and to correspond with the children's level of development. For example, if the children are learning to sort by the attributes big and little, a spinner divided in half with *Big* written on one side and *little* on the other can be used. If the children are learning to sort by color or shape, the spinner can be divided into wedges of color or sections with shapes pictured. Sitting in a circle around the pieces and spinner, children enjoy taking turns spinning, reading the spinner, and selecting the indicated pieces.

For a greater challenge, the children can use more than one spinner. That is, the child spins one spinner for size, another spinner for color, and a third spinner for shape, then takes the piece described: for example, a little, red triangle. Play continues until the players have taken all the pieces. When all pieces are claimed, a spinner divided into *most* and *least* is spun. The winner of the game is the player with the most or least pieces, depending on the spin. To simplify the game or eliminate competition, this last step need not be used.

How Many Bird Wings?

Children enjoy learning about flying animals and insects, and this math activity is a good follow-up to an investigation of airborne creatures. The teacher wonders, "What if everyone in the class were a bird?" Children imagine they are birds and flap their "wings." The teacher points out that each bird has two wings and asks the children to guess the total number of wings there are in the class.

Kindergartners usually guess one more than the number of students in the class—each child realizes that he has two wings but does not take into account that everyone else does, too. To resolve this misinterpretation, each child draws a picture of a bird with two wings, the pictures are posted, and the class counts the wings aloud. Later activities can investigate similar patterns by counting eyes, hands, or feet.

Moon Charts

Two small, white paper plates are given to two different children every day for one month. The children are responsible for conducting a moon watch, cutting the plate to show the size of the moon that night and bringing it to class the next day. If the moon is not visible due to cloud cover, children can cover the plate with cotton balls or black paper, depending on the conditions.

The moons are posted daily on a calendar, and the children discuss the pattern. The teacher introduces the descriptive words *full*, *half*, and *new* as they relate to each phase of the moon. Even with many cloudy nights, children can usually see a growing pattern.

Children are generally conscientious about doing their "homework" and bringing in their moon assignments.

Dippy Patterns

Children fold white paper towels many times. They then dip the corners of the folded towels in water dyed with food coloring. After all the corners are dipped, they open the towels and set them out to dry. The dried towels are posted on a bulletin board.

Without indicating which towel is theirs, children take turns describing the pattern on their towel, from one top corner around to the other top corner while their classmates try to guess which towel is being described. Afterward the teacher prompts the children to look at the towels from a different perspective, such as diagonally from top left corner to bottom right corner, vertically from top to bottom, or horizontally from side to side. A new perspective often fosters new and varied descriptions.

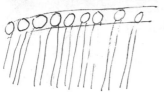

Photo Patterns

Photographs featuring patterns on buildings, sidewalks, and monuments around town are displayed in the block center. Children create their own versions of the structures in the photos by setting up block creations with similar patterns. They later draw the structures and post the drawings next to the appropriate photos. Photographs of the children's constructions can be taken to record the activity.

Children's creations are often remarkably similar to the buildings or structures in the photos. After doing this activity for a while, children find they can't go anywhere without seeing patterns inside and outside buildings!

Building Block Blueprints

After viewing real building plans, children enjoy making block buildings and creating their own blueprints using symbols and representations for their building block creations. These symbols may include a rectangle for a rectangular block or a square for a cube, as well as the child's own symbol for a doorway or stairs. (Younger children cannot be expected to create keys for their plans, although some second-graders may wish to do so.)

Using white chalk, children draw buildings on blue butcher paper. They eagerly read and share each other's symbols and pictures and use them later to recreate their constructions.

Pattern Dance

Children take turns creating a dance using three different motions in sequence—for example, kick-spin-wiggle. The steps are repeated over and over again in an *abc* pattern. The child who creates the dance serves as the class's dance director, teaching the steps to the other children. When the music is turned on, everyone hops, wiggles, spins, kicks, jumps, flaps, or shakes in accordance with the pattern dance!

Music Concert

Using musical instruments, children play an easily recognizable song featuring a pattern. "Bingo," for instance, is familiar to most children, and the chorus has a clear repeating pattern. Clap, clap, clap-clap-clap! represents the B, I, N-G-O! pattern and is easily grasped by children. Children enjoy hearing instruments playing in a pattern, and they enjoy performing songs with homemade instruments, such as banjos created from plates and rubber bands, and shakers made from popcorn kernels and plastic tubs.

Pattern Music

In the music center, children decorate particular instruments with designated colors. For example, drums might be covered with blue stickers. Children compose music by creating patterns with different color stickers on paper printed with a musical staff. Each instrument plays in the order indicated by the pattern. This activity is great for small groups of children.

The Lineup

In this activity, children see how a group (a *set* in mathematical terms) is formed from items that either have a particular characteristic or do not have this feature. It is a good introduction to the *not* concept. When it is time for children to line up, they are shown a card with a symbol to indicate who goes first. The cards include symbols for features such as shoe type, pet ownership, people wearing a specific color of clothing, and so on. Some cards have symbols with large, black **X**s through them, meaning *not*. For example, the teacher might hold up a card with a red blob covered with a large, black **X** and say, "Those children not wearing red should line up."

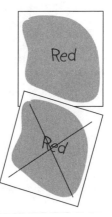

Initially, *not* characteristics are very difficult for young children to comprehend. To best teach this concept, select one characteristic and divide the children into two groups—one that has the characteristic and one that does not. Place signs labeling the characteristic in front of each group. After some practice, most young children master the *not* concept quite well.

Snake Patterns

After looking at pictures of snakes—or, better yet, an actual snake—and studying the snake's patterned skin, children make their own snakes from playdough or paper. Snakeskin patterns can be created using cookie cutters, plastic tools, color construction paper, and other art materials. The completed snakes are displayed around the room.

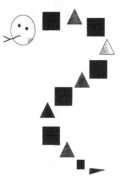

Snakes made from paper cut first into a circle or oval and then into a spiral hang especially well from the ceiling, providing a new way to look at patterns. (Remind children to make a pattern on both sides of a paper snake.)

Straw Constructions

Children choose a number of small stirring straws of different lengths and stand them up in a piece of foam, arranging them in a line in order of height. They can adjust the height of the straws by snipping off the tops as necessary.

Children can take as many or as few straws as they wish; most choose about ten straws. They tend to spend a long time making these constructions, reordering straws to make the pattern look just right.

Make an Equation

This activity helps children understand *equal* and *not equal* by comparing the quantities represented on two cards. The game also helps children recognize *true* and *false* equations.

Two decks of number cards are placed face down on the table. Each card represents a number using a numeral or another type of representation such as tally marks, pips like those on dominoes, or a 10-frame. The spinner is divided into halves, one featuring the *equal* symbol (=) and the other, the *not equal* symbol (≠). The spinner is placed between the two decks of cards.

A player turns over the top card from each deck and then spins the spinner. Viewed together, the number on the top card of the first deck, the symbol indicated on the spinner, and the number on the top card of the second deck make an equation. If the player makes a true equation, he keeps the two cards. If the equation is false, the cards are placed face down next to the two decks, and the same player continues taking his turn until he makes an equation that is true. Play continues, using the discard piles when the decks are gone, until there are no more cards.

Children make interesting discoveries playing this game. They find that the not equal symbol usually works better than the equal symbol. They also learn that equations such as 7 = 7 are true whether the numbers are expressed in numerals, tally marks, or pips.

Triangle Quilts

Children are given three paper squares of different colors. They fold the squares in half diagonally and cut each into two triangles. The children arrange the six triangles in patterns on a piece of paper and paste them down. They enjoy showing and describing the beautiful triangle "quilts" that result.

Covered Tiles

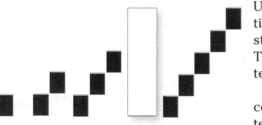

Using color tiles, groups of children create patterns with an additional property: The patterns become larger with each successive stage. Each pattern must have at least five terms laid out in tiles. The teacher can check that each pattern is consistent from one term to the next.

After the tile patterns are created, one term in each pattern is covered with a piece of paper. The groups view one another's patterns to try to figure out the missing term and then construct their guesses using tiles. The missing terms are then revealed and the children who guessed correctly explain the strategies they used.

Marble Races

One end of a piece of PVC pipe (approximately one foot long) rests on the ground, while a child holds the other end. The child rolls a marble through the pipe, and everyone observes as the marble rolls out the other end and across the floor. The children record how far each marble rolls and how high the pipe was held, and then they raise or lower the pipe and try again. They take turns, seeing whose marble rolls the farthest. A discussion ensues about the best way to hold the pipe, and in the process, children learn about angles and functions.

In this beginning activity demonstrating function, children typically believe that the higher the pipe is held, the farther the marble will roll. This is not always the case. In fact, when the pipe is held almost vertically, the marble travels only a short distance due to its impact with the floor as it reaches the end of the pipe.

The children's recordings are highly dependent on their developmental level. Some may simply draw pictures of how high the pipe is held and then state that the marble went far or not as far. By second grade, children have developed measuring skills and some are able to give fairly accurate measurements for how high the end of the pipe is as well as how far the marble rolls. A child may make standard measurements with rulers if she is able, but she may also measure in relative terms. For example, a child might find that the end of the pipe was "as high as three books" and "the marble rolled five footsteps."

Geometry and Spatial Sense
in the Early Childhood Curriculum

Geometry is foundational to an understanding of mathematics and especially important to young children. The study of geometry involves shape, size, position, direction, and movement and is descriptive of the physical world we live in. Children's spatial sense is their awareness of themselves in relation to the people and objects around them.

Historically, geometry was one of the first areas of mathematics taught to young children. In the 1850s, Friedrich Froebel, "the father of kindergarten," designed a curriculum suggesting instructional practices based on the use of geometric forms and their manipulation in space. In this curriculum, Froebel designed "gifts" for kindergartners—special materials to enable them to explore and grasp basic forms and relationships. The first six gifts included balls of different colors, cubes, spheres, cylinders, and complex sets of geometric blocks that children manipulated and observed in a series of progressive tasks (Balfanz 1999).

As kindergarten has evolved over the last 160 years, this geometric focus has largely been lost. In fact, in many recent international comparisons, U.S. elementary school and middle school students score poorly (as compared with many peers, and across other math content areas) in geometry (Beaton et al. 1996; Lappan 1999; Gonzales et al. 2009; Sarama & Clements 2009). Many reasons have been suggested; but researchers, teachers, and policy makers acknowledge that the study of geometry and spatial sense has not been a focus in the typical elementary or secondary curriculum here. This is especially true in early childhood classrooms. Shape definitions ("This is a *square*") are typically the only prominent geometric ideas introduced, whereas manipulation of shapes and spatial exploration are generally neglected. Young children may work with shapes in art activities and puzzles and construct shapes with Legos and unit blocks, which offer rich opportunities to explore geometry and spatial relationships. But many teachers do not emphasize spatial concepts or take advantage of natural connections to such mathematics when they arise in their classrooms.

Curriculum Focal Points (NCTM 2006) lists topics in geometry as a focus for three of the four age groups (prekindergarten, kindergarten, and first grade), with specific connections from geometry to other math content areas mentioned for all four age groups. After number and operations, geometry should be the most emphasized content area in early childhood. Beginning in prekindergarten, children should identify shapes and use spatial vocabulary to describe their relationship to other shapes ("When I put the triangle on top of the square, it makes a pentagon!") and to other objects ("I see a cylinder shape next to the door") or to describe their orientation in space ("When the triangle is flipped over, one of the vertices is pointed up!"). In kindergarten, children's ability to identify shapes can be extended to describing shapes by their attributes and orientation in space ("I pasted the green triangle below the red square"). In addition, they should connect their understanding of spatial orientation to measurement and to number by following and creating simple navigational directions ("Everyone take six steps left, then hop over the line!").

In first grade, geometry learning involves the decomposition and composition of shape, along with the understanding of terms such as *symmetry* and *congruence*. Geometry connections to measurement and to number are emphasized in second grade, by focusing curriculum on the attributes of geometric shapes and connecting children's knowledge of shapes to measuring their dimensions.

The foundational nature of geometry is also apparent in the importance the NCTM Standards (2000) place on additional key aspects of geometry and spatial sense that would, by twelfth grade, enable students to—

- analyze characteristics and properties of two- and three-dimensional geometric shapes and develop mathematical arguments about geometric relationships;
- specify locations and describe spatial relationships using coordinate geometry and other representational systems;
- apply transformations and use symmetry to analyze mathematical situations;
- use visualization, spatial reasoning, and geometric modeling to solve problems. (96)

Familiarity with shape, structure, location, and transformations as well as development of spatial reasoning enable children to understand not only their spatial world but also other mathematics topics. As children count the sides of two-dimensional shapes or the faces of a cube, they learn about number relationships. Facility with patterns, functions, and even rudimentary algebra is also at work when children identify patterns in space or when they see the relationships between the number of faces, edges, and vertices of three-dimensional figures. When children compare shapes, directions, and positions in space, they develop concepts and acquire vocabulary that they also put to use in measurement. Grouping items, sometimes by shape or by another geometric feature, is a skill also fundamental to data collection, and children can record and report shapes they encounter in an activity or in their environment.

Spatial sense and construction come into play in art, science, social studies, movement and music, and reading. For example, spatial-thinking skills emphasized in geometry are critical to the making and reading of maps—essential skills in social studies. Children notice shapes in natural objects of all kinds. They discover many things about shape and geometry in their block play. Manipulating shapes in space introduces children to vocabulary words about position as well as other words necessary for reading and language arts. Even distinguishing between letters of the alphabet involves paying attention to shape and position. In art, spatial relationships and geometric forms are critical elements in making both two- and three-dimensional creations.

Young children enjoy manipulating shapes in space, and their spatial capabilities often exceed their numerical skills (NCTM 2000). Three-year-old Jeffrey in chapter 1 has a strong intuitive knowledge about shapes and how they relate to his world. While most of his knowledge is perceptual in nature, he is able to relate a two-dimensional circle to his uncle's basketball and to recognize that, unlike a basketball, the circle will not bounce.

As in the other math content areas, the teacher's role is to bridge the young child's informal knowledge to formal school mathematics. This bridging often means using the child's own language and relating it to formal terms and definitions. For example, the teacher might decide to provide the word *sphere* for the basketball and engage Jeffrey in considering other differences between a ball and a two-dimensional circle. It may also mean offering a position or shape word that describes what the child is doing or attending to. Jeffrey's teacher, for example, later referred to the "piece of pizza" shape, as Jeffrey called it, and compared it with a triangle.

Children engage with geometry in a variety of contexts

This first vignette, Look, Make, and Fix, demonstrates a thinking activity designed to foster children's shape awareness, spatial visualization skills, and problem-solving skills. Using a magnetic display board, first grade teacher Mr. Quintanilla shows the children a model he has created from several magnetic tangram pieces. They study the configuration of shapes on the board and then take a given amount of time to duplicate the model picture with their own tangram pieces, look again, and fix their figures to match the teacher's. Mr. Quintanilla encourages the children to help each other. As the configurations increase in difficulty, he gives the children as many tries as they need to fix their pictures to match his.

Playing Look, Make, and Fix in small groups allows children who have difficulty with spatial skills to get more practice and learn new strategies. The game can also be played with attribute or pattern blocks. Children enjoy the activity so much that they like to play it on their own when they have the chance.

Look for the video clip of "Look, Make, and Fix" on the DVD!

Look, Make, and Fix

Children are getting settled in the classroom as the school day begins. The message on the chalkboard directs them to get a set of tangrams. Seeing the display board, the children anticipate one of their favorite thinking activities and each excitedly gets a tangram bag—containing seven tangram pieces that can combine to make a large square.

Mr. Quintanilla: Today we are going to get your thinking started by playing Look, Make, and Fix. First, let's check our tangram bags to see if we have all the shapes. Who remembers what we should have in our bags?

Tanya: Two big triangles and two little triangles.

Stanley: And one medium triangle. Five triangles!

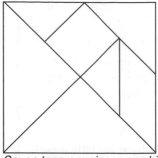

Seven tangram pieces combine to form a large square.

Mr. Quintanilla: Right. That covers the triangles. What about the other shapes? There are seven shapes altogether, so how many more do we need to find?

Jane: There's a square, and that funny shaped one, a squashed rectangle. I forget. . . .

There is some discussion as the teacher pauses, listens, and observes children finding the parallelogram. Although the children have heard the words *parallelogram*, *rectangle*, and *quadrilateral*, they are not sure what they mean or how they relate to one another or to the particular "squashed rectangle" in the tangram set.

Mr. Quintanilla: Let's everyone look at Jane's squashed rectangle. Hold it up, and let's trace around it with our fingers. [models with his parallelogram shape as he speaks] Side . . . stop, tip [touches the vertex, the point where two sides meet]. Side . . . stop, tip. Side . . . stop, tip. Side . . . stop, tip. How many sides?

Children: Four.

Mr. Quintanilla: Then, although it can be called different things, like *squashed rectangle*, let's call it a *quadrilateral*. A quadrilateral is any shape that has four sides. In fact, let's use one of Jane's words and call it a squashed quadrilateral. . . . Can you say it fast? *Squashed quadrilateral, squashed quadrilateral, squashed quadrilateral* [lots of laughter].

Mr. Quintanilla decides not to further define a quadrilateral or identify the square as a special quadrilateral. Geometry and spatial sense are skills that develop over time, and those ideas will be introduced in future lessons. For the moment, the children have the words to help them identify the shape, and that is enough.

Mr. Quintanilla: All right. Check your shapes and see if you have every shape [places the seven shapes on the board for children to see as he says the words]. Five triangles, two small, two large, and one medium; and one square and one squashed quadrilateral. A total of two, four, five, six, seven pieces. . . . Is everyone ready?

One child locates a missing triangle on the floor and another gets a square from the box of extra pieces. Everyone is now ready.

Mr. Quintanilla: Place your pieces in a pile at the top of your table. Hands in your laps! Don't move them until I tell you to. Eyes down. Here we go.

Selecting the medium triangle and the square, Mr. Quintanilla uses them to make a shape configuration on the magnetic board.

Mr. Quintanilla: Look!

Children stare at the shape for a few seconds, but don't touch their pieces. Mr. Quintanilla then turns the board over.

Mr. Quintanilla: Make!

Children select pieces from their piles and use them to make the picture at their tables. Some look at their neighbor's and copy or compare pictures. Most children make the picture correctly. A few use a different-size triangle. Mr. Quintanilla waits about 30 seconds while some children continue working and then he turns the board to show the picture again.

Mr. Quintanilla: Fix!

Children check their creations against the model shape. Most of the children who used the wrong triangle see their error and change pieces. Two children do not. Mr. Quintanilla reminds everyone to help each other, so one child helps the first of the two with the configuration, and Mr. Quintanilla quietly changes the incorrect piece of the second child himself.

Kimberly: [raising her hand] Mr. Quintanilla, Sara is looking at my picture and copying!

Mr. Quintanilla: That's okay, Kimberly! Remember, this is not a test; it is a game where we all help each other. Sara, I'm glad Kimberly has a good picture for you to look at. Thanks, Kimberly! . . . Now let's try another one. This next one is harder!

Mr. Quintanilla repeats the process with three more model pictures. They get progressively harder, each including more pieces in different configurations. The last task takes many "fix" steps for everyone to complete.

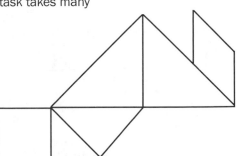

Mr. Quintanilla: Whew! That last one was a lot of work. Thanks for helping each other fix that picture. I noticed that Fernando was excellent at solving this one. Fernando, can you help us understand how you did it?

Fernando, whose home language is not English, tends to have difficulty verbalizing his thoughts. After a long pause, he shrugs and responds.

Fernando: I just thunk and thunk!

Mr. Quintanilla: I could see that you did! Did you think of a picture that the shapes made? Did it look like anything to you? A *gato*, maybe?

Fernando: [laughing] Not a cat. . . . Maybe a turtle with no legs!

Mr. Quintanilla: Oh, what a good idea. What about you, Gina? You helped lots of people on that one. How did you do it?

Gina: I just worked on one part at a time. First I made the mountain [points to the two large triangles] and then I added the other stuff. The hardest part was that weird piece.

Mr. Quintanilla: The squashed quadrilateral?

Gina: Yeah. I looked at that a lot before I got it.

The discussion continues a few more minutes, then the tangram pieces are put away. Mr. Quintanilla will discuss more varied spatial tasks, strategies, and geometric terms at another time. Spatial sense takes a long time to develop, and this is just a beginning exploration.

Mr. Quintanilla's class does this basic activity in varied settings—large groups, small groups, and learning centers. Families can also play Look, Make, and Fix and other games relating to space and shape. During holiday time, Mr. Quintanilla sends two die-cut tangram sets home as a gift so children can teach their families the game.

Interestingly, Mr. Quintanilla, like many teachers, would say that he has never found spatial sense activities easy. Some teachers with this difficulty might say to themselves, "Some people have spatial sense and some just don't," and either neglect spatial activities or convey a negative, defeated attitude toward them. Instead, Mr. Quintanilla highlights the importance of effort rather than luck or intelligence in demonstrating spatial sense. He talks about how hard children are working, and he offers the "fix" component of the activity as many times as needed to allow children to succeed. Believing that spatial sense activities are important for all children to experience, Mr. Quintanilla has made sure to include plenty of them and become comfortable doing them.

Young children naturally love to explore geometric and spatial aspects of the world around them. There are many opportunities for teachers to scaffold children's understanding by asking questions, suggesting other activities, showing various transformations (such as two same-size right triangles forming a rectangle), and providing additional materials.

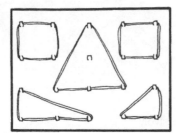

Denise, age 4, excitedly shows her teacher some shapes she has drawn in her journal. Mrs. Stipe gives her a geoboard with bands and asks if she could copy the shapes on her board. Denise proudly demonstrates the result.

Ms. Patterson finds three large, plastic mirrors at a garage sale and places them in the housekeeping center. She listens as a verbal 3-year-old gives everyone a guided tour: "Look in here. I can see two me's and two you's. These are called magic windows." For weeks children experiment with their mirror images and reflections.

Geoboard with bands

Creations in the block center provide many opportunities to enhance children's understanding of geometry. Questions such as "How is your tower different from Joe's?" or "What will happen if the bottom block is removed?" or "What if I try to make a building like yours without looking? Can you tell me what I need to do to make mine just like yours?" or "It will soon be time to clean up. How will you remember what you have built?" can facilitate thinking and experimentation.

As a result of the teacher's questions and discussion with 7-year-old Frank, for example, the balance and symmetry of his block creation (shown here) were enhanced and noted more consciously by Frank—and by the other children looking on.

General learning paths and development

Learning paths (or trajectories) in geometry and spatial thinking are detailed in *Learning and Teaching Early Math* (Clements & Sarama 2009). Children's skill development in geometry is not governed by their specific ages but rather by a range of ages that typically indicates specific developmental benchmarks. Below, general age ranges are defined with the caveat that they are approximate, because skill development is largely dependent on children's experiences. General learning paths are described for five areas: (1) recognizing and comparing shapes, (2) composing and decomposing three-dimensional shapes, (3) composing and decomposing two-dimensional shapes, (4) spatial orientation, and (5) spatial visualization.

Recognizing and comparing shapes. As early as ages 1–2, children begin to compare real-world shapes and match identical shapes. From ages 3–4, they recognize and match typical two-dimensional shapes (e.g., circle, square) by size and orientation. They also begin to recognize less typical squares and triangles and may recognize some rectangles. As they get older, they can compare shapes by constructing the whole shape from parts and classify parts by their attributes. By ages 6–7, children can identify and classify most common shapes by their geometric properties ("This shape has three sides and three angles, so it is a triangle").

Composing and decomposing three-dimensional shapes. This is an important aspect of geometry. With three-dimensional shapes, children first begin stacking blocks and then progress to making lines of blocks. Then, around age 2, they stack blocks that are congruent (i.e., the same shape and same size) and begin building simple structures. Their building then progresses to making representations of actual structures with blocks (e.g., stacking many rectangular prisms on top of one another to make a tall apartment building; placing a triangular prism on top of a cube to represent a house) and substituting blocks for other blocks. From ages 6–8 and beyond, they make more complex shapes using three-dimensional solids.

See the Focal Points charts for first and second grade on the DVD!

The Young Child and Mathematics

Composing and decomposing two-dimensional shapes. This skill follows a pattern similar to three-dimensional shapes. Children first experiment with individual shapes and draw pictures, with one shape representing one object. Then, by age 5, they begin making pictures by putting two or more shapes together to make other shapes and completing puzzles with only an outline. They can decompose shapes into smaller shapes and compose shapes knowing what the result will be. By ages 7–8, children are able to substitute shapes for other shapes; they also can construct and duplicate shapes using units, a process known as *tiling*.

Spatial orientation. Young children begin to understand the meaning of landmarks and spatial orientation vocabulary (*on, inside, under, over, next to, between*) at a very young age. Their ability to orient to space progresses from ages 3–5, as they gain experience locating objects after movement and using landmarks. By ages 6–7, they can use maps and read coordinates on maps, a skill that results in the ability to follow a simple map route by age 8 or older.

Spatial visualization. The ability to look at a group of shapes, look away, and then remake the shape is one that is important to the skill of spatial visualization (see the activity Look, Make, and Fix earlier in this chapter). As early as age 3, children can duplicate a simple picture or block structure that they have seen. With experience, they can begin to slide, flip, and turn shapes to match the shapes they have visualized, and they understand that a shape must be flipped over to match on the diagonal. Finally, around the age of 8, they can move shapes based on their mental images.

Geometry and Block Play

Using blocks presents children with many opportunities to make discoveries about two-dimensional and three-dimensional shapes. A multitude of configurations appear from children's spontaneous arrangements.

• Four of the small triangular prisms can make a cube.

• Four of the large triangular prisms can result in a face that is a rhombus.

• Two cubes and two triangular prisms form a face that is a hexagon.

• Two triangular prisms joined to a rectangular prism can make a face that is a parallelogram.

• Two small triangular prisms and a cube create two faces that are trapezoids (the long side of the trapezoid may be at the top or bottom; if the long side is at the top, the children may call it a boat).

Children also make many discoveries about shape when constructing objects they use in creative play.

Adapted from E. Hirsch, ed., *The Block Book,* 3d ed. (Washington, DC: NAEYC, 1996), 57–58.

Promoting development of key skills and concepts

Although young children often demonstrate intuitive spatial abilities, many teachers virtually ignore geometry and spatial thinking. In addition to the emphasis in *Curriculum Focal Points*, geometry and spatial thinking are highlighted in *Principles and Standards for School Mathematics* (NCTM 2000) as an important content area for children, beginning in prekindergarten.

Let's take a closer look at the specific expectations for young children in geometry.

Shape concepts

Children begin to form shape concepts in the years before school, and these concepts are fairly stable by the time children are 6 or 7. Clements (1999a) suggests that an ideal period to learn about shapes is between ages 3 and 6. For the most part, young children do not develop their concepts of shape from looking at pictures or merely hearing verbal definitions ("A triangle has three sides and three angles"). Rather, they need to handle, manipulate, draw, and represent shapes in a variety of ways.

The study of shapes should focus on the attributes and properties of both two- and three-dimensional shapes. Initially, children must be given many opportunities to manipulate and sort shapes according to their own criteria. Teachers can easily highlight particular sorting clues as children sort blocks and put them away on shelves by marking the shelves with outlines for each type of block, or by some other system. For example, tubs can be provided for children to sort pattern or attribute blocks according to number of sides (quadrilaterals vs. triangles). Matching or classifying objects by such properties helps children to focus on the critical attributes of each shape.

Research strongly supports the use of a wide variety of manipulatives to help children understand geometric shapes and develop spatial sense. Manipulating geometric solids helps children learn geometric concepts. Solid cutouts of shapes are more conducive to shape learning than are printed forms (Greabell 1978; Clements & McMillen 1996; Clements & Sarama 2007; Martin, Lukong, & Reaves 2007).

Computer programs that allow children to manipulate shapes have specific advantages because, if designed correctly, they offer great flexibility (Clements & McMillen 1996; Clements 2003). The best software programs allow children to instantly change the shape and the size of forms, as well as to save and later retrieve their work.

Beginning with shapes they can pick up and handle, children can familiarize themselves by tracing the outline of a shape with their fingers. When the child gets to the end of a side (reaches a vertex), the teacher notes this verbally and then the child follows. For example, in tracing a rectangle they might say, "Side, stop, vertex, turn; side, stop, vertex, turn; side, stop, vertex, turn; side, stop, vertex." By stopping, saying "vertex," and then turning the shape in a very pronounced way, the teacher draws the child's attention to the attributes of a rectangle. When they turn, they are representing the angle; and when they trace each side, stopping and saying "vertex," they are identifying that a rectangle has four sides. This same procedure can be used as a whole-body kinesthetic activity, in which children walk large shapes drawn outside on the blacktop, using a long sliding step on a side, then stopping and turning at the vertex. Children can also use one of the corners of an index card to identify right angles; experiencing the pronounced manner in which the right angle "turns" will help them see right angles in their environment.

At first, children recognize a shape by its appearance as a whole. Children may know that "a triangle has three sides," and perhaps recognize the familiar equilateral triangle, yet be unable to identify other triangles within a group of figures. Having a limited understanding of "triangleness," young children often do not recognize triangles that depart from the equilateral version they know and love!

> Four-year-old Daniel recognizes both the regular and irregular triangles in a group containing all triangles, but he declares, "These are the really *good* triangles" [pointing to the equilateral triangles resting on one of their sides] . . . "And these ones are *bad* ones!" [pointing to the long, skinny, or irregular triangles with their vertices pointing toward him]

Similarly, children may see a triangle standing on its vertex as "wrong" and call a square sitting on its point a "diamond."

Children most readily learn the critical attributes of a geometric shape when they see a variety of examples and nonexamples (Clements 1999a). Examples of triangles shown in a variety of positions and sizes, as well as nonexamples (e.g., triangle-like shapes but with curved sides, without closed sides, or with too many sides), should be shown, manipulated, and discussed. Most important, children benefit from practice in telling why a particular shape does or does not belong in a group.

At their level of development, young children do not easily categorize shapes in more than one way. Children tend to see squares and rectangles as two discrete categories; rather than seeing squares as a subset of rectangles, they expect a rectangle to always have two long sides. A square is a special rectangle, of course, one that has four equal sides. A square is also a quadrilateral, a parallelogram, and a rhombus. Introducing all these words and concepts to young children is probably premature. However, teachers should themselves have the real meaning of such terms clear in their own mind to avoid giving children ideas that are actually wrong (e.g., by saying, "No, that's not a rectangle—it's a square").

In Look, Make, and Fix, as Mr. Quintanilla uses the words *side* and *tip*, he models tracing the parallelograms with his finger to clarify their meanings. He discusses with the children Jane's "squashed rectangle" terminology and introduces a new word, *quadrilateral*. Mr. Quintanilla combines tangram shapes, placing them in a variety of positions for the children to replicate. To be successful, a child must not only recognize various shapes but also note their positions in space. At this point in their development he does not ask the children to draw the shapes, but he has this planned for later in the year.

Spatial sense

Thinking spatially—that is, visualizing objects in different positions and imagining their movements—is important to young children's development as mathematical thinkers. Specifically, teachers need to help children "develop a variety of spatial understandings: direction (which way?), distance (how far?), location (where?), and representation (what objects?)" (NCTM 2000, 98). Of course, learning to think spatially is an evolutionary process. In their early childhood years, children's experiences with simple maps, hearing position words in context, and opportunities to manipulate shapes into various positions are important to their development of spatial sense.

These skills can be emphasized during classroom routines or in specially planned activities.

> The kindergartners love finding their class puppet every week by reading a map Mrs. Mason gives them. The map includes direction words and arrows, geometric shape landmarks, distance between landmarks in number of footsteps, and a pictorial representation of the puppet to be found. Later in the year, the kindergartners make the maps themselves.

The creative dramatics center is a good place to emphasize spatial vocabulary (see the activities Reenacting Stories and Treasure Map later in this chapter). As children act out stories such as "The Three Billy Goats Gruff" or "The Three Bears," position words can be used as prompts for their movements. During guided reading activities, position words can be emphasized and used in context in other meaningful situations. Also, language expressing how something is moved (*right, left, up, down*) and what it looks like after it is moved ("standing on one tip, with the big part on the top") should accompany actions that involve moving objects in space. Using children's language combined with meaningful definitions, the teacher and the children can describe how movements are made and the resulting effect. Here is more spatial vocabulary:

- **Location/position words**—*on, off, on top of, over, under, in, out, into, out of, top, bottom, above, below, in front of, in back of, behind, beside, by, next to, between, same/different side, upside down*

- **Movement words**—*up, down, forward, backward, around, through, to, from, toward, away from, sideways, across, back and forth, straight/curved path*

- **Distance words**—*near, far, close to, far from, shortest/longest path*

- **Transformation words**—*turn, flip, slide*

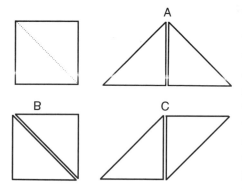

Transformations

Young children are often unable to visualize what the shape will look like when it is turned, flipped, slid, or transformed in some other way. When 4-year-olds fold a square diagonally and cut it in two, they often giggle in surprise when they can use the two halves to make a triangle [A] or move the two halves back to make a square again [B]. Similarly, when they flip up and slide half of the triangle [A] to make a parallelogram [C], they are delighted at the transformation and may practice it over and over again to see the changes. Moving puzzle pieces and making shapes fit exactly into frames requires children to transform shapes by sliding, flipping, or turning them.

Lines of symmetry

A *line of symmetry* divides a figure into two parts that are mirror (reversed) images of each other. To further their understanding of symmetrical relationships, children can draw half of a picture—half of a person, half of a house, half of a flower. When they place the edge of a mirror (held at a right angle to the paper) against the unfinished edge of the picture, the resulting image will look whole.

Another way for children to explore symmetrical relationships is to cut out two identical geometric shapes (squares are easy), then fold each shape along the same line of symmetry (for squares, the line can be vertical, horizontal, or diagonal, as long as it divides the squares perfectly in half). When they hold one folded square against the other, axis to axis, children can see that the matching halves form a whole. Children also experiment with balance and symmetry while building with Legos, wooden blocks, and other materials. For young children, exploration should be the primary focus of experiences with symmetry.

Providing a mathematics-rich environment

More than any other content area, geometry requires certain, specific types of manipulatives to help children learn. Attribute blocks (in different colors with shape, size, and thickness attributes), pattern blocks (red trapezoids, orange squares, green triangles, yellow hexagons, blue and white rhombi), and tangram pieces are important shape models that are helpful to children as they develop their understanding of shape and space.

Three-dimensional models are also important. A variety of wooden blocks with unusual shapes, along with the more typical shapes, helps children develop their perceptions of three-dimensional shapes in space as they view them from different perspectives. In addition, children can use clear containers (spheres, cubes, cones, rectangular prisms, pyramids) filled with water to explore the water surface and provide opportunities for explorations of moving shapes.

Everyday objects also contribute to children's understanding of geometry and spatial sense. The young child's world is filled with natural geometric shapes in different sizes

---

Getting Children Thinking about Geometry and Spatial Sense

Although experienced early childhood teachers ask many questions, they often overlook questions relating to spatial sense and shape. Here are some possibilities:

How is that shape like this one? How is it different?

Why isn't this shape [an oval, a square]? What makes it [a circle, a rhombus]?

What if I turned this shape? What if I flipped it? What would it look like if I slid it from your paper to my paper?

Where have you seen this shape before?

Can you find something like this at home?

(When a child has made a picture out of shapes) How did you decide to use this [triangle] for the [roof]?

How did you decide what to copy/draw?

Can you tell me how to get to [the cafeteria, the library] from here?

Can you tell me about the neighborhood you built with blocks? I'm going to draw a map of it without looking. So tell me what it looks like and what I should put where.

Do you think this shape would roll? Slide? Could we stack these?

How could you cut this paper to make another shape?

What shape could you make out of these shapes?

Could we make the cone roll straight, or would it roll crooked? What about the cylinder?

What would happen if I dropped [a cube, a cylinder] and it broke in half? What would the parts look like? Could it break in half another way?

Have you found all the ways to put those shapes together? How do you know?

What would happen if I cut off an end of this? What would it look like?

Can you think of another name for this shape?

Can you make [a square, a triangle, a rectangle] with pipe cleaners? How about [a ball, a box, a cone]?

---

and orientations. Basketballs, cereal boxes, and cans are examples that children can compare with classroom models such as blocks. Patterned fabric or artwork with shapes positioned in unusual ways can be displayed on classroom walls. Children can use string, pipe cleaners, and yarn to create the outlines of shapes or shape sculptures. Teachers can share books that involve children in looking at objects from different perspectives, or children can create books of this kind of their own. Objects that children bring from home to share may be excellent examples of shapes and may add to a mathematics-rich environment.

Young children also benefit from having many opportunities to climb in and out of big boxes or on or around climbing equipment, going *under*, *over*, *around*, *through*, *into*, *on top of*, and *out of* different things to experience themselves in space. With an assortment of large hollow blocks, boards, sawhorses, and the like (Cartwright 1996), children can build structures big enough to get inside, which allows them to experience their constructions from a very different spatial perspective.

Literature connection

Jack the Builder, by Stuart Murphy, is a highly imaginative book that focuses on both geometry and the number skill of *counting on*. On the first page, the young boy, Jack, uses two blocks from his pile of seventeen to make a building, which he then imagines is a robot. As the story continues, Jack adds more blocks, and he imagines a new creation each time. On the final pages, seventeen blocks become a many-staged rocket ship, which blasts off into space and becomes the original pile of seventeen blocks.

This book can be used to help children visualize three-dimensional solids when they are put together, and as a model for a class project. Photographs can be taken of children's own block constructions, and then these pictures can be placed in a class book that the children can use to communicate what their constructions "looked like." Drawings of the constructions, captioned with the imaginary descriptions, can then be added to the block center for others to duplicate. A class book also can be made, similar to *Jack the Builder*, that includes the photographs, the "looked like" descriptions, and the children's matching drawings.

In-class assessments

The best in-class assessment for geometry is active observation during center time. Children in the block center demonstrate an understanding of shapes and shape attributes as they stack blocks, compose buildings made of blocks, and test the blocks' stacking properties. Children who can describe their buildings using geometric and spatial terms indicate their mathematical understanding and vocabulary. Similarly, children working puzzles of increasing difficulty can be observed for particular abilities and skills.

In giving children specific clues ("Turn over the blue shape" . . . "Flip it over on its side"), the teacher can observe each child's ability to understand directions and compose shapes to make a whole.

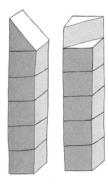

Look for the video clip of "Block Towers" on the DVD!

> Douglas and Kurt are building matching towers in the block center, but Douglas keeps putting a triangular prism on the top of his tower. Kurt motions and says, "Turn it, turn it! Then you can build more on top. Get rid of the point!" Douglas keeps trying to turn the last block, but each time he does, the pointed edge is still facing up. Finally, Kurt goes over to the tower and turns the block so its triangular face is up and provides a good building surface. The teacher notes that Kurt knows the attributes of a solid that work best for stacking and that he can use and model some spatial-thinking skills.

*   *   *

Some activities based on geometry and fostering spatial sense follow. While these activities are roughly listed in order of difficulty, many can be expanded to be more challenging or can be streamlined to simplify them.

String Shapes

Three or four children hold a large string loop. They make a variety of shapes by adding or taking away a vertex or a side, changing the size of an angle, or increasing or decreasing the area of a shape.

Children enjoy making shapes as the leader of the activity names them. They find that a triangle is easy to make because it can be skinny, fat, or "just right" and still be a triangle. A square is harder because all the sides must be exactly the same. Children are often surprised that a circle is one of the hardest shapes to make with string, as it is easy to draw. As one child explained, "Circles are easy to draw because you don't have anyone holding the line and making a point. They are much harder to hold."

Reenacting Stories

Children act out stories they have heard recently using position words such as *above*, *below*, *down*, *up*, *right*, *left*, *under*, *top*, *bottom*, *side*, *beside*, and *through*. Children either represent the characters in the stories themselves or they model the stories by using storyboards.

The storyboards depict settings of recently studied themes or projects and can be used as backdrops for a variety of stories. Using objects to represent characters, children model stories by placing items appropriately on the storyboard. They use position words to describe the characters' actions.

"The Three Billy Goats Gruff" is a great story for children to perform; it is especially popular with prekindergartners. A small table can be used as a bridge. The narrator emphasizes many position words (such as *under*, *over*, *after*, *next*, *between*) and size words (such as *big*, *medium*, *little*) to describe the action as children act out the story. Afterward, the story can be rewritten with the characters in different locations (the troll *on top of* the bridge, the billy goats trotting *under* the bridge), which children often find amusing.

Kitchen Prints

Children use a variety of kitchen utensils to make paint prints in the art center. The imprints must fill up an entire piece of paper, but the individual imprints on the paper may not touch one another. Forks, spatulas, handles, plastic lids, the tops of pans, cheese graters, slotted spoons, and food brushes create unique prints in a variety of shapes and partial shapes.

Children generally take great care in spacing the individual "stamps" so they do not overlap. When finished, they describe the paint prints using shape and position words and have fun guessing which tools made the prints in each other's pictures.

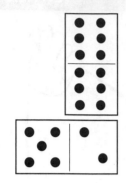

Domino Flash

With half of it covered, the pip side of a large domino is quickly shown to the children. Based on their fleeting view of the pattern of the pips, children use spatial recognition skills to decide what number is displayed on that part of the domino. When children become comfortable with this activity, both halves of the domino face are shown and children must add the two amounts. (It is best to use a domino set with "double-six"—six pips on each half—as the highest value, as this activity may be too difficult for young children if higher values are used.)

Children quickly learn what the arrangement of pips for 1, 2, 3, 4, 5, and 6 look like. When asked how they recognize the numbers so quickly, their responses reveal their understanding of number as well as spatial sense:

> When Allen was asked how he knew five pips stood for 5, he said, "It's one in the middle and two up and two down. You don't even need to count—it's just there!" Jelani said that 2 was "so easy—there's one in one corner and one in the other corner. Easy!"

Treasure Map

Eric Carle's book *The Secret Birthday Message* is a delightful story about a boy searching for his birthday surprise: a new puppy. The book uses many direction and shape words. A map at the end of the book visually represents story events, using shapes and arrows to indicate directions.

After listening to the story and studying the map, children make their own maps of the classroom, complete with shapes, arrows, and a hidden puppy. These wonderful maps can be created entirely using construction paper shapes. For example, the teacher's desk becomes a rectangle; the clock, a circle; the doorway, a rectangle; and the cabinet door, a square. A puppy can be constructed by using two circles and cutting one in half to make ears.

When the classroom maps are finished, children "read" each other's to see if they can find the puppy. The maps are saved and often shared with other classes.

Quick Draw

Children are briefly shown one or two shapes, which they quickly draw. Afterward, children discuss and describe the shapes or draw pictures using them. These pictures can be kept in a special "shape journal."

This activity is especially well suited to prekindergarten classes, although older children also enjoy it. After drawing a shape, children often create more pictures to put in their shape journals by drawing patterns featuring that shape. Other shapes can be included in the pictures, as well. Some children prefer to draw the circle because "it's easy." Other shapes such as hexagons are harder for children to draw, but after tracing cutouts of these shapes, children recognize them more readily and their drawings improve.

Guidelines in Action: Geometry and Spatial Sense

The classroom examples and activities throughout this chapter reflect some of the curriculum, instruction, and assessment guidelines from chapter 2 that form the basis for teaching mathematics effectively to young children. To clarify how specific guidelines look in practice, this chart highlights four instances in which they are evident.

Curriculum Guideline 3— Emphasize the processes of mathematics	Many of the activities in this chapter involve problem solving, communicating, and representing. Children draw pictures of their building constructions, solve spatial problems by putting shapes together to make larger squares in quilts, and communicate what they have built or made with shapes.
Curriculum Guideline 4— Create a mathematics-rich environment	The geometry activities in this chapter occur throughout the classroom, in centers, outside, and in small groups. The materials used are books, manipulatives specifically designed for geometry, and a large variety of real-life tools. All of them combine to make classrooms that use these materials in ways that are mathematics rich.
Instruction Guideline 1— Plan experiences	A child-centered approach is demonstrated frequently during the tangram activity as Mr. Quintanilla uses children's vocabulary to describe shapes, values children's strategies for replicating shapes, and joins in the laughter when children play with the words *squashed quadrilateral.*
Instruction Guideline 4— Interact with children	Mr. Quintanilla promotes children's interactions when he changes Kimberly's focus on Sara's copying to helping, while emphasizing the importance of learning from others.

Making Cone, Cylinder, and Cube Books

Tana Hoban's book *Cones, Cylinders, and Cubes* is a wordless book that contains real-life photographs of cones, cylinders, and cubes. Using toy catalogs or grocery ads, children can cut out pictures of cones, cylinders, and/or cubes. These pictures can be labeled and become pages in a class book entitled "Cones, Cylinders, and Cubes We Have Discovered." This activity helps children visualize three-dimensional shapes as they appear two-dimensionally.

Finding Circles and Rectangles

Children identify circles in their environment and place adhesive dots on all circles they identify. Before they can place the dot sticker, they must trace the circle, slowly saying "Rroouunnd!" They also find rectangles in their environment and use rectangle-shaped adhesive notes to identify the shapes they discover. Before they can place the note sticker, they must trace the rectangle saying, "Ssiiiide, stop, turn; ssiiiide, stop, turn; ssiiiide, stop, turn; ssiiiide, stop."

Shape Pictures

In this excellent learning center activity, children compose pictures using specified numbers of circles, triangles, and rectangles. First, children cut multiples of these shapes in various sizes from construction paper. Using a spinner divided into thirds (labeled *circle*, *triangle*, and *rectangle*) and a die with one through six pips, children spin the spinner and roll the die, select the appropriate number of the shapes indicated, and repeat the process once more. They then make pictures using the shapes they selected. Children display their pictures and describe their constructions using shape and position words.

The pictures can be quite interesting. Squares might become animals, houses, or robots. Circles are often used as parts of flowers, the sun, or spots on a dog. Triangles become people's heads, tops of buildings, or race cars.

Quilts

Quilt making is an excellent activity to encourage young children to compose whole shapes using smaller ones. To make the easiest quilt, children fold square adhesive notes in half, matching the corners so that they make long rectangles. Each child uses eight multicolored rectangles with different orientations to totally cover one square. These squares are then put together into a large, multicolored quilt. A more difficult quilt can be made with the same materials, only children fold the square notes in half to make triangle shapes, again using eight triangle shapes to totally cover one square. Both the quilt made with rectangles and the one made with triangles are beautiful when the squares are put together as big quilts. Children love to describe their particular squares and their placement in the large quilt.

Tangram Creations

Using one or more sets of construction paper tangram pieces, children can create original designs or follow pictures from tangram shape books. Creations are named, described, and displayed for everyone in the class to see. This is a great activity for 4-year-olds, as long as they have enough time to experiment with the shapes.

Secret Socks

Children create their own "secret socks," which contain several mystery shapes. A child threads two or three shape beads onto a pipe cleaner, folding the ends so the beads will not fall off. He places the pipe cleaner and beads in a secret sock. The secret socks are then traded.

Children feel the shapes inside the socks without looking, and in their own words, they describe what they think is inside. Children's descriptions are typically connected to everyday objects. They describe the sphere as a round ball, the cube as a box, and the cylinder as round and flat like a can. Using another pipe cleaner and shape beads, the children then make a copy of the shapes they believe are inside. Finally, answers are checked by opening the secret socks. (The teacher may need to explain that beads of the same shape match even if they are different colors!)

Picture Pie Books

Ed Emberley's series of *Picture Pie* books are filled with pictures made from circles, squares, and partial shapes. He gives step-by-step directions for making insects, puppies, flowers, letters of the alphabet, and a variety of real and pretend characters.

Children view the directions and make the pictures of their choice, tracing the shapes needed or following the templates provided in the book. The pictures are easy to adapt or simplify. When associated with a particular theme or story the children encounter in any part of the curriculum, these pictures help them make connections between mathematics and other areas—social studies, science, art, and so on.

Mystery Shapes

The teacher or a child hides a three-dimensional shape in a box. The teacher or child gives clues, and children try to guess the hidden shape. For example, a child's clues for a rectangular block might include, "It's shaped like a cereal box. What shape do I have?"

Bubble Wands

Children bend pipe cleaners into bubble wands of different shapes, predict what shapes the bubbles blown with these wands will be, and then blow bubbles. How surprising that all the bubbles are spheres! The children try over and over again to make cube or pyramid bubbles. Alas, bubbles are always spheres!

This activity provides useful experience in constructing shapes and recognizing spheres, but at this level the children are not given any scientific explanations of this phenomenon.

Aka Backa Soda Cracker

This game helps children learn to recognize shapes and pass an object from right to left. It may also help the teacher to assess children's understanding of shape words.

Children sit in a circle and pat their legs in time to "Aka Backa Soda Cracker." The chant goes: "Aka backa soda cracker, aka backa BOO"—at BOO, everyone claps his or her hands in the air—"Aka backa soda cracker, pass to you!" After learning the words and rhythm of the chant, each child gets a manipulative shape. The teacher models how to pass from right to left. (The teacher may also wish to explain that moving from right to left inside the circle is like the movement of the hands of a clock, and that this circular direction is called *clockwise*.) When the words "Pass to you!" are sung, children pass the shape they are holding to the person on their left and receive a new shape from the person on their right. If done correctly, all pieces move one at a time in a clockwise direction. The game continues for as long as the class wishes.

Once the passing motion is error-free, the children are ready for a modification of the game. A leader for the activity is selected. Periodically, the leader says, "Stop!" at the end of a verse and then calls out the name of a shape. Anyone who has that shape holds it up in the air. Using descriptive terms like *side* and *corner*, the children holding that shape trace around it and describe it in unison, led by the leader. Those who do not have the shape can hold their fingers up in the air and trace an imaginary shape.

Teachers should not teach this game too quickly, or the children may not master the passing motion. If passing from right to left is modeled step-by-step, then children learn it easily and never seem to tire of the game.

Bubble Windows

In this popular activity, children form quadrilaterals from string and straws. After dipping these frames in a bubble solution, children investigate *planes*, as well as the many different shapes that can be made from two or more bubble windows that intersect. Because of the surface tension of soapy water, bubble windows can be combined in interesting and unusual ways and can be manipulated easily. The children make fascinating discoveries about shape properties and planes.

What Am I Seeing?

Three-dimensional shapes—pyramids, cubes, spheres, cylinders—are placed on the overhead projector and covered with a thin piece of paper. The children try to guess what shape is on the projector by looking at the image on the screen. If a dark circle is on the screen, children may guess that a cylinder is on the overhead projector, since they know that cylinders have circles on both ends. Shapes such as a pyramid are more challenging; a pyramid can be set on its square base or on a triangular side on the projector, so either a triangle or a square may appear on the screen.

This activity for learning about the relationship between two- and three-dimensional shapes is generally appropriate for children in second grade, or perhaps at the end of first grade. Children are able to see that three-dimensional shapes are made up of faces of different geometric shapes.

Straw Towers

Groups of children are challenged to "Make a tower one meter tall that can withstand a hurricane and an earthquake rated 7.5 on the Richter scale." The hurricane strikes when everyone blows as hard as possible on one side of the tower and then on the other side. The earthquake hits when the teacher shakes the tower's cardboard base as hard as possible seven-and-a-half times. The tower is made with a maximum of twenty-five straws, ten paper clips, a foot of masking tape, and one cardboard base.

The teams design, build, and name their towers. The children are given many opportunities to try out their ideas before testing the towers against the elements. When one of the towers withstands the weather, the architects are very proud.

After analyzing the results, children typically hypothesize that triangular bases are the strongest. They begin to observe other buildings and structures to validate their findings.

Creating a New Playground

Second-graders design their ideal playground by constructing a model using blocks and other materials. The children draw building plans for their model, using a key of their own design with symbols that can be easily interpreted. Symbols might include a green rectangle to indicate a wooden plank or a red line to represent a metal bar. This activity is a good early exercise in symbolic reasoning.

Cube Constructions

Children are challenged to build different constructions from five cubes that attach to each other. There are twenty-nine possible constructions. Each construction must be built so that it can be picked up, flipped, or moved in any way and not match any other construction. All cubes in a construction must be connected.

This is a good group problem-solving activity, as children can work in teams to make the different constructions. Children often find twenty-nine ways to connect the five cubes, but upon closer inspection the constructions they create may not all be different. Unique constructions are displayed so children can compare their efforts. This is an excellent task for persistent builders!

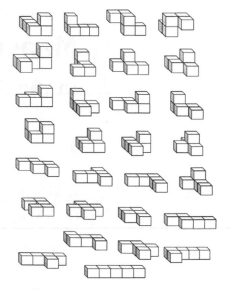

Chapter 7

Measurement
in the Early Childhood Curriculum

Even during the preschool years, children begin to encounter many situations in which they want to compare things or judge *how big*, *how long*, or *how deep* they are. And they also hear adults talk in terms of *feet*, *quarts*, *miles*, *minutes*, *hours*, and dozens of other units of measurement. My 4-year-old daughter once came home from preschool complaining everyone else at school was "4-and-something" years old and she was "only 4." In her mind, that made her *shorter* than everyone! When I informed her that she was really "4 and $^1/_8$" she was quite proud of her new measurement, and her smile reappeared.

Young children are continually measuring how big, how tall, how much, how far, how old, and how heavy they are compared with their friends. In daily experiences such as choosing the biggest brownie or pouring juice into too small a glass and spilling all over the counter, children use and develop their intuitive notions of comparing volume, area, length, and other attributes they will eventually learn to measure. Adults often think of measurement in terms of formulas, rulers, and graduated cylinders. But young children encounter measurement every day in many contexts as they explore and try to make sense of their world.

Measurement is an important area of investigation and learning across the entire span of early education, prekindergarten through second grade, and NCTM lists it as a focal point at three of the four grade levels. Beginning at the prekindergarten level, children directly compare objects and identify specific measurement attributes such as length or weight. In kindergarten, children continue to compare objects; however, these comparisons are done both directly (by comparing two objects) and indirectly (by comparing two objects with a third object). Although measurement itself is not a focal point for first grade, teachers should incorporate measuring activities (such as measuring length using rods made of ten cubes by laying them end to end and then counting them by 10s and 1s) into the study of number and operations. All these measurement experiences then culminate at the second grade level, where measurement returns as an important focus and children more fully develop an understanding of linear measurement, especially the processes of measurement. These processes include the use of equal-size units, an understanding of the inverse relationship between the size of a unit and the number of units used, and *transitivity* (described in greater detail later in this chapter).

In the discussion of the Measurement Standard in NCTM's *Principles and Standards for School Mathematics*, the guidance for teachers states,

Children should begin to develop an understanding of attributes by looking at, touching, or directly comparing objects. They can determine who has more by looking at the size of piles of objects or identify which of two objects is heavier by picking them up. They can compare shoes, placing them side by side, to check which is longer. Adults should help young children recognize attributes through their conversations. "That is a *deep* hole." "Let's put the toys in the *large* box." "That is a *long* piece of rope." In school, students continue to learn about attributes as they describe objects, compare them, and order them by different attributes. Seeing order relationships, such as that the soccer ball is bigger than the baseball but smaller than the beach ball, is important in developing measurement concepts. (2000, 103)

Although researchers still have much to learn about children's development of measurement concepts and skills, recent work has identified specific learning paths that children follow (see the General Learning Paths and Development section later in this chapter). Piaget's work (for an overview, see Ginsburg & Opper 1988) shows that young children's intuitive concepts of *quantity*, *volume*, *weight*, and *length* are rather different from those of older children or adults. As in previous chapters, the focus in this chapter is not on when children acquire particular mathematical concepts; rather, it is on the experiences that facilitate acquisition.

As in other mathematics content areas, it is important that teachers not underestimate young children's measurement capabilities and, as a consequence, limit their learning. Instead, recognizing that even young children have some understanding of measuring and comparing things, teachers should provide a variety of experiences, use specific measurement vocabulary, and ask questions that require comparisons to help children explore and reflect on their understanding of measurement.

Young children construct measurement concepts over an extended period of time, and their process can be quite complex. The box Steps in Comprehending Measurement gives an overview.

Steps in Comprehending Measurement

An effective teaching sequence for measurement skills and concepts follows the five basic steps in children's learning about measurement (Inskeep 1976; Driscoll 1981; Hiebert 1984; NCTM 2000). Within any of the areas of measurement—length, area, volume, weight, and so on—children tend to follow these steps:

1. Recognize that objects have measurable properties and know what is meant by "How long?" or "How heavy?" and other expressions referring to properties

2. Make comparisons (*shorter than*, *longer than*, etc.)

3. Determine an appropriate unit and process for measurement

4. Use standard units of measurement

5. Create and use formulas to help count units

Research evidence (Clements & Sarama 2007) suggests that teachers of young children should primarily promote mastery of the first two steps, as well as plan some activities to encourage exploration of unit, which is an aspect of the third step. Children typically progress through the last two steps in the upper elementary grades. However, exposure to standard measuring tools is certainly appropriate throughout the early childhood years.

Children engage with measurement in a variety of contexts

In the Watering Hole vignette below, children in Mrs. Wong's kindergarten class are engaged in a thematic unit on animals. In terms of mathematics learning, they are investigating numbers, telling animal number stories, and designing zoos using geometric shapes. They are enthusiastic about solving problems and have had some experiences making best guesses (or "estimates") of amounts.

For this lesson, children work in a large area that has room for movement and is separate from their regular classroom. The activity integrates creative dramatics, physical movement, time measurement, estimation, science, and language arts.

Watering Hole

Mrs. Wong has a bag of finger puppets: butterflies, bats, caterpillars, mice, and dragonflies—enough for every child. In addition to a bucket of Unifix cubes, she has five separate bags of the cubes. (Unifix cubes are important props because they stack well.) Children sit on the floor around the reading chair.

Mrs. Wong: Today we are going to pretend to be animals and move like they do. Let's practice!

Mrs. Wong reads a poem by Evelyn Byer, "Jump and Jingle," from *Another Here and Now Story Book*, by Lucy Sprague Mitchell. Children use their hands and voices to act out the movements described in the poem.

Mrs. Wong: Now I think you're ready to pretend and do something else, something that you are getting so good at: estimating. Does anyone remember what *estimating* means? [She waits while children look at each other or talk about ideas.] We estimated a few days ago when we were deciding about how many weeks we had until vacation. We estimated when we tried to decide if we had enough money to go on our field trip. We estimated when we told Mrs. Miller about how much carpet we needed for our library. We estimated in our store when customers wondered if they had enough money to buy their groceries. Do you remember what we did?

Children: We counted. . . . We guessed. . . . We said how many. . . . We bought groceries. . . .

Mrs. Wong: Yes, we made "good guesses" about how many or how much. Remember, a good guess is a guess that you think about. A good guess is an *estimate*. Today you will be estimating in a game. Each of you will pretend to be an animal going to the watering hole. This bucket [holds up the bucket of Unifix cubes] will be the watering hole, and every cube is one drink of water. The watering hole is over here [points to a spot about twenty feet from the group] and all of you animals will go to the watering hole to get a drink. Each time you get one, you'll bring it back here, and then you can go back for the next one.

Children: Can I be an elephant? . . . I wanna be a python! . . . a bee . . . an alligator . . . a vampire bat . . . a gorilla. . . .

Mrs. Wong: I have a finger puppet for each of you in my bag to help you pretend to be an animal. We want to give everyone a fair chance to choose the animal they want to be. How do we usually do that?

The children review the rules for fair chances, and with eyes closed everyone chooses a puppet from the bag. No complaining is allowed. When everyone has a puppet, the children form groups: all the bats are together, all the dragonflies are together, and so on.

The groups discuss and practice how their animal might move to the watering hole. When children seem ready, Mrs. Wong gets their attention.

Mrs. Wong: Remember I said you were going to estimate today? When it's a group's turn to go to the watering hole, all the other groups are going to estimate how many drinks of water the animals in that group will be able to take in thirty seconds. Let's look at the clock and I'll show you how long thirty seconds is [indicates thirty seconds on the analog wall clock]. Now, before I give each group a bag of cubes to show your estimates, I'm going to pretend to be an animal and we'll see how many drinks I can get.

Mrs. Wong pulls out her turtle finger puppet, selects a child to act as timer, and slowly moves across the room toward the watering hole. In thirty seconds she doesn't even reach the watering hole.

Children: You were slow! . . . Not even one drink! I thought there would be more. . . . My animal is faster than that!

Mrs. Wong: Well, let's see. Butterflies, come to this side of the room. [That group of children moves as she thinks aloud.] How many butterflies are there? Four. I wonder how much water they will drink altogether? There was only one of me, and I didn't drink any. Of course, I was very slow. I want to make a good guess, an estimate. . . . So, butterflies, could you show us how butterflies move, please?

The butterflies flit around the room and over to the watering hole. Mrs. Wong distributes one bag of Unifix cubes to each group.

Mrs. Wong: It is your job to estimate how many drinks of water this whole group of butterflies is going to take in thirty seconds. Each cube is one drink. Talk about it, count out cubes, and make one tower showing how many drinks you think the butterflies will take.

Groups begin talking while Mrs. Wong rotates among them, helping with rules and listening to their ideas.

Bats: It's gonna be more than Mrs. Wong, she was slow. . . . Okay, let's make two. . . . But there's more people. . . . So? It's still just a little more. . . . Let's make it a lot. . . . Use all of our cubes, then we will win!

The bat group makes three different towers: one with two cubes, one with six cubes, and one with all the remaining cubes in their bag, about twenty.

Mrs. Wong: Hello, bats, where is your tower? The butterflies can't begin until your estimate is ready.

Sewnet: James wouldn't do what I wanted, so he made the big one. Some of us thought little, and some thought bigger, so we have all three.

Mrs. Wong: Well, I only want one estimate from your group, so I guess we could just stack all of them together. Is that okay? [Some children nod; others look worried but want the game to begin.]

Soon every group has its estimate tower. Mrs. Wong comments about each group's estimation. The groups' estimates are very different: The bat group's tower is the tallest, containing more than twenty cubes; one tower contains only three cubes; another, between ten and fifteen; and the two others, sixteen to twenty.

Once all the towers are finished, the game begins. The butterflies start when the Timer says, "Begin!" Moving like butterflies, each gets a drink of water, brings it back to the other side of the room, then returns for more water. When time is called, each butterfly has gotten two drinks of water, a total of eight cubes. Mrs. Wong asks a butterfly to stack the eight cubes in a tower to show the class.

Mrs. Wong: Well, here it is. [She carries the butterfly group's tower around, comparing it with the estimation towers each other group made.] Ooh, close! . . . Your estimate was too much. . . . Too short. . . . Almost. . . . Whoa, way too big! . . . Okay, now let's try the dragonflies. There are only three of them!

This time, before the dragonflies begin, Mrs. Wong asks every group to explain or defend the height of its estimation tower. Here is their reasoning:

Caterpillars: [showing a tower of fifteen cubes] Dragonflies are really fast, so it is big!

Bats: [a tower of eight cubes] They will get just like the butterflies.

Butterflies: [a tower of six cubes] See, everyone will get two drinks, so [taking off two cubes, two more, pointing to the last two] this is water for one . . . water for another one . . . and water for the last one!

Mice: [showing a tower of seven cubes] We did that, too.

Mrs. Wong: Oh, how interesting! [points to the six- and seven-cube towers] But if you did that, too, why is yours one more?

Abdul: Well, see, dragonflies are just a little bit faster, so one of them will get just one more drink. Aaron didn't want to say seven, but I told him to!

The activity continues. Each time, children check their estimates against what actually happens. The five caterpillars move so slowly that they don't get any water. The bats have to sleep upside down when the lights are on, so estimating their number of drinks is very hard. And the mice run fast but get frightened and stop to look around.

Caterpillars: We think eight drinks for the bats because James and Karie thought nine and Shary and Arien thought seven, so we just kinda put our guesses together!

Mice: We just decided it. . . . It's like theirs! [pointing to a group that was correct last time]

Bats: We just think this because it's almost as tall as the butterflies, and the caterpillars are slower, so it will be little.

Butterflies: We think everyone will get three, and that's three [one butterfly demonstrates, showing three fingers] . . . three more [six fingers] . . . three more [nine fingers] . . . and then three more [holds up one more finger then stops to look at the ten fingers]. . . . So it's ten! Or maybe more. So we just made it this tall. [Their tower has thirteen cubes.]

From group to group, even though the animals' movements and the number of animals change, children's estimates and reasoning improve as the game progresses.

The Watering Hole game called on children to relate an action to the time it takes to perform—that is, how many times a given action can be repeated in a fixed amount of time. Further, because different pretend animals moved over the distance at different speeds, children needed to take that into account in predicting how many drinks each set of animals, whether fast-moving or slow-, could take in a thirty-second period. Using cube towers both to record the children's predictions and to show the actual number

The Young Child and Mathematics

of drinks made the two quantities concrete. Children were able to make a direct, visual comparison ("Did we guess too many, or not enough?") and then make adjustments in their subsequent predictions. At a practical level, children relate time, distance, and number as they participate in the Watering Hole game.

Opportunities to talk about measurement concepts occur on a regular basis. In the vignette below, children discovered the problem caused by using unequal measuring tools:

As Mrs. Freehand's kindergarten class is returning from their physical education period, she overhears Sari and Cori discussing the unfairness of the Best Sport award. Upon questioning them, Mrs. Freehand discovers that when children demonstrate good sportsmanship in physical education, they are allowed to reach into the pretzel jar and put one handful of pretzels in a bag for later. Sari and Cori won for the week; now, however, they are upset because their bags contain noticeably different amounts. Sari states, "Look, I have a little bag. Cori has a lot more. It isn't fair!" Cori counters with, "You just didn't use your whole hand."

While Mrs. Freehand recognizes that these comparison arguments are common between young children, she decides to use the opportunity to discuss *capacity* (how much a hand can hold) and the importance of fair measures (different hands don't always hold the same amount). She also introduces hand investigations in the math center. Children count the amount of pretzels their hands could hold and record the results in their journals. A few weeks later, the class writes a letter to the physical education teachers to suggest a fairer way to make the award.

What my hand can hold:

nine cotton balls

six teddy bear counters

six wooden blocks

five Unifix cubes

Measurement opportunities also occur in children's creative dramatics. In one early childhood classroom, four 3-year-olds prepared to enact the story "Goldilocks and the Three Bears" in the dramatic play center.

Blake is setting the table, Ashley is putting pillows on the chairs, and Valerie and Brandon are making the (pretend) beds. To aid their play, their teacher introduces materials of different sizes into the center: big and small plates, cups, and saucers, as well as big and small pillows. She uses descriptive and comparative words for the items as she places them in the area. Responding excitedly, the children promptly designate the big items Father Bear's, the items already in the center Mother Bear's, and the little items Baby Bear's. Then the children enact their roles using the materials of different sizes and their "big" and "little" voices.

Asking questions such as, "Is Mother Bear's bowl *bigger* than Baby Bear's bowl? . . . But is it the *biggest* of all?" and "Why does Father Bear have a *large* pillow and Baby Bear have a *small* one?" the teacher provokes further thinking about relative size.

General learning paths and development

Learning paths (or trajectories) for measurement in length, area, and volume are detailed in *Learning and Teaching Early Math: The Learning Trajectories Approach* (Clements & Sarama 2009) and summarized here. Children's skill development in measurement is not governed by their specific age but rather by a range of ages that typically indicates specific developmental benchmarks. Because skill development is largely dependent on children's experiences, general age ranges are given below, with the caveat that they are approximate.

Children begin to recognize *length* as an attribute around age 3. By age 4 they directly compare the lengths of two objects by matching them and can indirectly compare lengths using a string. Around age 6, they order lengths, place units end to end to measure lengths, and begin to use repeated units to measure lengths. With experience they recognize the need for identical units to measure lengths, and by age 8 children can use a ruler with understanding.

An understanding of *area* begins around age 4, with simple comparisons and covering a rectangular space with tiles. At this age, children may attempt to fill a region but will leave gaps. By age 8 they progress to making rows and columns with accuracy in order to measure area and make arrays.

The measurement of *volume* begins early, with children as young as 2 or 3 identifying *capacity* ("How much does this hold?") as an attribute. Children can directly compare capacities of containers at age 4 and make indirect comparisons by pouring water from two containers into a third container by age 5. This understanding progresses to measurement with cubes to fill boxes. By age 8, children can compute the capacity of a container by counting the number of cubes in one row and then adding rows together, or by multiplying to find the total volume.

Promoting development of key skills and concepts

In the early childhood math curriculum, measurement provides an ideal bridge between geometry and number, one that comes up frequently in everyday situations. To wrap a package, the right amount of paper (the surface area of the rectangular prism) must be estimated. To cover a table, the right size tablecloth (the area of a rectangle) must be found. To pour a glass of orange juice, the appropriate glass (one with a capacity that is not too small) must be selected. To send a package through the mail, one must gather the right amount of money, depending on how heavy the package is. When selecting a new pair of shoes, shoe size (the width as well as the length) is important for a proper fit. All of these examples and countless others illustrate the use of numbers to measure the size of geometric figures.

Even young children have some intuitive notions of measurement, and the curriculum can build on these. Measurement activities in the early years should focus primarily on providing opportunities for children to identify and compare attributes of length, area, weight, volume, temperature, and time. As children learn measurement vocabulary and explore a variety of measurement tools and materials, they begin to develop a more formal understanding of measurement and the components of *conservation*, *transitivity*, and *unit*. The use of appropriate measurement tools to measure height, length, weight, size, volume, time, or temperature comes later as children practice their skills using nonstandard and standard measurements.

Comparison and ordering

To lay the foundation for measurement, teachers involve young children in a lot of comparing. In fact, comparison is the core activity and concept that starts children on the path to fully developed understanding and use of measurement. Children should have opportunities, for example, to compare two things with respect to length (*longer, shorter*); area (*covers more, covers less*); capacity (*holds more, holds less*); and weight (*heavier, lighter*). They can also compare with respect to time/duration (*longer, shorter*) and temperature (*warmer, colder*). After comparing two items, children then can compare three or more items and put them in order from *shortest* to *longest*, from *covers the least* to *covers the most*, from *holds the least* to *holds the most*, from *lightest* to *heaviest*, from *shortest* to *longest* in duration, and from *warmest* to *coldest*.

To compare objects, children begin by using nonstandard units ("My table is more than four hands long") and then move to using standard units ("The table is almost three feet long"). *Comparing fairly* is an important concept for young children. They may mistakenly say that two objects are the same in length or the same in weight because they consider only part of the object to be measured or weigh two of an object rather than one. Until children learn to *conserve* in the Piagetian sense, their comparisons may be distorted by one perceptual factor or another.

Length and area

Linear measurement typically receives the most emphasis in the early grades. For young children, length concepts involve *how long, how high, how far, how wide*, or *how far around* something is. Rulers, measuring tapes, or meter sticks provide numerical measurements for length.

Area concepts are much more difficult for children because they require that children consider more than one dimension. How much two-dimensional space is covered (i.e., the *area*) depends on both the height (or length) and the width. However, even prekindergartners are able to understand that although they can measure length with linear tools such as rulers, they cannot directly measure area this way (NCTM 2000). With appropriate learning experiences, they grasp that to measure area they need to use a unit of area, such as a square tile.

Capacity and volume

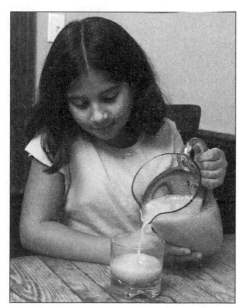

Although capacity and volume do not receive as much emphasis as other measurement topics in many early childhood classrooms, they have many everyday applications. *Capacity* describes the maximum amount that can be held by a container such as a bucket, and often refers to liquid measurement. *Volume* is the space occupied by a three-dimensional object (its height, width, and length) and is often described as the number of cubic units it takes to fill a figure (such as a wooden block) or a container.

Young children often explore capacity and volume in the classroom. As they carefully stack books on shelves, they are exploring the capacity of the shelves. As they pour sand from one cup to another, they must notice and compare the volumes of the two containers. When they combine cups of red and blue liquids in a pot to cook an imaginary recipe, they try to stop just before the pot overflows. Although young children do not yet use numerical measurements for determining capacity or volume, teachers can introduce common terms such as *liter*, *pint*, and *gallon* in context to describe items children see daily, such as a gallon of milk or a liter of soda. In cooking and science experiences, children begin to learn the names of common measures of volume such as *teaspoon*, *cup*, and *ounce*.

First-graders were asked to compare a tall bud vase with a wide, short dish to see which could hold more water. Like the children of whom Piaget and Inhelder (1941/1974) asked similar questions, most of them focused on the height of the bud vase:

> Most of the children tell Mrs. Albert that the tall container can hold more because "It looks like it" or "I just think so" or "It's tall!" But Ronnie, a 6-year-old who always asks questions, says, "I don't get it. Do you want the one that's tall [showing height with his hands] or the one that's like this [showing width with his hands]?" The teacher repeats, "I want to know which one will hold more water." Ronnie looks frustrated, and the other children seem irritated with his questioning.

Ronnie was beginning to see that there are different ways of measuring a container; most of the other children had not even considered the possibility. By providing many more opportunities for children to measure capacity and volume at the water and sand tables and sometimes asking questions, as she did here, their teacher will foster the children's continued thinking about these aspects.

Weight

Weight is determined by the mass of an object and the effect of gravity on that object. For example, an object that weighs ten pounds on Earth would have different weights on planets other than Earth because of their differing forces of gravity. An object's *mass*, in contrast, is not affected by gravity; it is simply the amount of matter in the object. With young children, comparing the weights of objects to see which one is heavier or lighter should be the primary focus.

Balances provide good measuring tools for comparisons ("We know this rock is heavier than that rock because the balance goes down on this side"). Scales allow children to put a numerical value to a weight ("Amir weighs sixty-five pounds because the scale shows that number").

Time

Because time concepts and measurements are very difficult for young children, teachers often do not emphasize time measurement in the early years. The Watering Hole game described earlier in this chapter is an example of a planned learning experience that engages children in exploring aspects of time, such as the relationship of *time, distance*, and *speed*. Activities like this, planned and led by teachers, are helpful in introducing concepts and extending children's thinking; children then explore these ideas further in their play.

For the most part, however, young children learn about time in everyday routines and conversation with adults and other children. Teachers use various types of time vocabulary, as Charlesworth and Lind describe (2010, 271):

• **general words**—*time, age*

• **specific words**—*morning, afternoon, evening, night, day, noon*

• **relational words**—*soon, tomorrow, yesterday, early, late, a long time ago, once upon a time, new, old, now, when, sometimes, then, before, present, while, never, once, next, always, fast, slow, speed, first, second, third,* and so on

• **specific duration words**—*clock* and *watch (minutes, seconds, hours); calendar (date, days of the week, month, year,* and their names such as *Monday, September, autumn)*

Getting Children Thinking about Measurement

Many questions can facilitate a child's thinking about measurement concepts. Teachers need to be sensitive to the pace of children's thinking and exploration, taking care not to interrupt with rephrasings or follow-up queries while the child is still pondering the original question. Questions are listed here as they relate to the different areas of measurement.

Length

Which one is longer? Shorter?

Can you find something that is longer/shorter than this? How can you show me?

How much ribbon will you need to go around this? How can you figure it out by just looking?

Can you put these three straws in order from the shortest to the longest? Show me how you know your answer is right. Where would you put this fourth straw? How did you know?

[The table] is three licorice sticks long. A toothpick is a lot shorter than a licorice stick. Would I need more toothpicks than licorice sticks to measure [the table]? Would I need fewer toothpicks to measure [the table]? Why do you think so?

You are measuring how long [the desk] is. What are you counting? Show me how you are measuring.

Area

Which shape can you cover with the most/least number of blocks?

Will it take more blocks to cover the table or to cover the book? Explain how you know your answer is correct.

To cover this book, would it take more cubes or more blocks?

I need your help in measuring how much space the rug is covering. *(later)* What are you counting? Show me how you are measuring.

Weight

Which is heavier? Lighter? How do you know?

How can you show which person weighs more/less?

Put these three blocks on the balance, one at a time. How can you tell which block is the heaviest? The lightest?

You are measuring how heavy [the book] is. What are you counting? Show me how you are measuring.

Capacity

Which of these two containers holds more/less? Why do you think so?

How can you find out which container holds more water?

If you have three containers and you can only fill one of them, how could you find out which one holds the most water?

You are measuring how much [the cup] holds. What are you counting? Show me how you are measuring.

Time

Will it take longer to walk to the door or to write your name?

Will it take longer than a minute to walk to the park? Why do you think so?

What do we do when we come to school? What do we do after that? Before lunch?

What do you think takes longer/shorter?

You are measuring how much time it takes to [wash your hands]. What are you counting? Show me how you are measuring.

Temperature

Is [this room] warmer or colder than [the hallway]?

Was the weather warmer last month? Yesterday? On Thanksgiving? During the Fourth of July?

You are measuring how hot or cold [the window pane] is. Show me how you are measuring.

• **special day words**—*birthday, Passover, Juneteenth, Cinco de Mayo, Easter, Christmas, Thanksgiving, vacation, holiday, school day, weekend*

Concrete representations of time passing, such as sand running through an egg timer, help children get a sense of how long a given period of time is. For example, the teacher might tell the children that they have five minutes to clean up and that the sand will all be at the bottom when five minutes are up.

Working with the calendar gives children the opportunity to understand *yesterday, today, tomorrow, next week*, and so on, as they discuss recent and upcoming events. At first, young children use only general terms of comparison, describing one event as taking *longer than* another, for example, or perhaps as taking *longer than* a minute, an hour, or a day.

Adults frequently use time words inaccurately or in a casual, nonmathematical manner. For example, many adults tell a child they will "be back in a minute" to help with a particular activity. When that minute stretches to twenty minutes or an even longer time, the child may form an idea of *minute* that is quite inaccurate.

Temperature

Temperature, too, should be taught in the context of the young child's world. *Hot, warm, cold*, and *freezing* are temperature words that may describe the temperature of food, the weather, or even a child's warm or cool forehead.

Thermometers can be thought of as vertical number lines. Kindergartners in the upper peninsula of Michigan have no difficulty talking about the temperature being "below zero" and are developing a beginning understanding of negative numbers. Conversely, kindergartners in Houston, Texas, understand from firsthand experience that 100 degrees Fahrenheit is very hot, even before they really grasp the value of 100. Again, measurement vocabulary used in context is critical to children's understanding of temperature and to their ability to make comparisons.

Conservation

Piaget's term *conserve* describes a child's cognitive ability to understand that even if an object changes shape, its fundamental attributes stay the same. So, for example, even if water is poured from a tall vase to a squat one, or a line of blocks are pushed farther apart, or a pipe cleaner gets bent, the water's volume, the blocks' number, and the pipe cleaner's length don't change.

Based on his interviews with children, Piaget and his colleagues (Piaget & Inhelder 1941/1974; Piaget, Inhelder, & Szeminski 1960) concluded that most children become conservers of length and area between ages 7 and 9 and conservers of volume a few years later. Other researchers (e.g., Gelman & Gallistel 1978; Clements & Sarama 2007) have reported that with careful questioning, they find children able to conserve at an earlier age, and that conservation of length develops over time with supportive experiences.

Transitive reasoning

Transitive reasoning, or transitivity, is the understanding that if the measurement of one object (A) is, for example, longer (or heavier or holds more) than a second object (B), and if object B is longer than a third object (C), then object A will always be longer than object C. A child demonstrating transitivity can make inferences of this kind: "If Timothy is taller than James, and James is taller than Stephen, then Timothy must be taller than Stephen." Similarly, the two weight comparisons using balancing scales that are shown here illustrate transitivity in a comparison of the weights of scissors versus a pencil and then a book versus scissors. From these two direct comparisons, a comparison of the weight of a pencil versus a book can be reasoned.

Researchers have disagreed about the age at which children typically develop transitive reasoning (see Clements & Sarama 2007). Clements and Sarama (2009) report that children as young as 5 can indirectly compare the capacities of two containers by pouring the contents of the first container into a third container and noting where the liquid level is, then doing the same for the contents of the second—a process that demonstrates transitivity.

At whatever age it occurs, we can reasonably conclude that young children's progress toward transitive reasoning can be facilitated by experiences in their learning environment. Teachers can model such thinking by musing aloud—for example, "Let's see, your sister is older than your brother, and he's older than you. So I guess your sister's older than you, too, right?" Teachers can also provide situations that call for children to try working out such relationships themselves.

Unit

Critical to accurate measurement is consistency in the size of the unit used to make the measurement. In measuring and comparing, young children tend to consider only *how many* units, overlooking the lack of consistency in the size of the units used to measure. Say young children are measuring distances using licorice sticks as the unit of measurement. If one child has partially eaten his licorice stick (and therefore it is shorter than the other children's), they may not make the connection between the differences in their measurements and the differences in the lengths of their licorice stick tools (see the activity Balloon Rocket at the end of this chapter for another example). The box Understanding of Unit (below) briefly reviews research supporting this point.

Despite this, children are very concerned with fair measurements. In contest situations they may begin to see the importance of measuring with equal units. With first- and second-graders' natural love of competing with the teacher, appropriate contests engage their strong interest and provide opportunities for them to measure and thus encounter challenges and difficulties with measurement.

Understanding of Unit

To estimate reasonably and measure accurately, children must understand that the unit of measurement makes all the difference. A particular distance could be accurately described as 144 inches, twelve feet, or four yards. The differences in number derive from the use of different units of measurement.

The National Assessment of Educational Progress (NAEP) reported that 8-year-olds have difficulty with this concept (Kouba et al. 1988). When children were shown a picture of three boxes of equal size and told that one would be filled with softballs, one with marbles, and one with tennis balls, two-thirds of the third-graders correctly said that the one filled with softballs would contain the fewest objects. However, on a similar task involving length, only 8 percent of the third-graders answered correctly. Researchers note that children do not gain this concept with the activities and instruction commonly provided by schools (Carpenter 1975; Carpenter & Lewis 1976; Hart 1984; Clements & Sarama 2007). More focus on both the number and size of units in measurement is needed.

One such activity involves a distance competition between the teacher and the class using cars. In this activity, children release toy cars one at a time. The cars roll down a ramp and the distance traveled is measured and recorded for each car. In order to demonstrate the importance of fair measures, the teacher should begin by designing the activity so that the children's cars travel noticeably farther than his own. Then, when the teacher uses a four-link chain to measure his car's distance and the children use chains with ten links to measure theirs, the teacher will obtain a number (e.g., thirty "chains" traveled) that is larger than those of the children (e.g., fifteen or eighteen "chains" traveled). Wonderful discussions arise from this initially startling discrepancy. Cries of "That's not fair!" are typically heard, followed by "You have to measure using the same thing!" or "Do it again, and let's use something else than chains." The teacher can then help children clarify their reasoning and follow up with other experiences relating to units of measurement.

In one kindergarten class, the teacher focused children's attention on the need for consistent units of measurement with an exploration activity:

> Mrs. Knapp attaches a "totem pole" of medium-size teddy bear cutouts to the side of a door frame. Children measure themselves by standing next to the door frame and asking a partner, "How many bears tall am I?" Each child records his or her results on a poster sheet.
>
> Several weeks later Mrs. Knapp puts up a second totem pole, made from small bears, on the other side of the door frame. Again, children measure their height in bears and record the results. Because of the smaller size of the bears, these new numbers are almost twice those from the previous measurements.
>
> When Mrs. Knapp interviews the children, she asks about the two different measures. Five children refer to the size of the bears, noting that "They are different bears. . . . See, the big ones get this much and the little ones get this much!" The other children have very different responses: "I just growed!" or "I ate lots of food this week!" or "I have been exercising with my dad!" or "I don't know, but I'm gonna tell my brother I am getting taller than him!"
>
> A few weeks later, Mrs. Knapp hangs yet another totem pole on another door frame—this time of very large bears—and asks the children to measure their heights using the pole of their choice. Children measure themselves repeatedly against all three totem poles, exploring the differences. When Mrs. Knapp asks them to report their height in bears, almost all of them use the measurements from the small bears for their reports. However, more children talk about the differences in the size of the bears than previously.

Mrs. Knapp demonstrated a very important role of the teacher: She set up experiences that confronted the children with a discrepancy—dramatically different measurements of the same child. The discrepancy provoked them to think further and eventually to work out that unit size makes a big difference in measurement.

Measurement processes and procedures

Besides core concepts in measurement, there are certain processes children must learn in order to actually measure. These include choosing or devising an appropriate tool and then using it in a way that yields an accurate measurement—a task not as straightforward as it may seem to adults.

Choosing an appropriate tool. Using a ruler to measure length, a scale to measure weight, or a clock to measure time is second nature to adults—it just makes sense. For a young child, however, measurement tools are not necessarily part of their everyday experiences. They may never have seen a scale or used a ruler, and they may not know what the numbers on a clock stand for. It is not uncommon to overhear children boasting about how old they are when they are being weighed ("I'm older than you are. I'm 78!") or how long their bus is based on its route number ("Our bus is really long. It's 112!"). Again, teachers' appropriate modeling of tools in real settings is key. More important, the tools must be available for children's experimentation and use.

Learning to measure. The procedure of measuring can be rather complicated; teachers primarily begin by introducing children to length measurements. Two types of measuring can be used. The easier method for children involves using multiple physical duplicates of the unit of measurement (as with the multiple bear cutouts that made up a totem pole). In the other method, a single tool is used over and over again—an *iteration* process. For iteration, children must learn not to overlap the units or leave gaps between the units; they must note the exact spot where the first unit ended, even after picking up their measuring tool, to know where to place the tool for the next unit to begin. And they must mentally keep track of the number of iterations it took to measure the length. This type of end-to-end measuring can be done using nonstandard units (e.g., paper clips, licorice sticks, children's footprints, pencils) or with standard units (inch "worms," a 12-inch ruler, a meter stick).

Estimation

An *estimation* is "a good guess," meaning it is based on something we know and not just a random idea. Estimation is valuable in situations where exact measurement is not necessary or even possible (e.g., "How many stars are in the sky tonight?"). Estimation is also useful as a check on whether a result gotten from exact measurement is reasonable. Because estimating measurement focuses children's attention on what is being measured and how, it contributes to development of spatial sense, number concepts, and a variety of other skills relating to measurement (NCTM 2000).

Estimation often involves numerical values. Children may estimate how many paper clips long an object is or how many marbles will balance an object being weighed. With young children, the use of estimation vocabulary in the context of a measuring activity enhances understanding. Teachers can use words such as *about, close to, almost, just a little smaller, too much,* or *way too high,* making their meanings clear in context. For example, the teacher might ask the children how high the juice will fill up the pitcher when she pours every bit of it out of the carton, and then make her own prediction: "I think it will come almost to this line. Do you think that estimate is way too high, way too low, or close?"

Good estimations do not occur without exploration, many trial-and-error experiences, and numerous experiences in everyday situations. Estimation was a prime objective of the Watering Hole game earlier in this chapter. As Mrs. Wong did, providing opportunities for children to think about their answers helps them begin to construct estimation concepts.

Providing a mathematics-rich environment

Measurement tools are usually specialized for gauging length, area, weight, temperature, capacity, or time. Although measurement with standardized units is not the focus of young children's learning, standardized tools should be part of every classroom. Children should be given opportunities to explore with balances, weights, scales, clocks, rulers, meter sticks, grid paper, measuring tapes, thermometers, gallon containers, cups, teaspoons, tablespoons, and graduated cylinders. In addition, a variety of nonstandard measuring materials should be available. Children can use yarn, ribbon, blocks, cubes, timers, ice cubes, and a wide variety of containers to compare and measure to make sense of their world.

Literature connection

Guess How Much I Love You, by Sam McBratney, is a heart-warming story that provides a perfect opportunity to involve the young child, the family, and measurement. When Little Nutbrown Hare and Big Nutbrown Hare are describing their love for each other, they use a variety of measurement phrases to describe that love. They soon find out that "love is not an easy thing to measure." For a Valentine's Day celebration, children wrote "Guess How Much I Love You?" books to their families using a similar format:

> For one page, Ms. Mulder's first-graders measure how far they can jump using a long ribbon and record an accompanying number in inches. For another page, they use a long piece of yarn to measure how far they can throw a pom-pom and record that measurement with the yarn and an accompanying number. For still another page, they measure their own heights with a piece of adding machine tape and record it with the tape and an accompanying number. For the last page, they borrow a phrase from the story, "I love you to the moon and back" . . . adding "and that's just too far for me to measure!"

In-class assessments

Children's performance on specific measurement tasks provides an excellent assessment in measurement. Tasks at each grade level should focus on the focal point or connection suggested for that grade level (see the *Curriculum Focal Points* materials reproduced on the accompanying DVD).

For example, at the prekindergarten level, children should be asked to directly compare two lengths or weights using measurement terms (e.g., *about the same as, longer than, heavier than, shorter than, lighter than*) and then demonstrate the measuring processes they used. At the kindergarten level, children should order objects by a particular attribute and compare objects directly and indirectly. Again, they should not only demonstrate their procedures but also use measurement vocabulary to explain their results. At the first and second grade levels, children should demonstrate their skill at measuring lengths using both standard and nonstandard units. Their use of measurement vocabulary and processes, as well as their skill with the measurement tools, should be the focus of the assessment.

* * *

Activities

Some activities for measurement are described below in approximate order of difficulty. Many can be simplified or expanded to be more challenging. These activities, along with the classroom vignettes and other examples, emphasize the close connection between measurement and the content areas of geometry and of number. Children have an impressive intuitive understanding of measurement culled from informal experiences with measurement concepts. The teacher's role in teaching measurement is to build upon these experiences and help children as they apply their understandings of measurement.

Walking the Circle

This excellent transition or circle activity illustrates the meaning of comparison words, an important aspect of understanding measurement. Children walk in a circle. The leader of the activity calls out a certain style of walking, such as "Walk *faster!*" and everyone does as directed until the next direction is given. Other possiblities include walking *slower*, *higher* (on tiptoes), *lower*, *more heavily* (like an elephant), *more lightly* (like a mouse, like a butterfly), *noisily*, *quietly*, and swaying *back and forth*. For greater challenge, the children can hold dowels and combine different instructions, such as "hold the stick higher and walk faster!"

Family Links

Children bring photographs of their family to class. The children make paper or plastic chains to represent their family, with each family member being a colored plastic or paper link: a red link for an adult (male or female), a blue link for a boy, a green link for a girl, and a yellow link for a pet. The children display the chains next to their family's pictures. Children can then compare the lengths of their chains, or the chains can be combined into one large chain, representing the classroom family.

This activity, which connects number with length, can begin when children first come to school in the fall and continue throughout the school year. If the children's families grow, more links are added to represent a new pet, a baby, or another relative who joins the household. If a child moves away during the school year, she can either take the chain with her or leave the chain with the class to symbolize that she is still part of the classroom community.

Measuring Me

In this long-term activity, children measure themselves at the beginning of the school year and the end. The children measure how tall they are using yarn or ribbon, and they trace their hands and feet to record their size. At the beginning of the year, each child's measurements are placed in a time capsule marked with the child's name. At the end of the year, the children measure themselves again. The time capsules are opened and comparisons are made between the two sets of measurements.

This activity can also be used to connect school and home. A child's family can provide copies of his infant hand- or footprint and help the child measure a piece of string to show how long he was at birth. The prints and the string are added to the time capsule, providing another set of measurements for comparison.

Water Graph

Two clear, plastic cups are labeled "YES" and "NO." The teacher asks the class yes/no questions, and the children individually answer by using a turkey baster filled with colored water to place a drop in the appropriate cup. The water levels in the two cups are then compared to determine the most common answer.

This activity is relatively easy for children in kindergarten. For a greater challenge, an eyedropper can be used, but only to answer no. The turkey baster is still used for yes answers. The children then must decide if this is a fair system. Although they may be unable to verbalize their reasoning, children quickly decide that using both the eyedropper and the turkey baster is unfair. This indicates a developing understanding of the importance of a consistent unit of measurement.

Guidelines in Action: Measurement

The classroom examples and activities throughout this chapter reflect some of the curriculum, instruction, and assessment guidelines from chapter 2 that form the basis for teaching mathematics effectively to young children. To clarify how specific guidelines look in practice, this chart highlights four instances in which they are evident.

Curriculum Guideline 4— Create a mathematics-rich environment	Although the puppets used in the Watering Hole game are not typical mathematics materials, their use made the activity more realistic to the children. In addition, the Unifix cubes provided a perfect link between length, number, and measurement. While this activity can be effective without the puppets, the Unifix cubes are necessary to facilitate learning of measurement.
Instruction Guideline 4— Interact with children	The teacher began the Watering Hole game by modeling the process of estimation. She then asked children to estimate, talk about their decisions with friends, and listen to others' reasoning. She continually posed questions that prompted children's ideas yet did not give away answers or make corrections as they were exploring.
Assessment Guideline 1— Make child-centered choices	During the Watering Hole game, the teacher was able to observe different levels of development in the children. The caterpillars who figured averages to arrive at their answer and the mice who said their tower was a good answer because it looked like their neighbors' tower are at very different levels of understanding.
Assessment Guideline 4— Assess both children's learning and your teaching effectiveness	Because measurement has previously been an area of little research, many of the ideas in this chapter have been formed directly from assessing children's learning. Through observing children's learning and the effectiveness of teaching, instruction has been informed and changed.

Balance Scale Graph

The teacher marks one side of a balance scale "YES" and the other side "NO." In this variation of the Water Graph activity, children each answer the yes/no question posed by the teacher by placing a unit block on that side of the balance. The side most weighted down indicates the answer given most frequently. After the imbalance is analyzed, the blocks are taken off of the balance and stacked as two towers. Amazingly, the children find that the heavier pile of blocks always makes the taller tower!

Measuring Earthworms

Each child observes and cares for an earthworm. As part of the children's observations, the earthworms are measured, and their measurements are recorded. Children may measure and record in whatever way they wish. Some children measure their worms with string, while others draw life-size pictures. First and second grade children are often able to use rulers to make fairly accurate standard measurements.

One first-grader measured and recorded his earthworm by drawing the picture at left. When the teacher asked why he drew so many versions of his earthworm, he replied "Because it kept moving! So I just drew it the way it looked." When asked which picture showed the best measurement, he said, "The straight one, because it's easier to see how long it is."

Shoe Store

Transforming the housekeeping center into a shoe store provides 3- and 4-year-olds with many opportunities to measure. Children take off their shoes, and a shoe clerk measures and matches feet with shoes of the correct size. Purses and wallets may also be sold at the shoe store, and children can decide which purse or wallet holds the most. Boxes of various sizes can be used as shoeboxes. The shoe store employees must be sure that both shoes in a pair can fit into one shoebox. In addition to measuring, children also sort, count money, write receipts for purchases, and develop language skills in this activity center.

Coin Match

In this game for a small group of children, bags containing pennies, nickels, dimes, and quarters are prepared and distributed to the players. Each bag has the same number and type of coins. The children hold their bags of coins behind their backs. The leader of the activity picks one coin from her bag and displays it to the group. The other players try to find a matching coin in their bags, but they are not allowed to look—they must find the matching coin by touch only. Teachers can discuss with children how the size of the coin and the value of the coin are not always correlated (for example, the small dime is worth more than the large nickel).

Children quickly notice that the quarter is the easiest coin to find. It is biggest and, as the children say, "more different" than the other coins. The penny is often the hardest coin for the children to find.

Actual Size Footprints

Steve Jenkins's book *Actual Size* shows pictures of animals or parts of animals that are the actual size. One particular picture is of the foot of the largest land animal, the African elephant. Using construction paper and adding-machine tape, children make measuring tapes that illustrate their own footprints placed end to end, the estimated footprints of a baby placed end to end, and the footprints of the African elephant pictured in the *Actual Size* book. Children then measure their heights with all three footprint measures and compare their results.

Oobleck

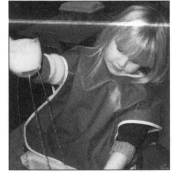

Children mix two parts cornstarch with one part water to make a substance called *oobleck*. Oobleck is a strange mixture that shifts between a liquid and a solid state—it can be temporarily molded into a solid shape, but within seconds reverts to a liquid form. The mixture is an excellent cleaner for children's hands and can also be used to clean water or sand tables.

When cornstarch and water are mixed together, children have an opportunity to measure both a powder and a liquid as accurately as possible. Then they can practice measuring various amounts of oobleck and explore its properties at the same time.

Sand Babies

Look for the video clip of "Sand Babies" on the DVD!

A favorite weight activity for young children involves children each filling a large plastic bag with sand until it is their approximate birth weight (PBS Mathline 2009). Children can then create a "baby" by putting their bag of sand into a large sock or wrapping it with a colorful cloth napkin. After a paper face and yarn hair are added, children love to directly compare their babies with others'. Margaret Miller's *Now I'm Big* is an excellent book to share with children and their sand babies, and similar class books can be written with the phrases, "When I was a baby, I . . . " and "Now I am big and I. . . ."

Cup Drips

In this comparison and timing activity, children poke holes of varying sizes in foam cups. They hold their fingers over the holes while the teacher fills the cups with water. When the teacher gives a signal, the children uncover the holes and observe how rapidly or slowly the water empties out of the cups. They compare which cups empty at what speeds and make predictions about which cups will empty fastest or most slowly the next time. Children in second grade and beyond enjoy more specific challenges, such as designing a water cup that will empty in exactly one minute.

Snapping

Second grade children estimate the number of times they can snap their fingers in one minute and record their estimates. Children then snap for fifteen seconds. The results are added together four times and compared with the initial estimates. Children are often surprised that their estimates are lower than their actual results.

Children love this type of activity and are eager to discover how many other things they can do in one minute.

Balloon Rocket

Using string, a plastic straw, a balloon, a chair, and a doorknob, this experiment is set up as shown in the diagram.

The teacher blows up a large balloon for the children, holds the end so that the balloon does not deflate, and tapes it to a straw according to the children's directions. The teacher lets go of the balloon and it blasts off along the string. Marking the balloon's highest point on the string, the children measure the distance the balloon traveled using a full-size licorice stick.

Next, the teacher inflates and blasts a much smaller balloon. This time, however, the distance the balloon travels is measured with a very small piece of licorice. The children loudly protest when the small balloon's measurement indicates that it traveled farther than the large balloon. In puzzling over the apparent discrepancy in measurement, children become more conscious of the importance of using a consistent unit to measure.

Chapter 8

Data Analysis and Probability
in the Early Childhood Curriculum

In almost every early childhood classroom, you find examples of children displaying, collecting, and analyzing data. Graphs hanging on the wall; information on a "This Is Me" bulletin board that lists everyone's favorite colors, foods, and books; pictures of families, marked with numerals indicating the number of siblings and pets; and number tallies showing how many children want milk, ride the bus, are in the block center—such are evidence of this mathematics content area. Directly related to the child's world and environment, the Data Analysis and Probability Standard (NCTM 2000) focuses primarily on different ways to help children collect, represent, analyze, and visualize information.

For the young child, the primary focus in this content area is informal experience with data collection and organization and the display of those data. Ideas about probability at this level are also informal. Probability vocabulary, such as *impossible*, *maybe*, and *certain*, can be introduced to describe likelihood in data collecting experiences such as throwing number cubes or selecting colored counters from a closed bag.

NCTM does not suggest data analysis be one of the main emphases in the early years, prekindergarten through second grade. So teachers would be giving it undue weight if they put data analysis on par with number and operations or geometry (or even measurement) in those grade levels. Yet there is a place in the early childhood curriculum for data analysis, which includes the kinds of collecting, organizing, and displaying of data that are described above. Important in connecting data analysis to content areas that *are* focuses for prekindergarten through second grade are problem solving, reasoning, and representation, all of which are very important mathematics processes.

Children are interested in and ready to do activities that meet the Data Analysis Standard. These activities are often drawn from other content areas; teachers can look out for opportunities to help children investigate data as they share stories.

> The preschoolers have just cooked and eaten "green eggs and ham" as part of a St. Patrick's Day celebration after reading the popular book by Dr. Seuss. Each child places a picture of green eggs or yellow eggs on a poster to show which color eggs he or she prefers. A discussion about their opinions ensues: "We don't like green food," "Green food is yucky," and "I always throw away stuff that is green!" are the most common comments.
>
> The children are fascinated by the effects of the green food coloring. The teacher asks if they would like the eggs better if they were red, purple, or blue. The children think about that for a while and decide that red food is "really, really good." To take

advantage of their interest in colored food, the teacher initiates an experiment to test their hypothesis about preferring red food. With some organizational help from the teacher and assistant teacher, the prekindergartners conduct a taste test.

They use vanilla instant pudding mix and just the right mix of food colorings to create red pudding, green pudding, and purple pudding. The puddings are placed in dishes outside the classroom, along with matching squares of red, green, and purple paper. The young scientists draft some kindergartners to be testers, giving each three clean spoons (no double dipping!) and directing them to the dishes of pudding. After each tester samples the puddings, he or she is to select a paper square to indicate the favorite. After the tasting is over, the 4-year-old scientists collect the squares and bring them back to their classroom for a lively discussion.

Although all of the colored puddings came from the same vanilla pudding mix, red pudding did turn out to be the kindergartners' favorite (i.e., the class hypothesis proved correct). Many family-school connections resulted as children began to request red mashed potatoes rather than white ones at home!

Children engage with data analysis in a variety of contexts

The following vignette illustrates a routine graphing activity. Individual graphing activities take place daily in this kindergarten. This lesson occurs in March. It is led by Paulie, who has the job of Class Grapher for the week.

"Graphing" with Blobs, Bars, and Circles

The classroom has a large circle area at the end of the room. There is also a free-form red "blob" of laminated construction paper on the floor in one corner and a similar blue blob in another corner. A red rectangle of laminated construction paper is on the floor near the door, with a blue rectangle next to it. The Question of the Week is on the board, and children study it as they settle in.

Paulie: The question is, "Do you have a cat?" Everybody, show your cubes.

Most children, knowing the routine, have already selected either a red cube for no or a blue cube for yes to show their response. The few who forgot go now to the cube box and select one.

Paulie: Okay, now let's get together in red blobs and blue blobs.

Children go to the red or the blue corner, depending on the color of their cube, and stand on the red or the blue blob, forming two groups.

Paulie: Point to the blob that looks like it has the most people.

Most children point to the red blob, which looks as if it has several more children than the blue. Paulie addresses the children standing on the red blob, asking them to move closer together. He asks the group standing on the blue blob to spread out.

Paulie: Now, point again to the biggest blob.

Again, most children point to the red blob, and Paulie looks at the teacher and says, "You can't fool us!" He refers to a time early in the year when the teacher used a similar activity relating to conservation of number. On that occasion many children were misled when the groups were rearranged to so that one group was crowded together and took up less space, while the other group was spread out and took up more space.

Paulie: Okay, now make bars.

The children excitedly line up either on the blue rectangle or red rectangle by the door.

Paulie: I am going to walk between the red line and blue line. Shake hands with a different color partner across from you after I go by.

Paulie walks between the two lines of children and children shake hands with their counterparts across the rectangles. Four children, all in the red bar, do not have someone with whom to shake hands.

Paulie: [after a short pause] How many people didn't shake hands?

Children: Four! [Paulie counts them to be sure.]

Mr. Jordan: So, how many more people are in the red bar than in the blue bar?

Children: Four!

Mr. Jordan: How many more people don't have cats?

Children: Four!

Mr. Jordan: Which group has more people?

Children: The red group—people who don't have cats.

Mr. Jordan: Good! Paulie, back to you.

Paulie: Okay, everybody make a circle divided into red and blue.

Red-cube children hold hands and blue-cube children hold hands. The two lines join and form a circle. The children then sit in a circle, putting their cubes on the floor in front of them. They are going to pretend their circle is a "pizza"—an analogy to a circle graph that is useful with kindergartners.

Paulie: [bringing a plastic crate with red and blue chains to the center of the circle] Blue kids, raise your hands.

Paulie takes a blue chain, attaches one end to the center crate, and gives the other end to a blue child sitting next to a red child, where the blue and red sections of the circle join. He then attaches another blue chain to the center crate and gives it to the blue child sitting at the other end of the blue section of the circle.

Paulie: Look how big the blue piece of pizza is. Now, red kids, raise your hands. [They repeat the process using the red chains.] Look how big the red piece of pizza is.

Mr. Jordan: Excellent job, Paulie! Before you go, boys and girls, let's look together at the red piece of pizza. Reds, raise your hands again. Can someone tell me about the red piece with words? I want to remember how big it is so I can make my pizza plate look like it.

Children: It's bigger. . . . It's more. . . . It's half of the pizza but just a little bigger. . . . It's smaller than the whole pizza. . . . It's how much I want if the pizza has pepperonis! . . . It's almost like the one we had when we counted brothers, see? [pointing to pictures on the board illustrating previous circle graphs]

Mr. Jordan: Fantastic! Now, everybody, put this picture in your mind. Got it? Go to your cubbies and get your pizza plates and let's make them look like our circle.

The children made "pizza plates" at the beginning of the school year from red and blue paper plates. In each plate they had cut a slit (slightly longer than the plate's radius) from the outside edge through the middle of the plate. Stacking the red plate on the blue, slits together, they can turn their red plate clockwise, making the blue edge overlap the red and forming a blue wedge of pizza in a red pizza pie.

Children get their plates and adjust the colors to look generally like the red and blue sections of the circle the class made. Talking together and giving feedback to those whose plates need adjustment, the children work to get all the plates right.

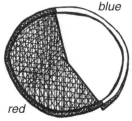

Finally, getting a sheet of paper with a large circle outline from the graph box, Paulie colors it red and blue to approximate the proportions of the red circle to the blue pizza slice indicated by his red and blue pizza plate. He tacks it to the bulletin board under the "Graph of the Day" sign.

From beginning to end, the graphing activity takes about twenty minutes. The teacher reminds the children that they will be exploring the cat question the rest of the week, representing the results with different graphs and activities (one of which is the YES/NO bags described in chapter 2).

Materials in the early childhood classroom provide children with many opportunities for practicing the basic concepts and processes that underlie data analysis, especially sorting and organizing. Unit blocks are a good example. They frequently need to be organized and put away; curved blocks, for example, may be stored on one shelf and straight blocks on another. Pictorial labels help children with the organization. When adding new blocks to the classroom supply, the teacher can ask, "Where should these new blocks be placed? Which blocks are they most like? Why would you put them there? Are there more blocks on the curved-block shelf than on the straight-block shelf?"

Sometimes the shelves need to be reorganized, and the children can help make decisions about rearranging materials. Telling the children that space needs to be cleared for new materials (e.g., water buckets and tubes), the teacher might ask them questions such as, "What blocks should we put away for a while? How can we find out which blocks everyone uses the most? You like the curved blocks the most, but does that mean everyone in the class does? How could we find out?"

Responding to questions like these, children are eager to help decide where and how new materials should be stored. When children have input about aspects of classroom organization, they feel greater responsibility for and ownership of the classroom—and they are learning about classifying and data collection in the process.

Teachers can use classroom routines, too, to give children experiences with the various skills and concepts of data analysis. During snack time, children can collect data to find out who prefers apple juice and who likes orange juice, whether more celery or carrot sticks are needed, or how many children use raisins or sunflower seeds on their cream cheese crackers. During circle time, data collection takes place as children post their names under an activity sign on the bulletin board to show which learning center they choose to work in. During cleanup, children classify and group items as they sort materials and put them away. Labeled shelves in each center help children organize materials and naturally allow children to see whether there are more big blocks than little blocks, more forks than spoons, and so on.

Question box

Children love to ask questions, but there is not always enough time to address them. A box for children's questions is a helpful addition to any classroom. Some of the questions children have may not lend themselves to data collection activities, but many will. The teacher can write out what children ask and put the questions in the box; she may add her own questions, as well. Some children may draw pictures of their questions, others may write only their names, and others may give brief statements and put them in the box for later interpretation—"I am getting a new baby" can translate into "Do you have a baby in your house?" Such questions are good for data gathering and can be used for weekly graphing activities, like the "Do you have a cat?" activity described above.

Children learn a great deal in thinking about and discussing how to collect data on questions that are important to them. One day a week, a period of time can be designated for talking about the questions in the question box. (The teacher may want to look through the question box beforehand and select particular questions.) The class can choose the question for the following week's graphing activity and then talk about other questions as time permits.

Data from the classroom

Early childhood classrooms abound with data that children love to count, sort, organize, or analyze. Children's center choices, the number of children riding to school in buses or cars, or "morning news" sharing during circle time are all examples that naturally contain data.

In Mrs. Chen's first grade classroom, children do a lot of counting, and each day a different child is named Counter of the Day. This classroom job provides another opportunity for data analysis. Each day, the Counter distributes a set of stacking cubes for that day's item to be counted:

Today's item to be counted is pockets, and Maddie, the Counter of the Day, places a cube in each pocket of all the children in the class—pockets in their shirts, pants, skirts, dresses, any item of clothing.

When Mrs. Chen announces that it's time to make the count, each child reports her or his own pocket count, and Maddie collects all the cubes and stacks them. Mrs. Chen places the tower of cubes on the chalk tray, with the label "Pockets" on the chalkboard above it. (Alternatively, a cube tower can be accompanied by a picture of the day's item.)

On Fridays, the children use these visual representations of their surveys to look at the results of a week's worth of counting and make comparisons and predictions:

Mrs. Chen's first-graders counted pockets on Monday (fifty-eight cubes), noses on Tuesday (twenty-three cubes), ears on Wednesday (forty-four cubes; someone was absent), and earrings on Thursday (twenty-four cubes). On Friday, the counting item will be shoes.

She asks the children questions about the data they have collected and displayed: "How tall will the tower of stacking cubes be when we count shoes later today? Which other tower will it be most like? Why do you think so?" . . . "Will the number of shoes cubes be even or odd? Why do you predict that?" . . . "What if five children were working in another classroom and were not in our classroom to be counted?"

Data from home

Once children have collected, organized, and analyzed data from their peers, they often are interested in how their brothers, sisters, parents, or neighbors will answer their questions. So data analysis activities are a natural link between classroom and home.

After the 4-year-olds complete "My Favorite Color" graphs in the math center, Ms. Abbott instructs the children to survey four more people at home about their favorite colors, using forms prepared by the teacher. The children ask each person they survey to write his or her name by the empty square drawn on the form. Then the children color in the square with that person's favorite color.

She is surprised when Robert returns his paper with a drawing of a dog next to a square he has colored red. She asks, "Whose favorite color does this red square represent?" Robert answers, "It's Champ's. He's my puppy and he doesn't talk to everyone. I asked him, and he told me his favorite color was red. Red's my favorite, too!"

Champ's favorite color was then added to the classroom graph, along with all the other home survey results.

Teacher questions

Teachers can facilitate an understanding of data analysis by interacting with children as they engage in activities in various centers in the classroom. Asking children to tell about their favorite stories, toys, or food is a good beginning. Then children can discuss methods of recording and displaying favorites within the group for some purpose, such as showing to other classes or to parents. The graphs or other representations can also be referred to later; for example, in planning foods for parties or selecting stories to read or act out.

Teachers will also find many opportunities to understand and extend children's thinking in situations in which they are grouping objects. Asking children to describe their choices is important: "Why is the circle in that group and not over here with these triangles?" . . . "How is the square like the other shapes in its group?" . . . "How is this square different from the oval over there?"

After children can organize the objects in one way (e.g., by size, by color), they can be asked to sort the objects on a different basis or to make more (or fewer) groups. For example, the teacher may ask such questions as, "Is there another way we could put these into groups?" . . . "What if this whole group of shapes were taken away; how would the rest of the shapes be sorted?" . . . "What if this square and triangle are in a different group; what could the name be?" . . . "If I sorted them this way, what group would this object be in? Why do you think so?" Such interactions help children learn to communicate their reasoning about sorting and organization and also provide meaning for data analysis.

General learning paths and development

Very little is known about young children's data analysis abilities because this content area has not been heavily researched for such a young age group. However, there is a developmental sequence for sorting, an important skill needed to organize and analyze data. In addition, many of the skills children need to analyze data have been discussed in previous chapters (e.g., in chapter 4, comparing numbers of objects involves analysis of sets of data; in chapter 5, finding geometric shapes in the environment involves collection of data and classifying).

The usual developmental sequence for sorting can be seen in young children's spontaneous behaviors (Markman & Subert 1976; Copley 1998; Langer et al. 2003). At first, a child will separate objects from a pile or collection because they share a common attribute—for example, they are all blue or fuzzy or round. Sometimes children can verbalize the reason for this selection; often they cannot. They do not apply one rule consistently throughout and may go on to separate objects based on reasons different from their original one (see the Reasoning section in chapter 3 for an illustration of this).

At the second developmental level, children are able to sort an entire collection of objects consistently by one attribute. They are capable of classifying things as having a certain attribute and as not having it; for example, sorting bears into "ones that are red" and "ones that are not red." This two-part type of classification—*has* versus *has not*—is fundamental in collecting certain kinds of data (children who have cats and children who do not have cats) and in graphing and other representations of data. Young children may need help to understand the meaning of *not*, so teachers should offer them many experiences with this.

At the third level, children are able to sort a collection of objects in more than one way (e.g., by color *and* size); for example, sorting a collection of attribute shapes into blue and not blue, then each resulting group into small and not small. A child approaching this level often shows confusion when another child uses a sorting rule that is different from his. Teachers may also be puzzled when viewing a child's collection and may need to ask the sorter to talk about how she sorted her objects. At this level, children need to hear other children's reasoning and sorting rules frequently.

The highest level of sorting reached by young children is to be able to state the rule that accounts for a grouping, even when someone else has done the sorting. To do this, the child must perceive one or more attributes common to all the objects in the group ("all these items are big, blue triangles") and also determine that the attribute(s) is not shared by objects outside the group ("none of these is a big, blue triangle"). A child at this level also is able to verbalize a rule to indicate whether a new object would be included or excluded ("It has to be a triangle that is big and blue" . . . "It can't be a red triangle").

Promoting development of key skills and concepts

Skills and concepts relating to collecting and analyzing data and considering probability apply widely across the curriculum. Among these skills and concepts are those appropriate for young children: posing questions and gathering data to answer them; organizing data, including by sorting and classifying; representing data; describing and comparing data; and beginning to grasp concepts and language of probability.

Sorting and classifying, for example, are important in every subject area: science, social studies, literacy, the arts. Language itself is based on classification. To learn a new word, we need to know which actions, descriptors, or objects the word applies to and

which it does not. The learner typically begins by getting a general idea and then refines his knowledge of what does and does not fit that category. When a young child first learns the word *dog*, for example, he may think *dog* refers only to his own collie and others of that breed. Gradually he broadens his conceptual category to include a wide range of assorted canines, perhaps overextending *dog* to include wolves and foxes but having no idea that a chihuahua belongs in there, too! Learning many new words every week, the young child is continually refining his knowledge of the grouping to which each of these words refers.

Skills and concepts relating to data analysis and probability can encourage children's language development in other ways, as well. Children reading and describing graphs or other representations from their own perspectives and explaining the advantages and disadvantages of specific representations is another example. Probability vocabulary, such as *certain* and *likely*, can be useful in contexts beyond mathematics. And the reasoning questions that naturally occur as children interpret data can help increase their use of precise and descriptive words.

Posing questions and gathering data

Young children have an endless supply of questions, and these questions often involve their own attributes or preferences: "Do you have any sisters or brothers?" . . . "Do you like green ice cream?" . . . "What kind of backpack do you have?" Often, however, children's questions are difficult or impossible to answer: "Why is the sky blue?" . . . "Why don't airplanes fall down?" . . . "Why do brown cows give white milk?" . . . "How high are the clouds?" . . . "Where did I come from?"

The teacher's role is to nurture children's curiosity, help them formulate questions (perhaps using the question box strategy described earlier in this chapter), and then

The Young Child and Mathematics

use these questions as catalysts for investigating and learning. Among the possible directions a teacher can take such queries is to engage children in data analysis experiences that can help children answer their own questions.

Children can begin to understand data gathering by conducting simple surveys of attributes of children in their class or other classes ("Do you have freckles?" . . . "Are you wearing white socks?") and using various forms of tally marks, check marks, or numerals in YES/NO columns to indicate answers. They can make counts of object attributes or even survey the preferences of family members and neighbors. Young children may better understand the concept of data gathering when it is demonstrated physically or concretely—for example, having children actually stand in one group or another (as they did in the "Graphing" with Blobs, Bars, and Circles vignette) to indicate their answer, or cast their vote by placing a marker or cube in a YES/NO box.

YES	No
⫕̶̶	|||
I∖I	¬|
✓✓✓✓✓	✓✓✓
5	3

Young children often pose questions that are not easily definable, and at first they certainly do not know how to get the data that would answer a question. But these are learnable skills. Teachers can introduce children to a variety of data collection methods and model and discuss questions appropriately. They can and should provide many data collection experiences involving children's own questions. These are all important roles of the early childhood teacher in this content area.

In the activities presented in the "Graphing" vignette, the teacher drew from children's natural questions to decide on the Question of the Week: "Do you have a cat?" Every Friday children were asked to suggest and discuss possible questions for the following week. The teacher helped them pose their questions appropriately, and he also facilitated their discussion.

Organizing data, including sorting and classifying

Sorting and *classifying* are important processes in many math content areas other than data collection and analysis. Particularly in algebra and the concepts that underlie it, classification is fundamental (see chapter 5). Sorting and classifying activities promote reasoning skills.

To help children develop basic sorting and classifying skills, teachers should use materials with easily identifiable characteristics. For example, there are many types of counters commercially available. The dinosaur, frog, or bug counters are excellent sorting materials if they have more than one attribute (e.g., different colors and sizes) and the attributes are easily identified (type, number of legs, tail or no tail). Children move forward in classification when they encounter challenges and questions such as the teacher asking, "Can you sort these another way?" or "What if they were all red—how would you sort them?"

There are many other methods for organizing data, and a number of these may be explored by young children. In an effort to help children be successful, some teachers predetermine how data will be organized by providing preprinted tally sheets or forms with labeled grids and titles. Children, however, miss a vital step in learning to handle data if they are sent directly to a more limited task such as coloring a chart made by someone else. For example, counting different color candies and then coloring corresponding squares on a preprinted form is an activity lots of teachers use. In one such classroom, when children were asked to explain what they were doing, the typical response was, "You color these squares and then you get to eat the candy." A limited understanding of mathematics at best!

A more effective exercise is for children to collect data and then to sort and organize it in ways they work out themselves. When a child complains, "This is a mess! I don't know what the answer is!" the teacher can seize the teachable moment to offer her ideas about how data can be organized and displayed so that someone can find the answers she's looking for at a glance. While the product might not be as polished or pretty as one that used a preprinted form, that child's graph or chart or drawing will be her own work and evidence of her budding understanding of organizing information.

Representing data using concrete objects, pictures, and graphs

Visual displays of data are actually direct extensions of sorting and classifying. With young children, the teacher's purpose is to help them see graphs and other such representations as ways of showing the organized information so that people can "read" it just by looking and use it to make comparisons.

Using concrete objects is an essential first step in learning to represent data. By standing with classmates in the YES group or the NO group, each child shows his or her own response, and collectively the different size groups form a simple physical representation of the data. Placing pattern blocks (or other items) in rows in ice cube trays (see, e.g., the Ice Cube Tray Graphing activity later in this chapter) or on 10-frames, one block per compartment, according to their attributes—orange squares, green triangles, and so forth—forms a representation of categories in a way that easily translates into horizontal or vertical bar graphs.

Teachers can have children make tags to indicate their opinions on an issue, with each child placing his tag by the answer he chooses. Another method is to create picture cubes by putting each child's photo on an empty carton (e.g., single-serving cereal boxes), then having children cast their votes by stacking their picture cubes next to the answer of their choice. Another example is having children place cubes or counters, all equal in weight, on one pan or the other of a balancing scale to represent their votes, YES or NO. This procedure creates a different type of visual model: The side of the scale that tips down has more votes. In all these examples, concrete objects (blocks, cubes, counters) represent data in a way that children can more easily see and describe.

Representations of data can also be made with pictures depicting children's choices or answers. For example, the teacher can give children cards on which to draw their favorite pet. With these cards, the teacher can have children explore various ways to organize and represent a collection.

Different questions can be answered using the children's pet cards, with the answers displayed in a horizontal or vertical bar representation, a blob representation, or a circle representation. A survey titled "Is a Dog Your Favorite Pet?" could result in a bar graph with picture cards of dogs making up one bar and picture cards of pets that are not dogs forming the second bar. For a survey of "What Is Your Favorite Pet?" the picture cards could be lined up as on a bar graph and displayed in categories such as Dogs, Cats, Fish, Gerbils, Rabbits, Iguanas, and anything else the children draw. Similarly, a graph showing responses to the survey "What Kind of Animal Makes a Good Pet?" could list categories such as Mammal, Fish, Reptile, Bird, and so on.

As young children work with organizing and representing data, they often reveal their misconceptions. When this happens teachers can take the opportunity to help children develop a better understanding.

> A group of children are using Lego pieces to make bar graphs to show the number of children in the class who have younger siblings and the number who do not. The boy making the Have bar counts out seven Legos; the boy making the Do Not Have bar counts out eleven, but his Legos are a smaller size. When the bar of seven looms over

the bar of eleven, and thus seems to contradict what the children know to be true, they protest, "But there aren't as many kids who have little brothers and sisters!"

This teacher was able to pose questions to help them recognize the problem, and the children gained an understanding of the principle that units of equal size are required for accurate comparison (see the section on Unit in chapter 7). The understanding they developed was far more solid than it would have been if the teacher had simply told them, "Always use equal-size units."

As they create representations using objects, pictures, or graphs, children also learn about labeling and describing parts of their representations. They learn that they need to write words and labels on graphs so that others can understand what the graphs say. When children create the labels for their own graphs, the graph and the graphing process become more meaningful to them as well as to others.

To help children learn how to label graphs, the teacher should emphasize the importance of being able to remember later what their graph is saying and also the importance of communicating to others about their graph. He can pose questions such as, "How can we remember what those Xs mean?" . . . "How will we remember what those bars are?" . . . "What should we call these marks here? What are those squares?" . . . "What should we call this graph? What was our question?" . . . "Who did we talk to when we made this graph?"

Having children experience a variety of graph types is important, even for the same data. The two figures (NCTM 2000, 112) shown here illustrate two very different representations (bar graph, line-plot graph) describing the number of pockets in a second grade classroom. Although the data are presented differently, both graphs contain numbers, titles, and labels. Even young children can see the information conveyed in pictures, bars, lines, or circles and recognize differences and similarities between these representations.

Young children like to share the graphs they make with others; for example, with parents or other classes in the school or center. At a large primary school, every week each class made one graph and posted it, untitled, in the hallway. The classes in the school had fun reading one another's graphs and guessing their titles just from looking at the organized and labeled data. In the process, children learned more about interpreting graphs and saw the importance of titling and labeling them.

Describing and comparing data

Comparisons are an important part of data analysis. To help children develop their skills, teachers can ask questions that require children to make comparisons based on information shown in a graph. They can ask about part of the graph; for example, referring to a

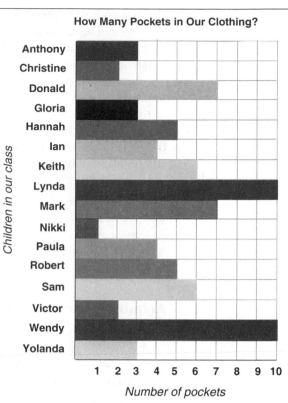

graph showing the number of bikes belonging to children in the school, "Do kindergartners have more bicycles than first-graders?" Teachers can also pose questions involving the data set as a whole, such as, "What is the most popular TV show?" . . . "What sport do most kids like best?" . . . "What is the least common way to get to school?"

Number lines also help children analyze and describe data. For example, in the estimation activity in chapter 2, children used a number line to find the mode and median of their answers to the question of how many finger snaps each child could do in one minute. Although the concepts of *mode* and *median* are often reserved for older children, the children in Ms. Henekee's second grade class easily understood these terms because she had presented them in a meaningful manner. Recall that—

> The children in Ms. Henekee's class lined up left to right, from smallest estimate to largest, forming a number line. Each child stated his or her number in turn, and everyone paid attention. The number they heard repeated most often they knew to designate as the *mode*. Then, when the children returned to their seats two at a time, one from each end of the number line, they knew the number of the last child left standing was the *median*.

Acquiring the concepts and language of probability

The early childhood curriculum focuses on only the most basic concepts of probability, such as *certainty* and *impossibility*, as well as the vocabulary used to express these ideas. Teachers can discuss situations where an event is *certain*, *impossible*, *more likely*, or *less likely* to occur, using those words in the context of experiences in everyday life as well as mathematical events. Teachers may comment on the weather ("Looking at those dark clouds, do you think it is *impossible* for it to rain today?"), class routines ("It is 12 o'clock; where do you think we will *probably* go next?"), or events ("We have twenty-two in our class. Do you think Ethan's mom is *likely* to bring 100 cupcakes for us?").

For a young child, difficulty in understanding probability words in their mathematical sense may result from the way adults often use them in casual conversation. Children may have learned at home that "You can probably go" will mean they will go, as long as Mom and Dad are in a good mood, but could mean something totally different if they are not. Likewise, Grandma's declaration of "Impossible!" rarely means that when directed at her two grandchildren.

Providing a mathematics-rich environment

In working with children on sorting and classifying, data collection and analysis, and probability, teachers find a variety of materials useful: animal counters, attribute blocks, buttons, plastic trees, cloth swatches, attribute people, sorting rings, graph paper, and prelabeled posters for graphs. Children can also use actual data (or themselves) to create real graphs.

Some mathematics supply products are quite helpful (especially attribute blocks), but many are not necessary. Instead, items purchased from dollar stores, old wallpaper samples, buttons, tops to milk containers, rocks and pebbles, old keys, garbage ties, straws, and so on, provide plenty of easily accessible and inexpensive opportunities, especially for sorting and classifying. Sorting trays can be purchased from restaurant suppliers, discount stores, or dollar stores.

Predrawn paper is not necessary when children create their own ways of organizing data. For example, children standing in a red bar graph representation who shake hands with corresponding children standing in a blue bar graph representation (as in the "Graphing" vignette) don't need a preprinted grid to tell them where to line up.

Getting Children Thinking about Data Analysis

Depending on the focus, there are many questions that can be asked to help children sort, classify, and analyze data. They include,

How are these alike? Different? The same?

Why do these belong here? Why does this not belong?

Is there anything that doesn't belong here?

Can you find (or make) another one that would go in this group?

What name could you give this group?

What if I asked you to sort the things in this group in another way? How would you do it?

(*with first- and second-graders*) Look at [Anne's] groups. How do you think these things were sorted? What was the rule [Anne] used to divide these into groups?

Which group has the most? How can you tell without counting?

Which group has the least? How can you tell without counting?

What does this graph tell you?

(*in experiences relating to bar graphs*) Which group has more children? How many more are in this group than in that one? How many people in these two lines don't have a partner?

(*in experiences relating to circle graphs*) Tell me about the red in the circle. Is it more than the blue? Less than the blue? More than half? Less than half?

Sticky notes are particularly useful for data collection. Each note can be used to record one piece of data, and then the individual notes can be moved and reorganized to form the best possible visual representation.

Literature connection

Information books can be used to make excellent connections between the content areas of data analysis and number and operations. *Tiger Math: Learning to Graph from a Baby Tiger* and *Chimp Math: Learning about Time from a Baby Chimpanzee,* both by Ann Whitehead Nagda and Cindy Bickel, are two examples of books that present real data that has been sorted, classified, and represented in graph and chart forms. Both books contain beautiful photographs, with explanations of the data collection providing all the context necessary for the data to be analyzed and represented in a classroom.

After reviewing information books such as these, children in a second grade science class created a book about Beaker, their colorful class bird. For the book, entitled "Beaker Math: Our Graphs and Charts about Our Class Cockatiel," they collected all types of data: how much he ate, the number of times he squawked in a day, his weight, his perching and flapping behaviors, and a time schedule for feeding and watering. The experience was very educational for all involved, especially when Beaker laid an egg and the class discovered that Beaker was, in fact, a female! (Beaker was quickly renamed Beakerina.)

*   *   *

A small selection of activities pertaining to data and analysis are listed below. They are roughly in order of difficulty, but the degree of challenge is highly dependent on the child's construction of the activity and the specific way the activity was introduced or extended.

Activities

Color Sort

Red, yellow, green, and blue boxes are placed in an activity center. Children cut pictures of different colors from magazines and place them in the matching box. Objects can also be used instead of pictures. This is an excellent activity for 3- and 4-year-olds.

Haves and Have Nots

This transitional or circle activity is a variation of The Lineup in chapter 5. The leader of the game (either the teacher or a child) selects a characteristic, such as red. She whispers her selection to one other person, who helps her remember what she has chosen—and ensures that the chosen characteristic will not change arbitrarily (this is often a problem with young children). The leader then tells each child whether he or she has or does not have the characteristic. If red is the attribute, then all children wearing red sit inside the circle (or line up, if the game is being used as a transitional activity), and those children not wearing red remain outside of the circle (or do not line up). Children try to guess what characteristic has been selected by comparing the children sitting inside the circle with those sitting outside.

Children soon realize that it is as important to observe those outside the circle as it is to observe those inside. Clothing color is often the first type of characteristic children select; however, they soon progress to other characteristics, such as tie or no-tie shoes, buttons or no buttons, earrings or no earrings. It is important to guide children away from selecting physical characteristics that may be tied to children's self-esteem (such as weight) or that may change before the end of the game (such as smiling).

Buried Treasure

Children in the sensory play center enjoy pretending to be archeologists as they search for creatures (plastic insects, spiders, or dinosaurs) in a sand table "dig." As archeologists, they carefully use shovels (plastic spoons) and brushes (small water color brushes) to search for the creatures and clear them appropriately so they can be analyzed. After they have found five creatures, they record exactly what they have found (a good representation activity) and use their words to describe their creatures. After many of the "archeologists" have completed the activity, the data can be sorted and classified and an archeological record can be compiled explaining their discoveries.

Marching Band

Children march in a band, playing homemade instruments such as rubber band guitars, percussion shakers, and kazoos. The musicians are grouped together by type of instrument, such as sound blowers (e.g., kazoos, homemade trumpets), string instruments, and percussion instruments. The conductor directs the band, having those in each group march in a particular way, such as swaying back and forth or taking giant steps, while playing.

The musicians sound their instruments when the conductor signals. For example, the conductor blows a whistle to signal the musicians: one whistle for the string players, two whistles for the sound blowers, and three whistles for the percussion players. Band members exchange instruments periodically.

This activity is very popular with 4- and 5-year-olds.

Guidelines in Action: Data Analysis and Probability

The classroom examples and activities throughout this chapter reflect some of the curriculum, instruction, and assessment guidelines from chapter 2 that form the basis for teaching mathematics effectively to young children. To clarify how specific guidelines look in practice, this chart highlights four instances in which they are evident.

Curriculum Guideline 2—Plan for connections	During the "Graphing" vignette, the children used circle graphs, which are not typically a part of the mathematics curriculum for young children. However, because of the meaningful presentation of the data, the children were easily able to handle this type of representation and discuss the results.
Curriculum Guideline 4—Create a mathematics-rich environment	In the "Graphing" vignette, the plates, chains, and color unit cubes all contributed to the success of "graphing" with blobs, bars, and circles. While the chains and cubes are generally viewed as mathematics manipulatives, the plates are not. Easily purchased, one set of disposable plastic plates generally lasts all year and can go home with children for further investigations.
Instruction Guideline 2—Orchestrate classroom activities	The teacher's consistent routine and good management skills in the "Graphing" vignette foster self-regulation in the children and promote a child-centered approach to learning. This is especially true for the Class Grapher; the child is able to direct the classroom activity through predictable and understandable questions and answers.
Assessment Guideline 3—Employ multiple sources of evidence	The graph documentation produced daily by the Graphers like Paulie in the "Graphing" vignette was a way for the teacher to document and collect children's representations. Later, these pages were made into a book that showed data collections over a month's time. Graphers always signed their work so it could be identified as theirs.

Sorting Collages

Each child divides a piece of paper in half and picks a category for each side. For example, the left side of the page might be for round items and the right side for rectangular items. From a variety of materials such as bottle caps, buttons, labels, and cloth pieces, the children select items that fit their categories and paste these items onto the paper.

Veggie Robots

Children bring a variety of vegetables to class, such as broccoli, carrots, celery, cauliflower, and sweet peppers. The children help clean the vegetables and, while the teacher cuts the vegetables into various size pieces, the class discusses which types of vegetables come from the flower, stem, seeds, leaves, or root of a plant.

Children then create veggie robots using toothpicks and pieces of vegetables. They describe their creations and classify the vegetable parts they used. The teacher asks questions such as, "Whose robot has a round head?" or "Does anyone have a robot with a body made from a triangle-shaped root?" If a child's robot has that characteristic, she stands up. After describing and classifying her creation, the child can eat the robot.

People Sort Book

At the beginning of the school year, each child creates a book about him- or herself. Each page of the book contains a different one of the child's attributes. For example, a child might draw a picture of himself with his two brothers on one page and with his goldfish on another.

During circle time or a transitional period, the teacher selects one book without revealing whose it is. The entire class stands up and, as the teacher reads or describes each page ("I have two brothers"), children who do not have that attribute sit down (or line up, if the game is being used as a transitional activity). Children enjoy seeing which of their classmates are similar to them. By the end of the book, only the author remains standing.

These popular books can be made in various ways; report covers with three fasteners work well because new pages can easily be added. Pages need to be updated as the children's lives change. Near the close of the year, the teacher can also make her own book about a child's attributes. For example, the teacher's book may describe a child who "works very hard," "is such a good scientist," or "is one of my favorite students." But each page in the teacher's book describes everyone, not just one child! Children of all levels can participate in this activity, but some may need more assistance than others.

Ice Cube Tray Graphing

Children use an ice cube tray to sort two different types of small objects; one object is placed in each compartment, with one type of object placed in each side of the tray. If a child has four ladybug magnets and two marbles, his ice cube tray would look like the one shown here.

A line drawn down the center of the ice cube tray helps children interpret the tray as a bar graph representation. If the tray is turned sideways, it can be interpreted as a horizontal graph. When placed vertically, it represents a vertical graph.

Counting Walk

With partners, children count objects in the school such as windows, desks, wastebaskets, chairs, flags, and chalkboards. Each pair of children counts a particular item. The children record their findings on sticky notes, making up to five tally marks per note. For example, a pair of children documenting the number of doors in the school may find that there are twenty doors. These children return to the classroom with four sticky notes labeled "Doors," each note having five tally marks.

When the children are finished counting, all of the sticky notes are stuck to the classroom's chalkboard, and the children discuss how to organize their results. The children assign items to categories such as Furniture or Things That Can Be Opened. The results are used to make graphs.

People in Your Hand

This probability activity emphasizes matching and introduces the concept of *impossible*. The attributes of a set of figurines are written on index cards. For example, attributes for the figurines below would include the colors *blue*, *red*, *yellow*, and *green*; words describing age and gender such as *girl*, *boy*, *woman*, and *man*; and adjectives describing size such as *big*, *medium*, and *little*. Besides these attributes, several others that do not belong (such as *dog* and *purple*) should be added to the list.

Each child selects a figurine and covers it with her hands. The teacher selects an attribute card that the children's figurines might have and shows it to the children. Children holding figurines with the selected characteristic say yes (or whisper yes if in a large group) and give the thumbs-up sign. After a period of play, the teacher selects an attribute that no figurine has, such as "purple polka dots." When every child says, "Oh well," the children soon realize that no figurines match the teacher's attribute. At this point, the teacher introduces the concept of *impossible*. The next time the teacher picks an attribute that no child's figurine has, the children reply, "Impossible!"

Children love the word *impossible* and use it often. Their knowledge of impossible is often transferred to other activities, such as the Haves and Have Nots activity described earlier. If "children who are dogs" are asked to line up, many children will reply, "Impossible!"

Minibeasts

This activity is a variation of the "Where Are the Minibeasts?" activity in chapter 4. Armed with magnifying glasses, children go outside to discover minibeasts—creatures smaller than a child's pinky finger. After observing the creatures in their natural environment, the children return to the classroom and draw pictures of the minibeasts they have seen. The children's minibeasts are named and classified into different categories, such as eight-legged spiders, six-legged ants, four-winged moths, and worms with no legs. Then children create their own minibeasts from playdough, classify them, and describe them in their own words.

Number Activities

Number activities are a natural place for introducing probability concepts in second grade or beyond. Tossing two cubes with faces numbered from 0 through 5, children predict the most (or least) probable sums to come up. Teachers encourage the investigation by challenging children to "keep rolling until you get a sum of eleven" (impossible with two dice numbered 0 to 5) or to "keep rolling until you get a sum of zero, one, . . . nine, or ten" (a certain event since all of the possible sums tossed would fall within this range). Children describe their tossed sums and share their frustrations with rolling a sum that is *impossible* or absolutely *certain*.

In addition to fostering skills pertaining to this content area, this activity offers many opportunities to facilitate language use. The mathematics processes described in chapter 3 are also evident as children communicate the results of their data analysis, discuss reasons for these results, and represent their findings so that others can understand them.

Sorting with Venn Diagrams

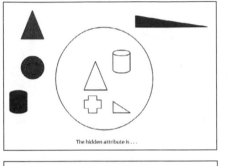

Many different sorting activities should be done using Venn diagrams as graphical models. In one-loop Venn diagrams, one characteristic is "hidden" that describes everything that would be inside the loop. Any object that doesn't have that attribute would be outside the loop. Children guess the attribute by asking the leader if a particular object is *inside* the loop or *outside* the loop. The goal of the activity is to guess the hidden attribute using as few clues as possible. The upper picture at left shows one such example.

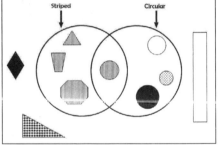

Two-loop tasks are more difficult and require reasoning and classification skills. To introduce the use of overlapping loops, it is helpful to have two separated loops. Then, when an object fits in both loops, children can conjecture methods of representation that would get the object in both loops at the same time. With a bit of scaffolding, children will be able to see how the overlapping loops represent an object that belongs in both circles. An example of a two-looped diagram is in the lower picture.

Chapter 9

Questions...
and Some Answers

I enjoy sharing my teaching experiences with other early childhood teachers. Every time I do, questions abound. The questions have remained similar over the past 30 years. But some of my answers have changed—or at least expanded—as I have continued to learn and to explore new ways of teaching various aspects of math. Because I study young children and listen to what they say and think, my teaching has become more child-focused and less directive, more holistic and less segmented, and more intentional and less spur-of-the-moment.

In addressing frequently asked questions throughout this book, I come from the perspective of someone who has spent many hours watching children as they experience math in various contexts, teaching and interacting with them, and observing other teachers in action. In the questions and responses collected here in this last chapter particularly, I also point out others' work that has been particularly valuable to me in relation to a given issue and that might be similarly valuable to you.

Like any dedicated educator, my own learning is very much a work in progress, so my answers are simply my best thinking at this moment. I offer them to you as personal perspectives to reflect on and perhaps synthesize with your own thinking and experiences.

I teach mathematics every day by using the calendar. Isn't that enough?

This is a familiar question. The best answer I know of appears in the National Research Council's 2009 book *Mathematics Learning in Early Childhood: Paths toward Excellence and Equity*. Based on current research regarding what is foundational mathematics for young children, the book answers this very question in a highlighted box entitled "How Using the Calendar Does Not Emphasize Foundational Mathematics":

> Many preschool and kindergarten teachers spend time each day on the calendar, in part because they think it is an efficient way to teach mathematics. Although the calendar may be useful in helping children begin to understand general concepts of time, such as "yesterday" and "today," or plan for important events, such as field trips or visitors, these are not core mathematical concepts.
>
> The main problem with the calendar is that the groups of seven days in the rows of a calendar have no useful mathematical relationship to the number 10, the building block of the number system. Therefore, the calendar is not useful for helping students learn the base 10 patterns; other visual and conceptual approaches using groups of 10 are needed because these patterns of groups of 10 are foundational.

Time spent on the calendar would be better used on more effective mathematics teaching and learning experiences. "Doing the calendar" is not a substitute for teaching foundational mathematics. (NRC 2009, 241)

What have you yourself learned in the past ten years that has influenced the way you teach young children mathematics?

One of my favorite quotes is from John Dana Cotton: "Who dares to teach must never cease to learn." I decided a long time ago that when I stop learning, I will stop teaching!

Recently, I have learned so much more about the predictable paths (trajectories) that children's mathematics learning typically follows (discussed in chapters 4–8). This new information has caused me to reflect on my practices and to reexamine the appropriateness of some of the activities I had been using for many years. Although I can think of many examples, let me respond with just one such reflection that has been particularly helpful to me.

For years, with first- and second-graders, I used an activity I called "Estimating Quantity" as part of a weekly routine. I would prepare and display a jar of objects, and children would guess the number of objects in it; at the end of the week, we would count how many were actually in the jar. Typically, there would be 100–200 objects. The children who came closest in their estimations I rewarded in some way, usually by placing their names on a "WOW" board. Children who guessed the exact number were starred.

Look for the video clip of "Estimating Quantity" on the DVD!

After analyzing the pertinent learning paths more carefully and thinking about another definition of *estimation* as "a range of values," I realized I was missing an opportunity to teach mathematics more effectively. To incorporate this aspect of estimation, the method I now use is quite a bit different. I still do the Estimating Quantity activity; however, now I have children estimate by selecting one of these *ranges*: (a) "fewer than 100," (b) "between 100 and 199," or (c) "200 or more." Then, to check the correctness of their estimation at the end of the week, I have children open the jar and organize the objects in sets of ten, so that we can all use a "quick look" and identify the exact number of objects that were in the container. This procedure gives them a chance to practice counting by 10s (a necessary skill for adding mentally), as well as uses another conception of *estimate* (as a range of values rather than "just one approximate answer").

I need to know more mathematics myself and to have a better attitude regarding math. My own experiences with mathematics in school were never good; how can I teach my young students better?

You are not alone! Mathematics is typically not a favorite of many early childhood teachers, and for good reason! Because of their own poor experiences of mathematics in school, they didn't get the opportunity to learn mathematics well and thus are not sure how to teach it well. Here are several possible sources of help.

First, if you can, take an early childhood math education course from your local community or four-year college. Also, visit the National Council of Teachers of Mathematics's excellent website (www.nctm.org) and view classroom examples and materials in its Illuminations section (http://illuminations.nctm.org). NCTM also is developing online courses that will focus on mathematics specific to the early childhood years, so check there in the future.

Second, many helpful print resources are available. For example, *Math Matters*, by Suzanne H. Chapin and Art Johnson, is a clearly written text for kindergarten through eighth grade teachers that can help you understand the math that you teach. Also, Great Source Education Group (www.greatsource.com) publishes a very helpful series it calls Math Handbooks, which contain easily understood definitions for mathematics vocabulary. The pictures and diagrams in the handbook for the first and second grades, *Math to Learn*, are particularly helpful to the teacher of young children.

Finally, look for professional development materials that specifically address the mathematics you need to know. Often your math program materials will contain some professional development concerning the content they cover. Workshops that present mathematics teaching ideas should include some mathematics content information, as well. That is, to be effective, professional development of any kind for early childhood teachers should teach actual math content, not just teach how to teach math content.

We early childhood teachers must know about and be able to do mathematics at a much higher level than the children we teach. If we don't, we will miss many opportunities to teach the math that is foundational for all!

What part should technology play in early childhood math programs?

NCTM's *Principles and Standards for School Mathematics* (2000) devotes one of six Principles for School Mathematics to this question: "Technology is essential in teaching and learning mathematics; it influences the mathematics that is taught and enhances [children's] learning" (24). Early childhood educators have had doubts about whether, how, and how much to use technology with young children, particularly in the prekindergarten years. Yet, positive results are reported by researchers and practitioners who make judicious use of developmentally appropriate multimedia tools (e.g., Davidson & Wright 1994; Clements 1999b; Haugland 1999, 2000). Weighing the evidence from research and practice, NAEYC adopted a position statement (1996a) in support of computers and other technology in early childhood classrooms, when these are appropriately and effectively used.

The tools of technology can enhance mathematical thinking and, also important, contribute to children's proficiency as users. So, clearly, the question of technology is not *whether* but *how*. For more on that, Clements (1999b) provides a useful synthesis of recent research on technology use in early childhood classrooms, with implications for practice.

To improve math curriculum and instruction here at our school/center, what is the best program we can adopt?

There is no one curriculum program that best fits the needs of young children as they learn mathematics. However, there are many good programs and resources that provide ideas and activities and also help teachers understand children's mathematical thinking. But there are also many resources about mathematics filled with activities only, with little or no connection to theory.

How can you know which are good? Something I find helpful in making such judgments is the "model of transformational curriculum" presented in NAEYC's two-volume guide *Reaching Potentials* (Bredekamp & Rosegrant 1992, 1995). As shown in the diagram opposite, the model captures "important perspectives on planning curriculum that help make learning meaningful for young children: integrated curriculum, whole child philosophy, intellectual integrity, and attention to individual children's needs and interests" (1995, 18).

In the diagram, the vertical axis represents knowledge that is meaningful to children; the horizontal axis represents our knowledge of child develop-

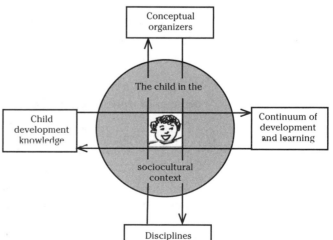

ment and learning. Below are questions, reflecting each part of the model, that can help you evaluate a teacher resource or math program:

"The child in the sociocultural context"

• Does the program

- take children's experiences and interests into account?

- allow children to make choices and contribute ideas about mathematics?

- suggest resources, games, experiences, and literature from various cultures?

- provide supporting research that was conducted in diverse settings?

Does it use approaches to make concepts meaningful, relevant, and accessible ("conceptual organizers")?

• How is mathematical knowledge introduced? Are math concepts and skills related to the real world of the young child?

• Do the curriculum and teaching strategies make mathematics content meaningful for young children? Do children explore concepts, use manipulatives, and connect their knowledge to more abstract forms?

• Are children given enough time to investigate and construct their ideas? Do materials give teachers useful and clearly described strategies for promoting children's learning?

• Is there research evidence that indicates young children's meaningful learning in this program?

Does it address key concepts of the mathematics knowledge base ("disciplines")?

• Does the program do justice to all the key *math content areas*, as defined by NCTM (2000) and elaborated in this book?

• Do its learning experiences and teaching strategies challenge children to solve problems, reason, communicate their thinking, make connections, and represent their solutions? Are these *math processes* (NCTM 2000) integrated with mathematics content?

Are its approaches and math concepts age appropriate ("child development knowledge")?

• Are its teaching strategies and activities consistent with the knowledge base about children's development?

• Are examples of children's work included in the program? Are activities described as they relate to young children's development and learning?

• What assessment strategies are presented in the program? Would they be helpful in considering children's development and mathematical thinking?

Are its rate and sequence of development/learning individually appropriate ("continuum of developmental and learning")?

• How does the program meet the individual needs of learners?

• Are there adaptations for children who have special needs and strengths? suggestions for children with different learning styles?

• Are there suggestions for integrating mathematics into circle time, centers, small groups, everyday routines, and other learning contexts?

How is math for preschoolers different from math for second- or third-graders?

Throughout this book I have emphasized the impressive mathematical understanding of young children, rather than their egocentrism or illogical reasoning. In fact, I would prefer to tell you about the *similarities* in effective mathematics education for young children of various ages. Common to all classrooms, prekindergarten through second grade, for example, are teachers' careful observing of children as they solve problems, teacher-child and child-child language that scaffolds and connects ideas, extensive exploration of mathematical concepts through play, and real-life contextual learning. Still, children's mathematical thinking does develop as they grow and learn.

As discussed in this book, the young child enters school, and even preschool, with considerable intuitive, informal knowledge of mathematics. The teacher's job is to build a bridge from this informal knowledge to the more formal knowledge of school (Ginsburg & Baron 1993; Ginsburg et al. 2006). The bridge is not the same for all children of a given age—for all 4-year-olds, say, or for all 7-year-olds. But there are predictable trajectories in cognitive development (just as in physical and social-emotional development) that need to be considered in math education.

Concepts and skills. Math concepts and skills build on previously acquired concepts and skills. Generally, mathematics in a prekindergarten classroom involves experiences with basic number concepts, counting and sorting objects, and building with two-dimensional and three-dimensional geometric shapes. Preschoolers can also find and create patterns, make comparisons, create simple graphs or other representations of information, and play reasoning games.

These same areas of mathematics—number and operations, geometry and spatial sense, and so on—are also present in the primary grade curriculum, but children work with the ideas on a different level. They are learning about place value; combining and separating larger numbers; identifying the attributes of shapes and their transformations; and estimating and measuring distance, area, weight, and volume. At age 7 or 8, children are able to generalize about patterns on the 100s chart; collect, analyze, and display data; and approach reasoning problems more strategically.

Materials and resources. The materials in the learning environment differ to an extent. For one thing, the fine motor skills of 3- or 4-year-olds are not as well developed as those of primary grade children. So materials in preschool settings tend to be somewhat larger and more easily manipulated. Very young children can handle things such as links, pattern blocks, unit blocks, and geometric shapes, and many of these materials are open ended in their uses. Although such versatile materials still have a place in the primary grades, older children begin to encounter more materials designed for specific purposes, such as base-10 blocks (with rods made of exactly ten cubes and flats made of exactly ten rods).

Language and thinking. With young children, teachers use many contextual references to concrete items and a wide variety of labels for concepts and ideas (e.g., "5 is a one-hand number; 10 is a two-hand number" . . . "It looks like a ball, but I call it a *sphere*"). They also make use of children's own descriptive phrases, rather than standard terms (e.g., "a box with one end squashed" to describe a square pyramid). With second- or third-graders, teachers make more use of conventional math vocabulary, and these words can be used in verbal explanations of math concepts. All verbal explanations, however, should be accompanied by concrete examples that illustrate the math concept; teachers should never rely on language alone to convey ideas. Older children's greater linguistic skills also enable them to explain their own concepts and reasoning—not with perfect clarity but far more effectively than younger children are able to do. Thus, a teacher can learn more about older children's (mis)understandings from their verbalizations and written language than is possible with younger children, and this changes the teacher's assessment strategies.

Between ages 4 and 7, children also become increasingly capable of abstract thinking and representation. In solving problems, for example, younger children are likely to use concrete objects to count, add, or subtract (e.g., moving counting bears from one pile to another). By second grade, children make greater use of simple pictures, tally marks, or other representations to work through a problem and its solution.

Teacher-child interactions. Here there is both continuity and change. Regardless of age, all young children should get opportunities to explore materials and generate their own activities and ideas. In preschool settings, teachers devote more time to exploration and play, and they look for opportunities to extend and connect the play to mathematics. Young children spend relatively less time than older children in planned activities. Although math-oriented small groups are a valuable learning tool throughout children's early childhood years, teachers typically make more extensive use of them in the primary grades.

How can I learn how to assess young children's mathematical understanding?

The primary purpose of assessment is to benefit children. My set of assessment guidelines presented in chapter 2 supports that purpose. They are based both on the position taken by NAEYC and the National Association of Early Childhood Specialists in State Departments of Education (NAEYC & NAECS/SDE 1990) and on NCTM's pertinent Principle for School Mathematics: "Assessment should support the learning of important mathematics and furnish useful information to both teachers and students" (2000, 22).

Of course, recognizing the importance of assessment is one thing; implementing effective assessment is quite another. Several sources have strongly influenced my perspective. Among these is the National Research Council publication *Early Childhood Assessment: Why, What, and How* (2008), which gives an excellent set of general guidelines for assessment. Another is Herbert Ginsburg's work, particularly *Entering the Child's Mind: The Clinical Interview in Psychology, Research, and Practice* (1997) and *The Teacher's Guide to Flexible Interviewing in the Classroom: Learning What Children Know about Math* (Ginsburg, Jacobs, & Lopez 1998), both of which emphasize the importance of interviewing children, listening to their responses, and planning instruction to build on their knowledge. In chapters 4–8 of this volume, I have included questions I find useful in getting children thinking about each math content area. Of course, it is essential not only to pose good questions but also to follow up after listening carefully to the child's response.

Many excellent strategies for documenting children's work are described in *Windows on Learning: Documenting Young Children's Work*, 2d ed. (Helm, Beneke, & Steinheimer 2007). These ideas, significantly shaped by the intensive use of documentation in Reggio Emilia, have further changed my teaching and helped me to focus on building the bridge between children's informal knowledge and more formal school mathematics. My own efforts to document children's work appear in the dialogues and work samples throughout this volume.

Finally, *Assessing and Guiding Young Children's Development and Learning*, 5th ed. (McAfee & Leong 2011) is very helpful in providing the organization and analytic strategies that teachers are looking for to improve the usefulness of their assessment. That book describes many different strategies and procedures for assessing young children's cognition and learning as well as physical and social development. The detailed procedures described by McAfee and Leong for collecting work over time, designing checklists, and interpreting anecdotal records provide practitioners with the specific, practical help needed to plan for the group as a whole and for each individual child.

Many parents believe that their child is learning more if he or she comes home with worksheets to complete. How can I explain why I don't assign worksheets, and get parents to share math experiences with their kid at home?

To start with, for many adults, their image of proper math instruction is based on recollections of their own school experiences. Those experiences were sometimes negative and often dramatically different from the kind of learning I present in this book. Even more problematic is that many parents have low expectations for their child's mathematical achievement because they themselves were "never good at math."

Just like teachers, parents need to be informed about key goals and learning experiences in mathematics. Regarding worksheets specifically, we need to emphasize to parents the value of *meaningful* learning—that is, experiences that connect math to children's lives, to what they already know and can do, to ideas they find interesting and that motivate them to learn more. Worksheets have none of these traits. When learning is meaningful, it sticks with children, enables them to solve real problems, and lays the solid foundation of understanding they will need in order to tackle more advanced mathematics later on.

These points can be communicated in parent meetings, workshops, parent-teacher conferences, and newsletters, as well as over the sharing of children's portfolios. Sources of help in getting families on board with math learning already exist. Among these are parent materials from NCTM (http://nctm.org/resources/families.aspx) and programs such as Family Math (Lawrence Hall of Science, UC-Berkeley; http://lawrencehallofscience.org/equals/aboutfm.html). Such approaches focus parents' attention on their child's learning and understanding, rather than on worksheets and the like. When they see evidence of children investigating, learning, and applying math concepts, both in and out of the classroom, they will value it.

Where can I find quality mathematics-related children's books?

Children's books can be excellent resources connecting children to mathematics. Over the past ten years, many children's book authors have written stories specifically directed toward concepts of number, geometry, or measurement. Many of these books are excellent, and teachers can easily use them to introduce and teach mathematics content.

I will not attempt to answer this question by giving you a set of criteria for high-quality children's books; I am not an expert in that area. Rather, on the DVD accompanying this book, I have included a list of children's books that I use, as well as a list of professional books that identify many children's books categorized for specific mathematics content. Please note that some of the books on my list do not address mathematics specifically. In fact, you may wonder why they are on the list! The reason they are listed is that I believe books of all kinds can connect to mathematics concepts—if they are integrated appropriately. Books with good stories can be a source of new mathematics word problems; children can analyze books with strong visual patterns for repeating or growing patterns; and the images in photo books can supply collections for classification activities involving shapes or numbers.

> See the Children's Book List on the DVD!

One professional book that has helped me identify new ways to integrate literature and mathematics is *Increasing the Power of Instruction* (2008) by Judith A. Schickedanz. Her suggestions for including texts that reinforce both literacy and mathematics concepts are important and worth reviewing. In fact, I will borrow from her title and say, "Children's math-related books, if used intentionally and appropriately, will increase the power of instruction!"

Using the Accompanying DVD

Hardware/software you will need:

• PC with a DVD drive. Operating system: Windows 2000 (or later version). Web browser: Internet Explorer 6 (or later version) or Firefox
or
Mac with a DVD drive. Operating system: Mac OS 9 (or later version). Web browser: Safari or Firefox

• Adobe Flash Player. Download at www.adobe.com/products/flashplayer/

• Adobe Reader. Download at http://get.adobe.com/reader/

To access the DVD files:

This DVD is a web browser–based program. The way it runs on your computer will depend on your settings and which browser you are using.

1. Insert the DVD into your computer's DVD drive

2. If you have a PC

   a. Typically, the DVD will run automatically. Depending on your settings, you may be prompted to click "Run autorun.exe"

   b. If the DVD does not run automatically, start it by going to "My Computer" (or to "Computer" in Vista), then double click on the DVD drive. Click on "Start_Here. html"

   c. The welcome page of the DVD should open in the browser window

If you have a Mac

   a. Double-click the DVD icon on your desktop to start it

   b. Click on "Start_Here.html"

   c. The welcome page of the DVD should open in the browser window

Learning Paths and Teaching Strategies

Excerpted from the 2002 NAEYC/NCTM Joint Position Statement "Early Childhood Mathematics: Promoting Good Begininnings." For the complete position statement, see the accompanying DVD or visit www.naeyc.org.

The research base for sketching a picture of children's mathematical development varies considerably from one area of mathematics to another. Outlining a learning path, moreover, does not mean we can predict with confidence where a child of a given age will be in that sequence. Developmental variation is the norm, not the exception. However, children do tend to follow similar *sequences,* or *learning paths,* as they develop. This chart illustrates in each area some things that *many* children know and do—early and late in the three-to-six age range. These are, then, simply two points along the learning path that may have many steps in between. For each content area, the Sample Teaching Strategies column shows a few of the many teacher actions that promote learning when used within a classroom context that reflects the recommendations set forth in this NAEYC/NCTM position statement. In general, they are helpful strategies, with minor adaptations, across the age range.

Content Area	Examples of Typical Knowledge and Skills From Age 3 ⟶ Age 6		Sample Teaching Strategies
Number and operations	Counts a collection of one to four items and begins to understand that the last counting word tells *how many.*	Counts and produces (counts out) collections up to 100 using groups of 10.	Models counting of small collections and guides children's counting in everyday situations, emphasizing that we use one counting word for each object: ♡ ♡ ♡ "One…two…three…" Models counting by 10s while making groups of 10s (e.g., 10, 20, 30…or 14, 24, 34…).
	Quickly "sees" and labels collections of one to three with a number.	Quickly "sees" and labels with the correct number "patterned" collections (e.g., dominoes) and unpatterned collections of up to about six items.	Gives children a brief glimpse (a couple of seconds) of a small collection of items and asks how many there are.

Content Area	Examples of Typical Knowledge and Skills From Age 3 ——————————⟶ Age 6		Sample Teaching Strategies
Number and operations	Adds and subtracts non-verbally when numbers are very low. For example, when one ball and then another are put into the box, expects the box to contain two balls.	Adds or subtracts using counting-based strategies such as counting on (e.g., adding 3 to 5, says "Five…, six, seven, eight"), when numbers and totals do not go beyond 10.	Tells real-life stories involving numbers and a problem. Asks *how many* questions (e.g., how many are left? how many are there now? how many did they start with? how many were added?).

Shows children the use of objects, fingers, counting on, guessing, and checking to solve problems. |
| Geometry and spatial sense | Begins to match and name 2-D and 3-D shapes, first only with same size and orientation, then shapes that differ in size and orientation (e.g., a large triangle sitting on its point versus a small one sitting on its side). | Recognizes and names a variety of 2-D and 3-D shapes (e.g., quadrilaterals, trapezoids, rhombi, hexagons, spheres, cubes) in any orientation.

Describes basic features of shapes (e.g., number of sides or angles). | Introduces and labels a wide variety of shapes (e.g., skinny triangles, fat rectangles, prisms) that are in a variety of positions (e.g., a square or a triangle standing on a corner, a cylinder "standing up" or horizontal).

Involves children in constructing shapes and talking about their features. |
| | Uses shapes, separately, to create a picture.

Describes object locations with spatial words such as *under* and *behind* and builds simple but meaningful "maps" with toys such as houses, cars, and trees. | Makes a picture by combining shapes.

Builds, draws, or follows simple maps of familiar places, such as the classroom or playground. | Encourages children to make pictures or models of familiar objects using shape blocks, paper shapes, or other materials.

Encourages children to make and talk about models with blocks and toys.

Challenges children to mark a path from a table to the wastebasket with masking tape, then draw a map of the path, adding pictures of objects appearing along the path, such as a table or easel. |

The Young Child and Mathematics

Content Area	Examples of Typical Knowledge and Skills From Age 3 ⟶ Age 6		Sample Teaching Strategies
Measure-ment	Recognizes and labels measurable attributes of objects (e.g., "I need a long string," "Is this heavy?"). Begins to compare and sort according to these attributes (e.g., *more/ less, heavy/light;* "This block is too short to be the bridge").	Tries out various pro-cesses and units for measurement and begins to notice different results of one method or another (e.g., what happens when we *don't* use a standard unit). Makes use of nonstandard measuring tools or uses conventional tools such as a cup or ruler in non-standard ways (e.g., "It's three rulers long").	Uses comparing words to model and discuss measuring (e.g. "This book feels heavier than that block," "I wonder if this block tower is taller than the desk?"). Uses and creates situations that draw children's attention to the problem of measuring something with two different units (e.g., making garden rows "four shoes" apart, first using a teacher's shoe and then a child's shoe).
Pattern/ algebraic thinking	Notices and copies simple repeating patterns, such as a wall of blocks with long, short, long, short, long, short, long....	Notices and discusses pat-terns in arithmetic (e.g., adding one to any num-ber results in the next "counting number").	Encourages, models, and dis-cusses patterns (e.g., "What's missing?" "Why do you think that is a pattern?" "I need a blue next"). Engages children in finding color and shape patterns in the environment, number patterns on calendars and charts (e.g., with the numerals 1–100), patterns in arithmetic (e.g., recognizing that when zero is added to a number, the sum is always that number).
Display-ing and analyzing data	Sorts objects and counts and compares the groups formed. Helps to make simple graphs (e.g., a pictograph formed as each child places her own photo in the row indicating her preferred treat—pretzels or crackers).	Organizes and displays data through simple numerical representa-tions such as bar graphs and counts the number in each group.	Invites children to sort and organize collected materials by color, size, shape, etc. Asks them to compare groups to find which group has the most. Uses "not" language to help children analyze their data (e.g., "All of these things are red, and these things are NOT red"). Works with children to make simple numerical summa-ries such as tables and bar graphs, comparing parts of the data.

References

Anderson, A., J. Anderson, & C. Thauberger. 2008. Mathematics learning and teaching in the early years. In *Contemporary perspectives on mathematics in early childhood education*, eds. O.N. Saracho & B. Spodek, 95–132. Charlotte, NC: Information Age Publishing.

Balfanz, R. 1999. Why do we teach young children so little mathematics? Some historical considerations. In *Mathematics in the early years*, ed. J.V. Copley, 3–10. Reston, VA: National Council of Teachers of Mathematics; and Washington, DC: NAEYC.

Ball, D.L., & H. Bass. 2000. Interweaving content and pedagogy in teaching and learning to teach: Knowing and using mathematics. In *Multiple perspectives on mathematics teaching and learning*, ed. J. Boaler, 83–104. Westport, CT: Ablex Publishing.

Barbarin, O., D. Bryant, T. McCandies, M. Burchinal, D. Early, R. Clifford, R. Pianta, & C. Howes. 2006. Children enrolled in public pre-K: The relation of family life, neighborhood quality, and socioeconomic resources to early competence. *American Journal of Orthopsychiatry* 76: 265–76.

Baroody, A.J. 1987. *Children's mathematical thinking.* New York: Teachers College Press.

Baroody, A.J. 2004. The developmental bases for early childhood number and operations standards. In *Engaging young children in mathematics: Standards for early childhood mathematics education*, eds. D.H. Clements & J. Sarama, 173–220. Mahwah, NJ: Lawrence Erlbaum Associates.

Baroody, A.J., M. Lai, & K.S. Mix. 2006. The development of young children's early number and operation sense and its implications for early childhood education. In *Handbook of research on the education of young children*, 2d ed., eds. B. Spodek & O.N. Saracho, 187–221. Mahwah, NJ: Lawrence Erlbaum Associates.

Baroody, A.J., & D.J. Standifer. 1993. Addition and subtraction in the primary grades. In *Research ideas for the classroom: Early childhood mathematics*, ed. R.J. Jensen, 72–103. New York: Macmillan.

Baroody, A.J., & J.L.M. Wilkins. 1999. The development of informal counting, number, and arithmetic skills and concepts. In *Mathematics in the early years*, ed. J.V. Copley, 48–65. Reston, VA: National Council of Teachers of Mathematics; and Washington, DC: NAEYC.

Beaton, A.E., I.V.S. Mullis, M.D. Martin, E.J. Gonzales, D.L. Kelly, & T.A. Smith. 1996. *Mathematics achievement in the middle school years: IEA's Third International Mathematics and Science Study*, 41. Chestnut Hill, MA: Center for the Study of Testing, Evaluation, and Educational Policy, Boston College. Online: http://timss.bc.edu.

Bergen, D. 1997. Using observational techniques. In *Issues in early childhood educational assessment and evaluation*, eds. B. Spodek & O.N. Saracho, 108–28. New York: Teachers College Press.

Boehm, A., & R. Weinberg. 1997. *The classroom observer: Developing observation skills in early childhood settings*. 3d ed. New York: Teachers College Press.

Bredekamp, S., & T. Rosegrant, eds. 1992. *Reaching potentials: Appropriate curriculum and assessment for young children, volume 1*. Washington, DC: NAEYC.

Bredekamp, S., & T. Rosegrant, eds. 1995. *Reaching potentials: Transforming early childhood curriculum and assessment, volume 2*. Washington, DC: NAEYC.

Caine, R., & G. Caine. 1994. Principles of brain-based learning. In *Making connections: Teaching and the human brain*. Menlo Park, CA: Addison Wesley.

Carpenter, T. 1975. Measurement concepts of first- and second-grade students. *Journal for Research in Mathematics Education* 6 (1): 3–13.

Carpenter, T.P., E. Fennema, M.L. Franke, L. Levi, & S.B. Empson. 1999. *Children's mathematics: Cognitively guided instruction.* Portsmouth, NH: Heinemann.

Carpenter, T.P., M.L. Franke, & L. Levi. 2003. *Thinking mathematically: Integrating arithmetic and algebra in elementary school.* Portsmouth, NH: Heinemann.

Carpenter, T.P., & R. Lewis. 1976. The development of the concept of a standard unit of measure in young children. *Journal for Research in Mathematics Education* 7: 53–58.

Cartwright, S. 1996. Learning with large blocks. In *The block book*, 3d ed., ed. E.S. Hirsch, 133–41. Washington, DC: NAEYC.

Cavanagh, M.C. 2006. *Math to learn: A mathematics handbook.* 2d ed. Wilmington, MA: Great Source Education Group.

Chapin, S.H., & A. Johnson. 2006. *Math matters: Understanding the math you teach, grades K–8.* 2d ed. Sausalito, CA: Math Solutions.

Chapin, S.H., C. O'Connor, & N.C. Anderson. 2009. *Classroom discussions: Using math talk to help students learn.* 2d ed. Sausalito, CA: Math Solutions.

Charlesworth, R., & K.K. Lind. 2010. *Math and science for young children.* 6th ed. Belmont, CA: Wadsworth/Cengage Learning.

Clements, D.H. 1999a. Geometry and spatial thinking in young children. In *Mathematics in the early years*, ed. J.V. Copley, 66–79. Reston, VA: National Council of Teachers of Mathematics; and Washington, DC: NAEYC.

Clements, D.H. 1999b. The effective use of computers with young children. In *Mathematics in the early years*, ed. J.V. Copley, 119–28. Reston, VA: National Council of Teachers of Mathematics; and Washington, DC: NAEYC.

Clements, D.H. 2003. Teaching and learning geometry. In *A research companion to principles and standards for school mathematics*, eds. J. Kilpatrick, W.G. Martin, & D. Schifter, 151–78. Reston, VA: National Council Teachers of Mathematics.

Clements, D.H., & S. McMillen. 1996. Rethinking "concrete" manipulatives. *Teaching Children Mathematics* 2 (5): 270–79.

Clements, D.H., & J. Sarama, eds. 2004. *Engaging young children in mathematics: Standards for early childhood mathematics education.* Mahwah, NJ: Lawrence Erlbaum Associates.

Clements, D.H., & J. Sarama. 2007. Early childhood mathematics learning. In *Second handbook of research on mathematics teaching and learning*, ed. F.K. Lester Jr., 461–555. Charlotte, NC: Information Age Publishing.

Clements, D.H., & J. Sarama. 2009. *Learning and teaching early math: The learning trajectories approach.* New York: Routledge.

Copley, J.V. 1998. Notes of classroom observations in sorting activities in kindergarten classrooms. Typescript.

Copley, J.V., ed. 1999. *Mathematics in the early years.* Reston, VA: National Council of Teachers of Mathematics; and Washington, DC: NAEYC.

Copley, J.V. 2001. *Mathematics institute for pre-kindergarten and kindergarten: A TEXTEAMS project.* Austin: University of Texas at Austin.

Copple, C., & S. Bredekamp. 2009. *Developmentally appropriate practice in early childhood programs serving children from birth through age 8.* 3d ed. Washington, DC: NAEYC.

Davidson, J., & J.L. Wright. 1994. The potential of the microcomputer in the early childhood classroom. In *Young children: Active learners in a technological age*, eds. J.L. Wright & D.D. Shade, 77–91. Washington, DC: NAEYC.

Denton, K., & J. West. 2002. *Children's reading and mathematics achievement in kindergarten and first grade*. Washington, DC: National Center for Education Statistics.

Driscoll, M.J. 1981. Measurement in elementary school mathematics. In *Research within reach: Elementary school mathematics*. Reston, VA: National Council of Teachers of Mathematics; and Washington, DC: National Institute of Education.

Duncan, G.J., A. Claessens, A.C. Huston, L.S. Pagani, M. Engel, H. Sexton, C.H. Dowsett, K. Magnuson, P. Klebanov, L. Feinstein, J. Brooks-Gunn, K. Duckworth, & C. Japel. 2007. School readiness and later achievement. *Developmental Psychology* 43 (6): 1428–46.

Flavell, J.H. 1985. *Cognitive development*. 2d ed. Englewood Cliffs, NJ: Prentice-Hall.

Fuson, K.C. 2004. Pre-K to grade 2 goals and standards: Achieving 21st century mastery for all. In *Engaging young children in mathematics: Standards for early childhood mathematics education*, eds. D.H. Clements & J. Sarama, 105–48. Mahwah, NJ: Lawrence Erlbaum Associates.

Gardner, H. 1983. *Frames of mind*. New York: Basic.

Gelman, R., & C.R. Gallistel. 1978. *The child's understanding of number*. Cambridge, MA: Harvard University Press.

Ginsburg, H.P. 1977. *Children's arithmetic*. New York: Van Nostrand.

Ginsburg, H.P. 1997. *Entering the child's mind: The clinical interview in psychology research and practice*. New York: Cambridge University Press.

Ginsburg, H.P., & J. Baron. 1993. Cognition: Young children's construction of mathematics. In *Research ideas for the classroom: Early childhood mathematics*, ed. R.J. Jensen, 3–21. New York: Macmillan.

Ginsburg, H.P., J. Cannon, J. Eisenband, & S. Pappas. 2006. Mathematical thinking and learning. In *The Blackwell handbook of early childhood development*, eds. K. McCartney & D. Phillips, 208–29. Malden, MA: Blackwell Publishing.

Ginsburg, H.P., S.F. Jacobs, & L.S. Lopez. 1998. *The teacher's guide to flexible interviewing in the classroom: Learning what children know about math*. Boston: Allyn & Bacon.

Ginsburg, H.P., & S. Opper. 1988. *Piaget's theory of intellectual development*. 3d ed. Englewood Cliffs, NJ: Prentice-Hall.

Goldin, G., & N. Shteingold. 2001. Systems of representations and the development of mathematical concepts. In *The roles of representation in school mathematics (2001 yearbook)*, ed. A.A. Cuoco, 1–23. Reston, VA: National Council of Teachers of Mathematics.

Gonzales, P., T. Williams, L. Jocelyn, S. Roey, D. Kastberg, & S. Brenwald. 2009. *Highlights from TIMSS 2007: Mathematics and science achievement of U.S. fourth- and eighth-grade students in an international context*. Washington, DC: National Center for Education Statistics. Online: http://nces.ed.gov/pubsearch/pubsinfo.asp?pubid=2009001.

Greabell, L.C. 1978. The effect of stimuli input on the acquisition of introductory geometric concepts by elementary school children. *School Science and Mathematics* 78 (4): 320–26.

Greenes, C. 1999. Ready to learn: Developing young children's mathematical powers. In *Mathematics in the early years*, ed. J.V. Copley, 39–47. Reston, VA: National Council of Teachers of Mathematics; and Washington, DC: NAEYC.

Hart, K. 1984. Which comes first—Length, area, or volume? *Arithmetic Teacher* 31: 16–18, 26–27.

Haugland, S.W. 1999. What role should technology play in young children's learning? Part 1. *Young Children* 54 (6): 26–31.

Haugland, S.W. 2000. What role should technology play in young children's learning? Part 2—Early childhood classrooms in the 21st century: Using computers to maximize learning. *Young Children* 55 (1): 12–18.

Helm, J.H., S. Beneke, & K. Steinheimer. 2007. *Windows on learning: Documenting young children's work*. 2d ed. New York: Teachers College Press.

Hiebert, J. 1984. Why do some children have trouble learning measurement concepts? *Arithmetic Teacher* 31: 19–24.

Hiebert, J., & T.P. Carpenter. 1992. Learning and teaching with understanding. In *Handbook of research on mathematics teaching and learning*, ed. D.A. Grouws, 65–97. New York: Macmillan.

Hirsch, E.S., ed. *The block book*. 3d ed. Washington, DC: NAEYC.

Howden, H. 1989. Teaching number sense. *The Arithmetic Teacher* 36 (6): 6–11.

Inskeep, J. 1976. Teaching measurement to elementary school children. In *Measurement in school mathematics (1976) yearbook*, eds. D. Nelson & R. Reys, 6–86. Reston, VA: National Council of Teachers of Mathematics.

Kouba, V., C. Brown, T. Carpenter, M. Lindquist, E.A. Silver, & J.O. Swafford. 1988. Results of the fourth NAEP assessment of mathematics: Measurement, geometry, data interpretation, attitudes, and other topics. *Arithmetic Teacher* 35 (9): 10–16.

Lambdin, D.V. 2003. Benefits of teaching through problem solving. In *Teaching mathematics through problem solving: Prekindergarten–grade 6*, ed. F.K. Lester Jr., 3–14. Reston, VA: National Council of Teachers of Mathematics.

Lappan, G. 1999. Geometry: The forgotten strand. *NCTM News Bulletin* 36 (5): 3.

Langer, J., S. Rivera, M. Schlesinger, & A. Wakeley. 2003. Early cognitive development: Ontogeny and phylogeny. In *Handbook of developmental psychology*, eds. J. Valsiner & K. Connolly, 141–71. London: Sage.

Lesh, R., & J. Zawojewski. 2007. Problem solving and modeling. In *Second handbook of research on mathematics teaching and learning*, ed. F.K. Lester Jr., 763–804. Charlotte, NC: Information Age Publishing.

Ma, L. 1999. *Knowing and teaching elementary mathematics: Teachers' understanding of fundamental mathematics in China and the United States*. Mahwah, NJ: Lawrence Erbaum Associates.

Markman, E.M., & J. Subert. 1976. Classes and collections: Internal organization and resulting holistic properties. *Cognitive Psychology* 8: 561–77.

Martin, T., A. Lukong, & R. Reaves. 2007. The role of manipulatives in arithmetic and geometry tasks. *Journal of Education and Human Development* 1 (1). Online: http://scientificjournals.org/journals2007/articles/1073.htm.

Mason, J. 2008. Making use of children's powers to produce algebraic thinking. In *Algebra in the early grades*, eds. J.J. Kaput, D.W. Carraher, & M.L. Blanton, 57–94. New York: Routledge.

McAfee, O., & D.J. Leong. 2011. *Assessing and guiding young children's development and learning*. 5th ed. Upper Saddle River, NJ: Pearson.

McClain, K., & P. Cobb. 1999. Supporting students' ways of reasoning about patterns and partitions. In *Mathematics in the early years*, ed. J.V. Copley, 112–18. Reston, VA: National Council of Teachers of Mathematics; and Washington, DC: NAEYC.

NAEYC. 1996a. Position statement: Technology and young children—Ages three through eight. *Young Children* 51 (6): 11–16.

NAEYC. 1996b. Position statement: Responding to linguistic and cultural diversity—Recommendations for effective early childhood education. *Young Children* 51 (2): 4–12.

NAEYC. 2009. Developmentally appropriate practice in early childhood programs serving children from birth through age 8. Position statement. Washington, DC: Author. Online: www.naeyc.org/positionstatements/dap.

NAEYC & NAECS/SDE (National Association of Early Childhood Specialists in State Departments of Education). 1990. Position statement: Guidelines for appropriate curriculum content and assessment in programs serving children ages 3 through 8. In *Reaching potentials: Appropriate curriculum and assessment for young children, volume 1*, eds. S. Bredekamp & T. Rosegrant, 9–27. Washington, DC: NAEYC.

NAEYC & NCTM (National Council of Teachers of Mathematics). 2002. *Early childhood mathematics: Promoting good beginnings*. Joint position statement. Washington, DC: NAEYC; and Reston, VA: NCTM. Online: www.naeyc.org/positionstatements/mathematics.

NCTM (National Council of Teachers of Mathematics). 2000. *Principles and standards for school mathematics*. Reston, VA: Author.

NCTM (National Council of Teachers of Mathematics). 2006. *Curriculum focal points for prekindergarten through grade 8 mathematics: A quest for coherence*. Reston, VA: Author.

Nelson, G.D. 1999. Within easy reach: Using a shelf-based curriculum to increase the range of mathematical concepts accessible to young children. In *Mathematics in the early years*, ed. J.V. Copley, 135–45. Reston, VA: National Council of Teachers of Mathematics; and Washington, DC: NAEYC.

NRC (National Research Council). 1989. *Everybody counts: A report on the future of mathematics education*. Washington, DC: National Academy Press.

NRC (National Research Council). 2001. *Adding it up: Helping children learn mathematics*. J. Kilpatrick, J. Swafford, & B. Findell (eds.). Mathematics Learning Study Committee, Center for Education, Division of Behavioral and Social Sciences and Education. Washington, DC: National Academy Press.

NRC (National Research Council). 2008. *Early childhood assessment: Why, what, and how*. Committee on Developmental Outcomes and Assessments for Young Children, C.E. Snow & S.B. Van Hemel (eds.). Board on Children, Youth, and Families, Board on Testing and Assessment, Division of Behavioral and Social Sciences and Education. Washington, DC: National Academies Press.

NRC (National Research Council). 2009. *Mathematics learning in early childhood: Paths toward excellence and equity*. Committee on Early Childhood Mathematics, C.T. Cross, T.A. Woods, & H. Schweingruber (eds.). Center for Education, Division of Behavioral and Social Sciences and Education. Washington, DC: National Academies Press.

Nummela, R., & T. Rosengren. 1986. What's happening in students' brains may redefine teaching. *Educational Leadership* 43 (8): 49–53.

Payne, J.N., & D.M. Huinker. 1993. Early number and numeration. In *Research ideas for the classroom: Early childhood mathematics*, ed. R.J. Jensen, 43–71. New York: Macmillan.

PBS (Public Broadcasting Service) Mathline. 2009. The Elementary School Math Project—Sand babies: Math grows up (Measurement). Online: www.pbs.org/teachers/mathline/lessonplans/esmp/sandbabies/sandbabies_procedure.shtm.

Piaget, J. 1965. *The child's conception of number*. New York: Norton.

Piaget, J., & B. Inhelder. 1941/1974. *The child's construction of quantities: Conservation and atomism*. Translated by A. J. Pomerans. London: Routledge & Kegan Paul.

Piaget, J., B. Inhelder, & A. Szeminski. 1960. *The child's conception of geometry*. New York: Basic.

Polya, G. 1957. *How to solve it; a new aspect of mathematical method*. 2d ed. Garden City, NY: Doubleday.

Renga, S., & L. Dalla. 1993. Affect: A critical component of mathematical learning in early childhood. In *Research ideas for the classroom: Early childhood mathematics*, ed. R.J. Jensen, 22–37. New York: Macmillan.

Sarama, J., & D.H. Clements. 2009. *Early childhood mathematics education research: Learning trajectories for young children*. New York: Routledge.

Schickedanz, J.A. 2008. *Increasing the power of instruction: Integration of language, literacy, and math across the preschool day*. Washington, DC: NAEYC.

Tang, E.P., & H.P. Ginsburg. 1999. Young children's mathematical reasoning: A psychological view. In *Developing mathematical reasoning in grades K–12*, eds. L.V. Stiff & F.R. Curcio, 45–61. Reston, VA: National Council of Teachers of Mathematics.

Van de Walle, J., & K.B. Watkins. 1993. Early development of number sense. In *Research ideas for the classroom: Early childhood mathematics*, ed. R.J. Jensen, 127–50. New York: Macmillan.

van Hiele, P.M. 1986. *Structure and insight: A theory of mathematics education*. Orlando, FL: Academic.

Index

activity ideas
    data analysis and probability, 149–50, 152–54
    geometry and spatial sense, 111–12, 114–17
    measurement, 132–33, 135–37
    number and operations, 69–71, 73–78
    patterns, functions, and algebra, 93, 95–98
addend, 54, 57
Adding It Up, 7, 10
addition. *See* change operations
age appropriateness. *See* curriculum
algebra. *See also* patterns
    definition of, 79, 85
algebraic thinking, 85–86, 89, 90–91
art, 28, 41, 74, 100, 111, 115, 117
Assessing and Guiding Young Children's Development and Learning, 160
assessment, 12, 22–26, 160
    checklists, 24, 30, 93, 160
    guidelines for, 13, 72, 94, 134, 151
    in-class, 68–69, 92–93, 110, 132. *See also* observation
    methods of, 24–26, 160
attitude. *See* disposition
Block Book, The, 105
bridging (informal to formal knowledge), 39, 45, 55, 100–01, 159, 160
calendars, 41, 66–67, 84, 92, 128, 155–56
change. *See* functions
change operations, 54, 62. *See also* number and operations
child-centered choices, 23
children's errors/misconceptions, 5, 107, 128
    learning from, 9, 23, 39, 51, 93, 146–47, 160
    not correcting, 3, 7
children's literature, 40, 42, 49, 53, 67–68, 73, 74, 75, 78, 92, 108, 110, 111, 112, 114, 115, 120, 123, 132, 136, 149, 161
    connecting to, 67, 92, 110, 132, 149
circle graph, 140–41
classroom environment, 15, 17, 19, 27–28, 66–67, 87–88, 92, 109–10, 131–32, 148, 160
communication, 37–39, 143, 160. *See also* processes
    classroom contexts and, 37–38
    teacher roles, 39
commutative property, 90
comparison, 54, 62–63, 91, 118, 125, 128–29, 133. *See also* measurement
compose/decompose
    number and place value, 55
    shapes, 100, 104, 105, 114
connections, 39–41, 80. *See also* processes
    across subject areas/grade levels, 15, 41, 73, 100, 115, 144
    planning for, 15
    to children's lives, 32, 65–68, 77, 79, 84, 92, 110, 113, 132, 142, 149, 161
    to focal points, 15

conservation, 6, 55, 124–26, 128, 139. *See also* Piaget
Cotton, John Dana, 156
counting, 57–59. *See also* number and operations
    activities for, 69, 70–71, 73–74, 75, 153
    books and, 73, 74, 78
    development of, 54, 57
    finger, 49–51, 56
    one-to-one correspondence, 58
    patterns and, 84
    skip, 54, 88
curriculum, 12, 14–18, 157–58
    age appropriateness in, 3–4, 159–60
    guidelines for, 13, 72, 94, 113, 134, 151
    planning, 16–18
    sequence of, 45–46, 48, 79–80, 99–100, 118, 119, 159
Curriculum Focal Points, 10, 14, 46, 48, 79, 99, 106, 132
data analysis, 138–54
    activities for, 149–50, 152–54
    classroom contexts and, 139–43
    comparison and description in, 147–48
    environment and, 141, 148
    gathering data, 141–43, 144–45, 149
    graphs and graphing, 139–141, 147, 152
    organization, 141, 143, 145–46, 153
    questions, "Getting Children Thinking about," 149
    representation and, 142–43, 146–47
    sorting, 95, 106, 141, 143–44, 145–46, 150, 152, 154
    standards, 138
developmental checklist. *See* learning trajectories
developmentally appropriate practice, 5, 10, 11, 13, 72, 157–58
disposition, 7–9, 19, 24, 29, 31, 103
dissonance, 3. *See also* Piaget
DVD
    how to access, 162
    resources on, 11, 12, 14, 104, 161
    video clips on, 30, 31, 49, 68, 74, 76, 101, 110, 136, 156
Early Childhood Assessment, 160
Early Childhood Mathematics Education Research, 45
effort. *See* disposition
egocentric, 37, 39, 159. *See also* Piaget
Entering the Child's Mind, 160
equations, 52, 89–90, 97–98
equity, 7, 19–22
estimation, 20–22, 65, 76, 120–22, 131, 156
families, 161
Family Math program, 161
FAQs. *See* questions (FAQs)
focal point(s), 10, 11, 14, 46, 48, 54, 55, 79–80, 99–100, 118
    connections to, 46, 79, 100
formal knowledge, 55, 59, 79, 80, 86, 90, 124. *See also* bridging

Froebel, Friedrich, 99
functions. *See also* patterns
    classroom contexts and, 91
    definition of, 79, 85
games. *See* activity ideas
geometry, 99–117. *See also* shape
    activities for, 111–12, 114–17
    classroom contexts and, 101–04
    environment and, 109–10
    guidelines for, 113
    levels of thinking, 101
    questions, "Getting Children Thinking about," 109
    spatial awareness and, 101–03
    spatial orientation and, 105, 110, 111, 117
    spatial visualization and, 105, 110, 114
    standards, 99–100
    symmetry, 108–09
    vocabulary for, 108
Ginsburg, Herbert, 55, 160
graphs. *See* data analysis
guidelines. *See* assessment; curriculum; instruction
Increasing the Power of Instruction, 161
informal mathematics knowledge, 3–4, 5, 55, 138. *See also* bridging
instruction, 12, 18–22
    expectations, 19–20
    guidelines for, 13, 72, 94, 113, 134, 151
intentionality, 18–22
intuitive knowledge, 3–5, 39, 100, 119, 159
Learning and Teaching Early Math, 10, 24, 45, 54, 104, 124
learning cycle. *See* teaching
learning expectations. *See* standards
learning formats. *See* classroom environment
learning trajectories, 24, 45, 156, 163–65
    data analysis and probability, 143–44
    geometry, 104–05
    measurement, 124
    number and operations, 54–55, 57
    patterns, functions, and algebra, 85
listening. *See* communication
literacy/language, 52–53, 64, 100, 144
manipulatives, 28, 60, 67–68, 81, 101–03, 106, 114, 148, 159
    age appropriateness of, 159
    types of, 15
math buddies, 27
math journals, 43, 65, 85
Math Matters, 156
Math to Learn, 157
Mathematics Learning in Early Childhood, 10, 155
mathematizing, 39
measurement, 118–37
    activities for, 98, 132–33, 135–37
    capacity and volume, 125–26, 127
    classroom contexts and, 120–23
    end-to-end, 124, 131, 136
    environment and, 131–32
    estimation in, 120–22, 131